JEWISH COOKING AROUND THE WORLD

JEWISH COOKING AROUND THE WORLD

gourmet and holiday recipes

BY

HANNA GOODMAN

Introductions by
PHILIP GOODMAN
•
Drawings by
GAYLE MILLER

THE JEWISH PUBLICATION SOCIETY OF AMERICA
Philadelphia

To PHILIP

Go, eat your bread in gladness,
and drink your wine in joy;
for your works were long ago approved by God.

ECCLESIASTES 9:7

CONTENTS

PREFACE

Jewish Cooking around the World: Gourmet and Holiday Recipes presents a variety of recipes from foreign countries and recipes for the Sabbath and festivals, all complying with the Jewish dietary laws. The introduction to the recipes of each land will help to demonstrate the role foods played in Jewish communal life of the past. The introductory notes for the holidays describe the background for the dishes that are traditional on these occasions. "Food for Thought," a miniature anthology of selections from the Bible, the Talmud, and other Jewish literary sources, presents the Jewish attitude toward foods and eating.

All products—meats, cheeses, and others—used in the recipes are kosher. The wines are from Israel. The margarine, nondairy creamer, and nondairy topping are pareve (neutral). Meats are all made kosher before cooking.

Every recipe has been tested by the author.

Part of this book, excluding the chapters on the holidays, was published by Women's Organizations' Services of the National Jewish Welfare Board in 1969. Acknowledgment is also due to *The Jewish Exponent* of Philadelphia and *Tarbut,* the publication of the America-Israel Cultural Foundation, in which some of the material first appeared.

Some holiday introductions and some of my recipes are reprinted from *The Rosh Hashanah Anthology* (1970), *The Sukkot and Simhat Torah Anthology* (1973), *The Purim Anthology* (1949), and *The Passover Anthology* (1961), by Philip Goodman, by courtesy of The Jewish Publication Society of America. Selections from *The Torah, The Holy Scriptures,* and Louis Ginzberg's *Legends of the Jews* are also reprinted with the permission of The Jewish Publication Society of America.

To David C. Gross and Dr. Chaim Potok, executive vice-president and editor, respectively, of The Jewish Publication Society of America, I offer my deepest appreciation for their keen interest in this book and for making possible its publication. The meticulous editing of Mrs. Kay Powell, the Society's copy editor, was a great boon.

I want to thank the many hundreds of women and the men who participated in the Jewish gourmet cooking classes at synagogues and Young Men's and Young Women's Hebrew Associations in the Greater New York area, where I taught and experimented with most of the recipes presented here. Their warmhearted response and spirited enthusiasm inspired me to prepare this book.

The abiding interest in Jewish cooking that I have always possessed stems from my family background. Among the fondest memories of my childhood in Jerusalem is the picture of my mother, Nechamah Rivkah, and sister Sarah, of blessed memory, and my sister Zvia preparing food for the Sabbath, festivals, and the numerous joyous occasions that occurred in a family like ours with eleven children. Not only they, but also my devoted sisters-in-law and aunts, joined in the preparations, for we had no commercial caterers. Mother taught us the art of traditional Jewish cooking, and from Zvia, a professional cook, we learned the science of cooking. The crowning glory of every Sabbath was my father's singing "A Woman of Valor" (Proverbs 31:10–31), which he addressed to my mother as the entire family stood around the table set with the lit candles, sparkling wine, fragrant hallot, and gefilte fish. All this and more is the legacy I inherited from my parents, and therefore I would like to share it with my dear children and grandchildren.

Last but not least, I offer my gratitude to the chief tester and taster: my husband, Philip. Without his help this book would never have seen the light of day.

HANNA GOODMAN

September 6, 1973
New York

JEWISH COOKING AROUND THE WORLD

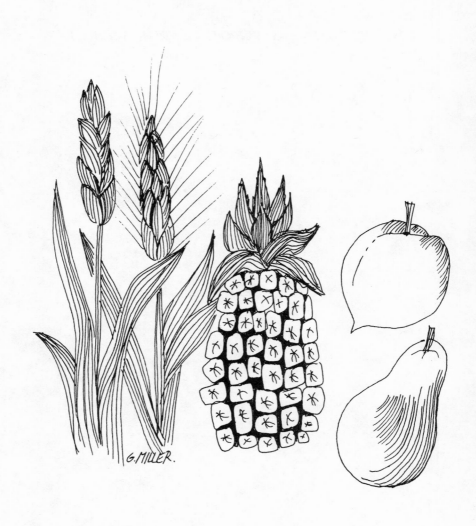

INTRODUCTION

Jews today are to be found scattered throughout the world. Although over 70 percent of Jewry live in three countries—the United States of America, the Soviet Union, and Israel—there are Jewish communities in at least eighty-five other countries. There are Ashkenazim, Sephardim, the Bene-Israel of India, Yemenites, Israeli sabras, and American Jews—all with obvious differences yet having much in common. Loyally identified with the nations among whom they live, Jews are bound together in a spiritual bond forged by a common origin, an ancient heritage, a great religion, and a noble history. While they share generic religious and cultural interests, it is undoubtedly true that the Jewish people exemplify diversity in unity. Since the environment influences all people, it is natural that in each land where they resided Jews should have acquired distinctive characteristics that are reflected in their social life, manners, speech, attire, and eating habits.

The history of the Jewish people is a saga of exile and wandering, of dislocation and resettlement. Starting with the biblical patriarch Abraham, the children of Israel have been wandering over the face of the earth. Following the dispersion from Palestine, where the Jews were a nation nearly two thousand years ago, they have been in constant motion. In the Middle Ages, Jews traveled from country to country either to escape oppression or for business or study. The czarist tyranny in the 1880s was responsible for a tremendous exodus of Jews from Russia, while this century witnessed other vast migrations resulting from the two world wars and Nazism.

In their wanderings throughout the world the Jews have taken with them the favorite recipes of the countries in which they sojourned. In each of their temporary dwelling places they learned to use the available foods and to cook the dishes that were prevalent. Notwithstanding the constant persecutions and civil and religious prohibitions to which the Jews were subjected, they mingled with their non-Jewish neighbors, maintaining frequent and regular contacts. Even though the ghetto, a creation of the European Middle Ages, confined Jews to limited residential quarters, they absorbed influences from the contiguous communities, especially regarding cuisine. Thus the Jewish culinary art was molded largely by the non-Jewish surroundings and environment. When Jews were banished from their adopted lands the extent of their cuisine was broadened, for they kept the old dishes while constantly adding new ones. The immigrants brought with them the foods and styles of cooking borrowed from neighbors in their old countries and assimilated into their own cookery.

A large number of dishes are part of the cuisine of Jewish households in many lands, while others are purely local. Because they lived in different areas of the world it is only natural that there would be substantial differences between the cuisine of the Sephardic and the Ashkenazic Jews. The Sephardim, who by and large resided in oriental countries, were accustomed to using an abundance of vegetables, olive oil, herbs, spices, and lamb—items that were not popular among Ashkenazic Jews. The names of Sephardic dishes are generally in Spanish, Arabic, or Persian, while the foods of the Ashkenazic Jews are usually called by Yiddish names—a further indication of the divergence between them. In Spain and Portugal Jews cultivated a taste for olives and for frying fish and other foods in oil; in Eastern Europe, where olive oil was not readily available, rendered fat was used. In Germany they learned to appreciate sweet and sour stews, while in Holland they developed a penchant for pickled cucumbers and herrings, butter cakes and *bolas* (jam rolls). Kasha and blintzes came from Russia; lokshen and gefilte (stuffed) fish from Poland; and *mamaliga* from Rumania.

Today the State of Israel is a large "melting pot" or, to use a modern term, a "pressure cooker," in more than one sense, for it has gathered in Jews from the four corners of the earth who have brought with them a wide variety of recipes and styles of cooking and are rapidly creating recognizably Israeli dishes.

Many foods have been a part of Jewish tradition for hundreds of years. Indeed, the Talmud discusses some dishes that are still part and parcel of Jewish cuisine. For example, fish has been a staple on the Jewish table from time immemorial. When the children of Israel left Egypt and were wandering wearily and hungrily in the desert, they yearned for fish, as the Bible states: "We remember the fish that we used to eat free in Egypt" (Numbers 11:5). The continued attractiveness of fish may be attributed to the facts that it does not require ritual slaughtering and it can be eaten with dairy or meat meals. While smoked salmon has recently become known as a Jewish delicacy, stuffed fish is traditionally eaten on Friday night.

Although there was generally a ready acceptance of the culinary patterns of the non-Jewish surroundings and of the available foods, this was always limited by two factors that made the Jewish cuisine different: adherence to the Jewish dietary laws, and the traditional culinary observances usually associated with the Sabbath, festivals, and other festive occasions, such as circumcisions, ceremonies of the redemption of the firstborn, weddings, and mourners' meals. These traditions are derived from laws relating to special days or events, historical episodes, and legends; or they may express symbolism.

The Jewish dietary laws created a marked distinction between Jewish foods, which have to be kosher (that is, properly or ritually prepared) and non-Jewish foods. The basis of these laws is found in the Bible: "You shall be holy to Me, for I the Lord am holy, and I have set you apart from other peoples to be Mine" (Leviticus 20:26). Hence, holiness is the fundamental reason for the Jewish dietary laws, although other purposes which are subsidiary to this primary, lofty aim have been expounded. The hygienic value of the laws is considered only incidental. According to the foremost medieval philosopher Maimonides, in his *The Guide for the Perplexed,* the purpose of the prohibition of certain foods is "to control the lusts and licentiousness evident in seeking what is most pleasant and the tendency to consider the desire for food and drink as an end in itself." The dedication inherent in the dietary laws has served to link Jews with their ancestral heritage and with their fellow Jews throughout the world. They have been a very potent force in the survival of the Jewish people and a formidable barrier against assimilation. Living among the nations of the world, Jews have been enabled to preserve their identity during many centuries by adherence to these culinary regulations rooted in the Bible and the Talmud and codified in the *Code of Jewish Law.*

The basic laws of kashrut (ritual fitness) are concerned with:

1. *PERMITTED AND FORBIDDEN ANIMALS. Animals that are cloven-footed and chew the cud, usually tame and passive, are permitted to be used as food. Carnivorous animals, such as beasts and birds of prey, are forbidden because of their cruel habits. All birds (fowl) may be eaten except the kind enumerated in the Bible. Fish with fins and scales are permitted but not shellfish (Leviticus 11).*

2. *PORTIONS OF PERMISSIBLE ANIMALS. It is forbidden to eat certain portions of permissible animals, particularly the blood of animals and birds and some of the fat of animals.*

3. *PREPARATION OF FOOD. There are conditions pertaining to the preparation of food from permissible animals. Animals must be ritually slaughtered by a qualified shohet (slaugh-*

terer). The blood of animals must be eliminated by a process of soaking and salting, usually called kashering.

4. PROHIBITION OF MIXING MEAT AND DAIRY FOODS. The biblical injunction that "you shall not boil a kid in its mother's milk" (Exodus 23:19) gave rise to an elaborate procedure to prevent the mixing of meat and dairy foods. Separate dishes, utensils, and other kitchen appurtenances must be provided for meat and dairy foods, which may not be eaten together.

The holiness inspired by the laws of kashrut is not asceticism but rather consecration, devotion to divine laws with a spiritual purpose. The dining table, according to the Talmud, is considered an altar of God, and the proper offering to be placed on it is food for the indigent. The grace that is recited after every meal by pious Jews includes the following words of the psalmist: "Yet have I not seen the righteous forsaken, nor his seed begging bread" (Psalms 37:25). Bread, called by some rabbis "God's gift," had to be shared with all who were hungry. The Talmud relates that when Rab Huna broke bread for a meal, he first opened his door and said, "Let every one in need come and eat" (Taanit 20b). It is also said that "he who does not leave some crumbs for the poor deprives himself of God's blessing" (Sanhedrin 92b). As God's gift should not be wasted, it was a tradition to gather the bread crumbs left on the table and feed them to the birds. These customs lent sanctity to the Jewish home and elevated eating to a plane of spirituality. In Jewish tradition, eating is only a means of existence; it is a necessity to give one strength so that he may engage in the higher pursuits of man. "If there is no bread, there is no learning" (Avot 3:21). Thus the Jewish housewife in the kitchen, providing for the needs of her household, is performing a sacred task.

JEWISH COOKING AROUND THE WORLD is designed to assist the Jewish woman in preparing a table that will be appetizing, interesting, and in conformity with Jewish tradition. Here will be found some of the most famous national dishes from many countries, adapted to Jewish cooking. All the food products and the recipes that are given comply with the dietary laws. The serving of these foods in the style hallowed by generations of Jews is an important link in the chain of the Jewish heritage.

THE COUNTRIES

G. MILLER

CHINA

According to some reports, Jews settled in China nearly two thousand years ago, eventually became separated from the mainstream of Jewish life, and through intermarriage became indistinguishable from other Chinese.

Kaifeng Fu had the most important Jewish settlement in China. Adjoining their synagogue, said to have been erected in 1163, was a place in which the sinews were extracted from the animals slaughtered for food (see Genesis 32:33). This so impressed the Chinese that they called the Jews *Tiao Kiu Kiaou*, "the people who extract the sinews." By the twentieth century the surviving Jews were distinguished only by their names and by the fact that they did not eat pork.

In later years two other major groups migrated to China. From the Middle East, and especially Iraq, came Sephardic Jews. After the Russian Revolution large groups of Russian Jews made China their home.

Israel Cohen, in his *The Journal of a Jewish Traveller*, described a domestic scene in 1920 in the home of Sassoon J. Solomon, in Shanghai: "The Sabbath table presented the traditional genial appearance, except that the 'loaves' were large, flat, blistered pancakes, though tasting unmistakably like bread. I was told that the Sabbath bread of this shape was baked in the home of all orthodox Eastern Jews. . . . Most of the dishes were of the Baghdad or Levantine school of cooking, which is faithfully preserved in most of the Sephardic households throughout the East, and there was an unusual abundance of fruit, with divers Oriental species such as the pawpaw and the pumelo."

Although there are very few Jews in China today, there is a synagogue with a kosher kitchen in Shanghai. A transplantation from China is found in New York City—Bernstein-on-Essex Street, a restaurant where kosher Chinese dishes are served by Chinese waiters wearing black skullcaps.

EGGS FOO YUNG

6 eggs, beaten
¾ cup mushrooms, sliced
½ cup scallions, sliced
½ cup bean sprouts
salt and pepper to taste
peanut oil
½ teaspoon monosodium
    glutamate (MSG) if desired*

SAUCE
1 cup soup stock
1 tablespoon cornstarch
3 teaspoons soy sauce
dash of sugar
salt and pepper to taste

Mix the eggs with the mushrooms, scallions, and bean sprouts (any mixture of vegetables may be used). Add salt and pepper. Heat a small amount of oil in a frying pan. When oil is hot, drop the mixture by tablespoons into the oil. Cook on both sides.

To make the sauce, mix the soup stock with the cornstarch and the rest of the ingredients in a small pan. Bring to a boil, stirring constantly. Cook a few minutes. Serve with the eggs. 6 servings.

*   *   *

EGG DROP SOUP

6 cups chicken soup
½ cup cooked chicken,
    shredded
¼ teaspoon powdered ginger

1 cup fresh spinach or
    watercress
3 eggs, well beaten

To the soup, add the chicken and ginger and bring to a boil. When soup boils, add the spinach or watercress. Then pour the eggs into the boiling soup, stirring for 1 minute. Remove from stove and serve. 6 servings.

*   *   *

EGG ROLLS WITH HOT MUSTARD SAUCE

1½ cups flour
1 teaspoon salt

1½ cups water
3 eggs, well beaten

Mix the flour with the salt and water. Add the eggs and mix well. The batter should be heavier than for blintzes.

Grease and heat an 8-inch frying pan. (To expedite the process, two

---

*A full teaspoon of MSG can be added to the main dishes in this section if so desired.

frying pans can be used.) When the pan is hot, pour in ¼ cup of batter, tilting to cover the bottom of the frying pan. Cook until it is easy to turn the pancake over. Cook for a few minutes on the other side, just to dry the top. Spread on paper towels. Continue with the rest of the batter. Allow the pancakes to cool.

FILLING

3 tablespoons peanut oil
2 cups cabbage, finely
   shredded
½ cup mushrooms, sliced thin
2 celery stalks, sliced
¼ cup water chestnuts, sliced
   thin

3 scallions, sliced
½ cup bean sprouts, rinsed
   and cut fine
1 cup cooked chicken, diced
1 tablespoon soy sauce
salt and pepper to taste
1 teaspoon sugar

Heat the oil in a large frying pan. Add the cabbage and stir-fry for 3 minutes. Add the rest of the vegetables and fry 2 minutes, stirring constantly. Add the chicken and continue stirring for 1 more minute. Add the soy sauce, salt and pepper, and sugar. Allow to cool.

When the pancakes and filling are cold, fill the pancakes. On one side of the pancake place a full tablespoon of the filling. Fold two sides of the pancake over the filling and roll up to the shape of a blintze. Heat oil in a deep fryer or in a frying pan, and fry the egg rolls on all sides until brown. Remove and drain on paper toweling. Serve hot with mustard sauce. 12 egg rolls.

HOT MUSTARD SAUCE

1 tablespoon dry mustard
1 tablespoon soy sauce
3 tablespoons water

2 teaspoons prepared
   horseradish

Mix all the ingredients together and serve over egg rolls.

CHICKEN WITH ALMONDS

2 pounds chicken breast
3 tablespoons peanut oil
1½ cups Bok Choy* (Chinese
    celery), diced
¼ cup canned bamboo shoots,
    diced
¼ cup water chestnuts, diced
½ cup onions, chopped
1 cup celery, diced
2 ripe tomatoes, cut in eighths

1 package frozen snow peas,
    thawed
1 cup chicken broth
salt and pepper to taste
2 tablespoons cornstarch
1 teaspoon sugar
½ teaspoon powdered ginger
2 tablespoons sherry
½ cup almonds, blanched,
    sliced, and fried

Bone the chicken, remove fat and skin, and slice very thin (partly frozen chicken is easier to cut). Heat the oil in a large frying pan. When the oil is hot, put in the chicken pieces, and stir-fry for 3 minutes, stirring constantly so that all the pieces are cooked. Remove the chicken. To the same oil, add the Chinese celery, bamboo shoots, water chestnuts, onions, and celery, and cook for 2 minutes, stirring constantly. Return the chicken to the pan, cover, and cook for 8 minutes. Add the tomatoes and snow peas, and cook for 2 minutes.

Mix the chicken broth with the salt and pepper, cornstarch, sugar, ginger, and sherry, and add to the pan, stirring until the mixture is hot. Add the almonds and serve immediately. 6 servings.

*Available in Chinese grocery stores.

*   *   *

FRIED RICE

3 tablespoons peanut oil
¼ cup onion, chopped fine
¼ cup celery, chopped fine
3 water chestnuts, chopped
½ cup bean sprouts

2 eggs, well beaten
4 cups cooked rice
½ cup cooked chicken, diced
1 tablespoon soy sauce
salt and pepper to taste

Heat the oil in a frying pan. Add the onion, celery, water chestnuts, and bean sprouts, and sauté for 2 minutes. Add the eggs and scramble them. Add the rice and sauté for 2 minutes. Add the chicken, soy sauce, and salt and pepper, and mix all the ingredients. 6 servings.

PEPPER STEAK

2 pounds flank (flanken) steak,
  sliced thin
3 tablespoons peanut oil
3 green peppers, sliced
2 onions, chopped
2 garlic cloves, chopped
salt and pepper to taste

1 teaspoon powdered ginger
1½ tablespoons cornstarch
⅓ cup sherry
½ cup broth
1 package frozen snow peas,
  thawed

Cut the meat into slivers (partly frozen meat is easier to cut). Heat the oil in a frying pan and place the meat in it. Stir-fry for 3 minutes. Remove to a plate. Place in the pan the green peppers, onions, and garlic, and sauté for 2 minutes, continuing to stir.

Add the salt and pepper, ginger, cornstarch, and sherry to the broth, mix well, and pour over the vegetables. Place the meat and the snow peas in the pan and bring to a boil. 6 servings.

* * *

MUSHROOMS WITH CELERY

2 tablespoons peanut oil
½ pound mushrooms, sliced
3 cups celery, sliced

2 teaspoons soy sauce
salt to taste
1 teaspoon sugar

Heat the oil in a pan over a high heat. Put in the mushrooms and celery, and stir-fry for 5 minutes. Add the soy sauce, salt, and sugar, and cook for 2 more minutes. 6 servings.

* * *

CHINESE DESSERT

Serve fruits, especially oranges and lichee nuts, for dessert. Chinese tea should be served throughout the meal.

EASTERN EUROPE

Jews have lived in various parts of Eastern Europe for more than two thousand years. It is believed that there was a Jewish migration to Rumania before the advent of the Common Era and to Hungary over seventeen centuries ago. Despite their long years of residence in the East European countries, Jews were generally treated as aliens and subjected to all types of discrimination, which, however, failed to inhibit them from developing organized Jewish communities and great institutions of learning. It is interesting to note how the overt prejudices against the Jewish population in these lands affected their livelihood and even their cuisine. In the seventeenth century the Christian butchers of Vilna, fearful that their own trade would decline because of Jewish competition, lodged a series of complaints against the Jewish butchers, resulting in a judgment which greatly restricted the latter and obligated them to pay contributions to the local church of Saint Casimir. In the same period Jews were excluded from the fishermen's guild, barred from the grain business, and in other ways subjected to difficulties in earning a livelihood. Unbelievable as it may seem, the Jews of Vilna were forbidden to purchase food from farmers in the marketplaces until nine o'clock in the morning so that Christians would have the first opportunity to satisfy their needs. Similar hardships were faced by Jewish communities in other East European cities.

For many generations the Jews in Russia have been subjected to anti-Semitic attacks and to this day live in danger of complete extinction as a result of the oppressive measures exercised by the government. For example, despite verbal denials, the Soviet Union uses various subterfuges to prevent Jews from having matzah for Passover. While according to law matzah can be baked in local government bakeries, or in those bakeries reserved specifically for Passover which adjoin some of the remaining synagogues, a permit for the purchase of flour must be obtained from the authorities. In most cases such permits are not forthcoming or are issued too late to be used for the festival. Nevertheless, many conscientious Jews find clandestine ways to purchase flour, albeit at exorbitant prices, and to bake their own matzah.

In contradistinction to the Soviet Union, the Rumanian Communist regime has recognized the Jews as a national minority and allows the production and distribution of matzah and kosher wine under the auspices of the government-supported Federation of Jewish Communities, which also regulates the slaughter and sale of kosher meat. The matzah factory is actually the major source of the federation's income. In Bucharest the Jewish community maintains a kosher restaurant. The decimated Jewish population of Budapest, Hungary, has two kosher restaurants as well as a kosher welfare kitchen for the needy that is supported by the Jewish community. It is estimated that in Poland today there are only fourteen thousand Jews, a mere remnant of a pre-Hitler population of three and a half million. Nevertheless, it is reported that in Warsaw there are still restaurants that specialize in Jewish cooking. For years the American Jewish Joint Distribution Committee (JDC) has provided free kosher meals in many cities behind the Iron Curtain and even distributed food in the Warsaw ghetto.

It is evident that the prospects for the remaining Jewry under Communist regimes are most bleak. But although Jews in Eastern Europe have endured more than their share of suffering throughout the generations, there have been some bright spots. A number of Jews achieved affluence. The Brodsky family in Zlatopol, Ukraine, for example, were known as the "Sugar Kings" of Russia until the end of World War I. Not surprisingly, Eliezer Brodsky died of diabetes.

It was in the inner spiritual life of their own communities, however, that the Jews achieved their greatest accomplishments, notably in Jewish scholarship and philanthropy. Widely practiced was the system of *essen teg* (eating days). Yeshivah students were assigned for one or more days a week to have their meals as guests of families; this was, in essence, a sort of scholarship program that enabled worthy students to pursue talmudic studies. It offered out-of-town students not only a satisfactory cuisine but also the opportunity for enjoying a home atmosphere.

In Eastern Europe the Jewish dishes were generally similar to those of the people among whom they dwelt, although some of these foods are now considered Jewish in the Western world. The Jews in Russia adopted borsht, kasha, and blintzes from the non-Jewish populace and *mamaliga* (cooked cornmeal) from the Rumanians. Popular among Lithuanian Jews were *kneidlach* (dumplings), often made with mashed potatoes and put in warm milk. Tzimmes, served with meat, was made in several ways: as a compote of cooked fruits, usually prunes or plums, or as cooked vegetables, mainly carrots, with spices. In Galicia and Rumania the ingredients of the tzimmes included apples, prunes, pears, and other fruits, while in Lithuania red turnips were used. Because Polish Jews tended to have a sweet tooth sugar was added to many dishes, while Russian and Hungarian Jews preferred spicy and peppery foods.

For many years Jewish cuisine in Eastern Europe was based on two staples—black bread and potatoes. Potatoes were the main ingredients in a variety of dishes prepared by the Jewish housewife. In the fall a large stock of potatoes was stored in the cellar to insure a sufficient supply for the cold winter months. Potatoes were often eaten two or three times a day in various forms—baked whole, cooked with onions and pepper, fried, and mashed with chicken fat. The virtue of the potato was hailed in the popular folk song *"Zuntig Bulbe, Montig Bulbe . . ."* (Sunday potatoes, Monday potatoes and on the Sabbath, for a change, potato pudding. Sunday again potatoes . . .). Workingmen often sated themselves with black bread, as it was believed to have strength-giving power.

Another mainstay of the Jewish diet was *zoiers* ("sours"), that is, borsht (beet soup), *schav* (sorrel soup), and cabbage soup. According to Hirsh Abramowicz in a Yiddish article, "Food among the Jews of Lithuania" in his *Fashvundene Geshtalten* (Buenos Aires, 1958), "sours" were especially well liked, probably because these were the most economical soups to serve and because they were the only appetizers, besides herring, that they allowed themselves. "Sours" were generally eaten with bread or potatoes at a brunch, although there was no set time for weekday meals: "A worry—as long as one eats and there is something to eat." In the springtime, *schav* with a little sour cream was served; in summer, borsht mixed with *schav;* and in the winter, cabbage soup. In cold weather, when milk was scarce, *russel* (fermented beet juice) was eaten with potatoes and chopped onions, considered by Jewish gourmets as the "dish of dishes." A staple in poverty-stricken Jewish households was *krupnik,* a thick soup that was made with potatoes, groats, and fat; well-to-do families added pieces of meat to this soup.

Herring was another favorite—perhaps the national—dish of Lithuanian Jews, and it was consumed with potatoes or bread. Herring was prepared in sundry ways—pickled, sweet and sour, baked, and chopped with onions. Piroshki, dough filled with chopped meat or potatoes and baked, and piroshkes (turnovers), small cakes fried in honey or baked and then dipped in molasses, were always welcome treats. In Poland delicacies were lokshen (noodles) with soup, gefilte (stuffed) fish, and stewed fish. Cucumbers in season were also popular among Jews, and they were eaten fresh with bread and salt or pickled. Affluent Jews pickled cucumbers and stored them for the winter. Also well liked were chick-peas, lentils, and beans, especially when cooked as soups.

More often than not the foods that comprised the weekday menus were potatoes, "sours," herring, and black bread. In contrast with the daily meals, those of the Sabbath were feasts which helped make the day one of exquisite pleasure even for the most indigent. Hallah, fish and meat, and often tzimmes, noodle pudding, kreplach, honey cake, torte, and other delicacies graced the table on the Sabbath and festivals.

Hayyim Nahman Bialik, who was reared in extreme poverty in Eastern Europe and later became the Hebrew poet laureate of Palestine, visited Lithuania in 1932. He was evidently entertained by some wealthy Jews, for he was so impressed with what he considered delicacies enjoyed by the Jews of Kovno that were unknown to him in his youth that he wrote his wife: "Lithuania has learned to eat. Here they eat! They eat even tomatoes! Without tomatoes they are no longer able to exist. They eat oranges and bananas. They eat salmon and caviar—indeed, the red caviar. I believe that soon they will begin to eat also olives. They will quickly learn to accomplish this. And there is no necessity to speak about meat, fish, and dairy dishes."

*   *   *

CAVIAR

fresh fish roe (carp roe)   *hard-cooked eggs, chopped*
oil   *onions, chopped*
lemon juice   *sour cream*
salt and pepper to taste   *dark bread*

Salt the roe, and refrigerate overnight. Remove the membranes from the roe.

Put the roe in the top of a double boiler, and place over boiling water. Stir the roe with a wooden spoon until it turns pink. Remove from heat.

Beat together the oil, lemon juice, and salt and pepper until well blended. Mix this dressing with the cooked roe, adding more salt if needed.

Serve the caviar with the eggs, onions, sour cream, and dark bread.

BAKED HERRING

2 herring fillets
3 tablespoons margarine
1 onion, sliced thin

1 tablespoon flour
pepper to taste

Soak the herring fillets in cold water, and refrigerate overnight.

Melt 2 tablespoons of margarine in a baking dish. Make a layer of onions, then a layer of fillets. Mix the flour with the pepper and sprinkle over the fillets. Dot the fillets with 1 tablespoon of margarine.

Bake the herring in a 375° oven for 20 minutes.

Serve hot with baked potatoes. 2 servings.

*　　*　　*

CHOPPED HERRING

2 herring fillets
2 hard-cooked eggs
1 medium onion
1 medium apple
⅓ cup bread crumbs

pepper to taste
2 tablespoons vinegar
1 tablespoon oil
tomato slices
black olives

Soak the herring fillets in cold water, and refrigerate overnight.

Remove the herring fillets from the water and put them through a grinder with the eggs, onion, and apple. Add the bread crumbs, pepper, vinegar, and oil. Mix well. Correct the seasoning. Serve with tomato slices and black olives. 6 servings.

*　　*　　*

QUICK BORSHT

1-pound can beets
1 carrot, grated
1 onion, grated
3 cups water
2 bouillon cubes
1 bay leaf

½ teaspoon powdered garlic
juice of 1 lemon
salt and pepper to taste
sugar to taste
1 can beef and cabbage soup

Shred the beets, reserving the juice. Place the shredded beets in a pot with the beet juice, carrot, onion, and water. Bring to a boil. Add the bouillon cubes, bay leaf, and garlic powder, and cook for 15 minutes. Add the lemon juice, salt and pepper, sugar, and soup. Simmer for 5 minutes.

Correct the seasoning. Serve hot with meat or potato piroshki. 6 servings.

PIROSHKI (Knishes)

DOUGH

3 cups flour, sifted
1 cup shortening (Crisco or
  Spry type)

½ teaspoon salt
½ cup orange juice
1 egg, well beaten

Mix the flour, shortening, and salt with a pastry blender. Add enough orange juice to hold the dough together. Refrigerate overnight.

Divide the dough into 3 parts. On wax paper roll out each part into an oblong ¼ inch thick and cut each in half.

Place some of the meat or potato filling at one end of a piece of dough, and roll the dough over the filling until it is covered (like strudel). Continue to fill the other pieces of the dough in the same manner.

Place the prepared rolls on a greased foil-lined baking sheet, and brush the top with the egg. Cut the rolls halfway down in desired portions.

Bake the piroshki in a 425° oven for 15 minutes; reduce oven temperature to 375°, and continue to bake the piroshki until nicely browned. 8 to 10 servings.

MEAT FILLING

2 tablespoons margarine
1 pound ground meat
½ cup onions, chopped

1 egg
salt and pepper to taste

Melt the margarine in a frying pan. Add the ground meat together with the onions; cook, stirring the meat, until brown. Add the egg and salt and pepper, and mix well.

POTATO FILLING

2½ cups boiling water
1 teaspoon salt
½ teaspoon pepper
1 envelope instant mashed
  potatoes (4 ounces)

½ cup onions, chopped
2 tablespoons margarine
1 egg, beaten

Bring the water to a boil together with the salt and pepper. Remove from heat. Add the instant mashed potato mix, stirring constantly.

Sauté the onions in the margarine until lightly browned, and add to the potatoes, together with the egg. Cool before using as a filling.

KRUPNIK

¼ ounce dried mushrooms
8 cups beef broth
⅓ cup barley
2 carrots, diced
2 celery stalks, diced

1 onion, diced
1 potato, diced
a few parsley sprigs
salt and pepper to taste

Soak the dried mushrooms in cold water to cover for 1 hour. Remove the mushrooms but reserve the water, which will be added to the soup. Cut the mushrooms in small pieces.

Place in a soup pot the broth, barley, vegetables, mushrooms, and reserved mushroom water. Bring to a boil. Lower the heat and simmer the soup for 2 hours. Add salt and pepper. Simmer for 30 more minutes. 8 servings.

*   *   *

HEART AND LUNG STEW

½ heart
½ lung
3 cups water
2 tablespoons margarine

2 tablespoons flour
2 garlic cloves, chopped
salt and pepper to taste

Cook the heart and lung in unsalted water until tender. Reserve 3 cups of water. Remove the meat and allow to cool.

Grind the meat coarsely.

Melt the margarine in a saucepan, and add the flour. Cook and stir until the flour is browned. Slowly add the reserved water, stirring constantly, and cook the sauce until it thickens. Add the ground meat with the garlic. Add salt and pepper. Serve as a first course. 8 servings.

*   *   *

SCHAV

1 pound schav (sorrel leaves)
½ pound spinach
6 cups water
½ cup scallions, sliced thin
2 teaspoons salt

4 tablespoons sugar
4 tablespoons lemon juice
2 eggs
sour cream
dill or scallions, chopped

Wash the schav and the spinach in cold water, changing the water a few times. Discard the stems. Shred the schav and the spinach, and put them in a large pot with the water. Add the scallions. Bring to a boil, reduce the heat, and simmer for 20 minutes. Add the salt, sugar, and lemon juice. Correct the seasoning.

Beat the eggs in a bowl. Slowly add 1 cup of the hot *schav* mixture to the eggs, and then return the egg mixture to the rest of the *schav*, stirring constantly. Allow the *schav* to cool. Serve it cold with sour cream and a sprinkling of dill or scallions. 6 servings.

*   *   *

VEAL PAPRIKASH

2 onions, chopped
2 tablespoons margarine
2 pounds veal, cubed
2 carrots, grated

salt and pepper to taste
1 tablespoon paprika
1 cup tomato juice

Sauté the onions in the margarine until brown. Add the veal, carrots, salt and pepper, paprika, and tomato juice. Cover and simmer until the meat is tender. Do not add water; if more gravy is needed, use more tomato juice. 4 servings.

Serve with cabbage and noodles.

*   *   *

BEEF STROGANOFF

1½ pounds tenderloin steak
3 tablespoons margarine
½ cup onions, chopped
1 cup broth

salt and pepper to taste
1 teaspoon mustard
2 tablespoons flour
⅓ cup nondairy creamer

Cut the tenderloin steak into very thin strips, about ½ × 2-inch pieces (partly frozen meat is easier to slice).

Melt the margarine in a pan, and heat until hot. Place half of the meat strips in the pan, and brown on both sides.

Remove the browned meat to a bowl. Then place the balance of the meat strips in the pan and brown on both sides. Add the first batch of browned meat strips to the pan. Add the onions and cook for 5 minutes. Remove the meat and onions.

Mix well some of the broth, salt and pepper, mustard, and flour; add the rest of the broth and pour the broth mixture into the pan in which the meat was cooked. Bring to a boil, stirring constantly until thick and smooth. Add the meat and onions and continue to cook over low heat for 10 minutes.

Before serving, add the nondairy creamer and reheat for a few minutes. Serve with kasha or rice. 6 servings.

* * *

CABBAGE AND NOODLES

2 pounds cabbage, shredded
4 tablespoons margarine
2 onions, chopped

salt and pepper to taste
½ pound broad noodles,
  cooked

Shred the cabbage, and salt it. Allow the cabbage to stand 1 hour, then squeeze out all the water.

Melt the margarine; add the onions and sauté them for 10 minutes. Do not brown the onions. Add the cabbage and continue to sauté until almost brown. Add the salt and pepper.

Cook the noodles according to directions on the package. Drain well, and add to the cabbage and onion mixture. Reheat and serve. 6 servings.

* * *

KASHA

1 cup medium kasha
  (buckwheat groats)
1 egg, beaten

2 cups boiling water
salt and pepper to taste
2 tablespoons margarine

Mix the kasha with the egg. Place the kasha in a frying pan over high heat and cook, stirring constantly. When each grain is separate and dry, transfer the kasha to a pot. Add the boiling water and salt and pepper; cover tightly and simmer for 30 minutes. Stir the mixture a few times while it cooks. Add the margarine and serve.

Sautéed onions and mushrooms can be added to the kasha. Serve as a side dish with meat. 6 servings.

* * *

PLAIN NOODLE KUGEL

½ pound medium noodles,
  cooked
5 eggs, beaten

salt and pepper to taste
6 tablespoons margarine,
  melted

Mix the noodles with the eggs, salt and pepper, and 3 tablespoons of melted margarine.

Grease a baking dish with the rest of the margarine. Heat it in the oven. When the margarine is hot, pour in the noodle mixture.

Bake in a 375° oven for 1 hour. 6 servings.

*   *   *

POTATO STEW

6 large potatoes
3 tablespoons margarine
2 large onions, sliced thin

salt and pepper to taste
1 cup water

Peel and quarter the potatoes.

Melt the margarine and add the onions. Sauté the onions for 10 minutes, but do not brown them. Add the potatoes, salt and pepper, and water. Cover the pot and bring to a boil; reduce the heat and simmer for 1 hour. Correct the seasoning. Serve hot as a side dish. 6 servings.

*   *   *

SWEET AND SOUR LIMA BEANS

2 tablespoons margarine
1 tablespoon flour
½ cup broth
2 cups cooked dried lima beans

juice of 1 lemon
½ cup brown sugar
a few whole cloves
salt to taste

Melt the margarine in a saucepan and add the flour. Brown the flour lightly in the margarine. Remove the saucepan from the heat, and slowly add the broth, stirring until well combined. Add the beans, lemon juice, brown sugar, cloves, and salt. Transfer the bean mixture to an ovenproof dish and bake in a 350° oven for 30 minutes. 6 servings.

*   *   *

CUCUMBER SALAD

2 cucumbers, sliced thin
1 onion, sliced thin
salt

DRESSING
⅓ cup vinegar
⅔ cup water
1 teaspoon sugar

To the cucumbers and onion add the salt; allow to stand for 1 hour. Squeeze the water out of the cucumber mixture.

To make the dressing, mix the vinegar, water, and sugar. Pour the dressing over the cucumber mixture, and refrigerate for a few hours. 4 servings.

*   *   *

KISEL

1-pound bag frozen
  blackberries or strawberries
2 cups water

1 cup sugar
3 tablespoons cornstarch
nondairy creamer

Cook the berries in the water for 10 minutes. Force the berries with the water through a sieve to remove the seeds. Add the sugar, and bring again to a boil.

Mix the cornstarch with a little cold water, and add it to the boiling berries, stirring constantly. Cook for 5 minutes. Mixture will be thin.

Pour the *kisel* into individual serving dishes or into a bowl, and chill for a few hours.

Serve with nondairy creamer or, for a dairy meal, with cream. 6 servings.

*   *   *

PIROSHKES

¼ cup margarine
½ cup sugar
2 eggs
2½ cups flour, sifted

1 teaspoon baking powder
dash of salt
2 tablespoons orange juice

Cream the margarine and the sugar until fluffy. Add the eggs, one at a time, and beat until well blended.

Sift the flour with the baking powder and salt. Add the flour and orange juice to the margarine and sugar mixture, and form into dough. The dough should be soft but not sticky.

On a floured board or on wax paper, roll out the dough to a very thin square. Cut the dough into 2-inch pieces.

Make the filling and the syrup (see next page).

Place some of the filling on each square of dough. Bring up the four corners of each dough square and pinch them together, leaving the sides open.

Place the filled squares on a greased foil-lined baking pan. Bake the piroshkes in a 375° oven until lightly browned.

Place the baked piroshkes upside down in the honey syrup and cook them a few at a time for 10 minutes. With a slotted spoon, remove each one to a plate. Continue with the rest of the piroshkes until all are covered with the honey. Allow the piroshkes to stand for a day before serving.

FILLING

3 cooking apples
½ cup brown sugar
½ cup chopped nuts

¼ cup white raisins
2 tablespoons candied lemon
    peel, cut fine

Peel and grate the apples. Put the apples in a saucepan with the sugar, nuts, raisins, and lemon peel, and cook over a medium heat until all the juice is evaporated. Stir the apples frequently while cooking so the mixture will not burn. Cool before using.

SYRUP

¾ pound honey

1 or 2 teaspoons powdered
    ginger

Bring the honey to a boil, lower the heat, and simmer for 5 minutes. Add the ginger. Use 1 or 2 teaspoons of ginger, depending on whether a mild or a more pronounced taste of ginger is desired.

*   *   *

CHOCOLATE NUT TORTE

7 eggs, separated
10 tablespoons sugar

2½ ounces bittersweet
    chocolate, grated
10 tablespoons nuts, chopped

Beat the egg yolks with 5 tablespoons of sugar until lemon-colored, and then stir in the chocolate and the nuts.

Beat the egg whites until stiff, and continue beating as you slowly add the rest of the sugar.

Blend the two mixtures together gently, folding the white mixture into the egg yolk and chocolate mixture.

Pour the mixture into a springform pan, and bake the cake for 1 hour in a 325° oven. Remove and cool the cake. When the cake is cold, run a knife all around the cake pan, and gently remove the sides of the pan. Transfer to serving dish, leaving the cake on the bottom of the pan.

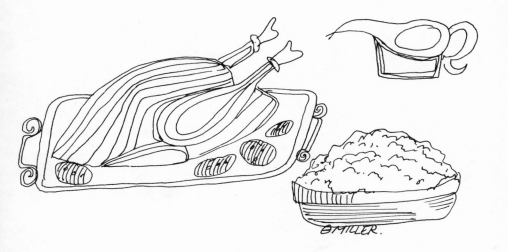

ENGLAND

There are records of ecclesiastical enactments against Jews in England as early as the seventh century. One church law stated: "If any Christian accepts from the infidel Jews their unleavened cakes [matzot] or any other meat or drink and shares in their impieties, he shall do penance with bread and water for forty days." However, when the Archbishop of Canterbury decreed that Christians could not sell any food to Jews so that they would not mingle with them, Henry III (1207–1272) countermanded the order. On the other hand, the following statement in a twelfth-century rabbinical work gives evidence that English Jews sought opportunities for social mixing with Christians: "It is surprising that in the land of the Isle [England] they are lenient in the matter of drinking strong drinks of the gentile and along with them. For the law is distinctly to forbid it on the ground that it leads to intermarriage. But perhaps, as there would be great ill feeling if they were to refrain from this, one must not be severe with them."

In 1836 Sir Moses Montefiore, the leading Jewish personality of England in the nineteenth century, wrote in his diary: "I had the honour of dining with their Royal Highnesses, the Duchess of Kent and the Princess [later Queen] Victoria. . . . There were thirteen at the table, and it was impossible for it to have been more agreeable. I never felt myself more at ease at any dinner party within my recollection." Sir Moses was able to have such inner security despite the fact that he was an observant Jew who at public banquets and receptions refrained from eating food that was nonkosher, partaking only enough to satisfy the social obligations. It is well known that during his many travels he always took along a Jewish cook and his own kitchen utensils.

The relationship between the Jewish community and the board of governors of London Hospital was so excellent that the hospital made special provisions to meet the kosher food needs of Jews. In the hospital's minutes of 1756 an item headed "Jews' Diet" appears, which states that Jews were "to be allowed Twopence Half-penny per Day in lieu of Meat or Broth, but to receive Bread and Beer like the other patients, according to the diet they are on." In Leeds, current British efforts to provide for Jewish hospital patients have resulted in a unique Jewish communal organization—Hospital Meals and Visitation. This agency maintains a kosher kitchen and, upon request, caters meals to the sick in any hospital of the city.

A striking example of British governmental cooperation to serve Jewish dietary needs is the Kosher School Meals Service organized during World War II. The scarcity of food prompted English authorities to set up a system of serving meals in schools, which continued after the war. The 1944 Education Act of England reinforced the practice and obligated the educational authorities to provide a wholesome and substantial meal to all pupils of schools maintained or aided by the state. In 1940, when large numbers of children were evacuated from London and other cities to Bishop's Stortford, a town in Hertfordshire, a substantial number of Jewish children were among them. A Kosher Canteen Committee was appointed by the chief rabbi of England to work with the authorities in providing kosher meals for these Jewish evacuees. Since the war the Kosher Canteen Committee has been operating in a number of other places and serving thousands of kosher luncheons daily. While the state pays the cost of the meals for the Jewish children, as it does for the non-Jewish children, the added expense of kosher meals and the initial cost of the equipment is borne by the Jewish community.

A Soup Kitchen for the Jewish Poor, established in London in 1854, is still functioning. It has ceased ladling out soup and now distributes canned soup and other food items.

An insight into the culinary interests of Jews can be gained from a visit to Whitechapel, the Jewish neighborhood in the East End of London. Similar in many respects to New York's Lower East Side of yesterday, Whitechapel still features open-air markets with a wide variety of food displays. The Jewish bagel woman with her sack or basket of the rings of baked dough was a familiar sight in the East End. One delicatessen shop, which sold kippered, schmaltz, chopped, and pickled herring, also advertised "pickled herrings in wine sauce." A food inspector, noting the absence of wine in the herring sauce, hailed the shop owner to court. The defendant claimed that the alcohol evaporated after several days. Thereupon the judge stated, "Apparently the fish swallowed the alcohol." This may be the origin of the colloquialism "pickled," meaning drunk.

In the eighteenth century, many turbaned Moroccan Jews were engaged in peddling spices and "Turkey" or "Russian" rhubarb. In the beginning of the next century Jews held a practical monopoly on the sale of nuts, lemons, and oranges. Well-to-do Jewish merchants were importers and wholesalers of these luxuries, and Jewish youngsters would hawk them. Some of these street vendors eventually became storekeepers and wholesale merchants. At this period Michael Myers was the leading fish dealer in London. Indeed, since his trade card boasted, "M. Myers, Fishmonger to His Majesty," he evidently had a royal appointment.

H. Mayhew, in his *London Labour and the London Poor* (1851), reported that there were twenty to forty Jewish sellers of pastry, who obtained their supplies from about a dozen Jewish pastrycooks in Whitechapel. Among the delicacies they handled were "bowlers": round tarts made of sugar apples and bread. Mayhew claimed that "the articles vended by the Jews are still pronounced by many connoisseurs in street pastry to be the best."

The earliest Jewish cookbook in English was published in London in 1846, entitled *The Jewish Manual: Or, Practical Information in Jewish and Modern Cookery, with a Collection of Valuable Recipes & Hints relating to the Toilette*. The title page reveals that this volume was "Edited by a Lady."

A favorite dish of English Jews is salmon—fried, white-stewed, or brown-stewed. A specifically Jewish preparation is white-stewed fish with lemon and bread balls. Israel Zangwill, British author of the classic *Children of the Ghetto* (1892), wrote: "Other delicious things there are in Jewish cooking—but fried fish reigns above all in cold, unquestioned sovereignty. No other people possesses the recipe."

*   *   *

WELSH RAREBIT

½ pound cheddar cheese, diced
2 tablespoons butter
½ teaspoon dry mustard
¼ teaspoon paprika

1 teaspoon Worcestershire
   sauce
¼ cup milk

Put all the ingredients in the top of a double boiler, and place over hot but not boiling water. Keep the water simmering over low heat and stir until all the cheese is melted and the mixture becomes the consistency of heavy cream. Pour over hot toast. 4 servings.

FISH AND CHIPS

½ cup flour
salt and pepper to taste
2 pounds fillet of fish
   (flounder, cod, or haddock)
oil for frying

1 package frozen French fried
   potatoes
lemon slices
parsley

Mix the flour with salt and pepper. Dip the fish into the flour and coat it on all sides. Fry in either deep or shallow hot oil until golden brown on both sides. Be careful not to overcook the fish. Drain on paper towels.

While the fish is frying, place the frozen potatoes on a foil-lined cookie sheet, and bake in a 375° oven for 20 minutes. Serve with the fried fish and lemon slices, and garnish with the parsley. 4 servings.

*   *   *

STEWED FISH

3 pounds salmon, sliced
2 medium onions, sliced
2 cups water
½ cup vinegar
a few cloves
a few peppercorns
4 bay leaves

⅓ cup raisins
½ cup brown sugar
¼ cup lemon juice
1 tablespoon flour
½ teaspoon powdered ginger
lemon slices

Salt the fish, and refrigerate it for a few hours.

Place the sliced onions and water in a pot, and cook for 10 minutes. Add the vinegar, cloves, peppercorns, bay leaves, raisins, sugar, and lemon juice. Put the fish in the pot and bring to a boil. Lower the heat and simmer for 20 minutes. Carefully remove the fish to a serving dish. Mix the flour with a little cold water, and add it and the ginger to the fish sauce. Stir and cook over low heat for 15 minutes. Pour the sauce over the fish. Garnish with lemon slices. Serve hot or cold. 6 servings.

STEAK PIE

1 ½ pounds shoulder steak (3
slices)
½ cup flour
salt and pepper to taste
3 tablespoons margarine
2 onions, chopped
1 bouillon cube

1 cup boiling water
1 bay leaf
5 peppercorns
2 celery stalks
1 large carrot, diced
½ pound mushrooms, sliced

Cut the steak in small pieces. Put the flour and salt and pepper in a paper bag, and mix. Put the meat in the bag and shake the bag to coat the meat with the flour.

Melt 2 tablespoons of margarine in a large fryer. When the margarine is hot, put in the pieces of meat and brown on all sides. Remove the meat. Add another tablespoon of margarine and the onions, and cook until soft, but do not brown. Return the meat to the pan.

Dissolve the bouillon cube in the boiling water and pour it over the meat and onions. Add the bay leaf, peppercorns, and celery. Cover the pan and simmer 1 hour. Allow to cool. Remove the bay leaf, peppercorns, and celery. Add the carrots and mushrooms. Transfer to a casserole.

Make the pie crust (see below). Roll the pie crust so that it will cover the casserole. Make slits in the crust and put it on top of the meat, crimping to the edge of the casserole. Bake in a 425° oven for 15 minutes, then reduce to 375° and bake for 30 minutes or until crust is browned. 4 servings.

The meat for the casserole and the pie dough can be prepared in advance. The pie dough will even be flakier if chilled overnight.

PIE CRUST

1 ½ cups flour, sifted
½ cup shortening (Crisco or
Spry type)

¼ teaspoon salt
¼ cup orange juice

Put the flour into a mixing bowl, and add the shortening and salt. Blend well with a pastry blender. Add the orange juice and mix lightly. Wrap in wax paper and chill.

The top of the pie can be glazed with an egg mixed with 1 tablespoon of water.

YORKSHIRE PUDDING

1 cup flour
salt to taste
2 eggs, beaten

1 cup water
4 tablespoons margarine

Put the flour and salt in a bowl, and, with mixer at low speed, add the eggs and water slowly. Mix until the batter is smooth. Let stand for a few hours.

Preheat oven to 375°.

Put the margarine in a 9 × 9-inch baking dish, and heat it in the oven until hot. Pour the batter into the dish, and bake for 30 minutes. Break into pieces to serve with roast beef. 6 servings.

*   *   *

DUNDEE CAKE

½ cup currants
½ cup raisins
¼ cup candied orange peel,
  chopped
¼ cup candied lemon peel,
  chopped
¼ cup candied cherries,
  chopped

½ cup almonds, chopped
2 cups self-rising flour
¾ cup (1½ sticks) margarine
1 cup sugar
4 eggs
½ teaspoon almond extract
½ teaspoon lemon extract

Line a 3 × 6½ × 10½-inch loaf pan with foil and grease well.

Mix all the fruits and the almonds with ¼ cup of flour.

With a mixer, cream the margarine with the sugar until fluffy. Add the eggs, one at a time, with a little of the flour. Add the almond and lemon extracts and the balance of the flour. Mix the dredged fruit into the batter, and then pour into the loaf pan.

Bake for 1½ to 1¾ hours at 325°. Remove from oven and allow to stand in pan until cool.

The cake, if wrapped well in foil, can be kept in the refrigerator and served as needed.

MERINGUE CAKE

4 egg whites (at room
   temperature)
¼ teaspoon salt
1½ cups sugar

1 teaspoon vinegar
1 teaspoon vanilla
1 tablespoon cornstarch

Beat the egg whites with the salt, and add the sugar a little at a time, beating constantly. Add the vinegar, vanilla, and cornstarch. Beat until all the sugar is dissolved and the mixture is thick and shiny. Shape the meringue into an 8-inch circle on a baking sheet covered with oiled foil. Bake for 1 hour at 250° and then leave in oven for 30 minutes. Cake will expand a little. Remove from foil, and put meringue cake on a large serving dish.

TOPPING

1 cup heavy sweet cream or 1
   container nondairy topping
1 large can crushed pineapple,
   well drained

1 cup sliced peaches, well
   drained
a few red and green
   maraschino cherries, well
   drained

Beat the cream or topping until thick. Add the pineapple to half of the cream, and put on top of the cake. Then spread the rest of the cream or topping on the cake and sides. Decorate the top with the drained peach slices. Garnish with the cherries.

Cover the cake with plastic wrap and allow it to mellow in the refrigerator for 24 hours.

The meringue cake without the topping can be baked as much as two weeks before serving. It should be wrapped in foil and stored in a tin.

FRANCE

While it was not until the French Revolution of 1789 that Jews were granted equal rights and citizenship, they had long participated in many aspects of life in France. Although the number of Jews who lived in the country during the first six centuries of the Common Era was not large, they evidently enjoyed good relationships with the general community, for we find that the church councils came to frown upon fraternization with Jews. Concerned with safeguarding Christians against Jewish influence, the councils prohibited certain contacts with Jews. They were zealous in protecting the prestige of the church, which, it was thought, suffered when Christians ate Jewish dishes while Jews considered Christian food to be ritually unfit. The church councils repeatedly decreed that members of the clergy were forbidden to partake of meals prepared by Jews or to serve them as guests in their own homes.

It is interesting to note that in the eleventh century it was a custom for non-Jews to send their Jewish neighbors gifts of leavened cakes, eggs, and other foods on the last day of Passover as they knew that the Jews did not have any leavened products throughout the festival.

During the Middle Ages many Jews were active in the manufacture of wine in France. Rabbi Solomon ben Isaac of Troyes (popularly known as Rashi), the great scholarly luminary of medieval French Jewry whose influence reached far and wide, earned his livelihood by cultivation of the vine. His intimate knowledge of vintage is found in his extensive commentaries on the Bible and Talmud. Among the outstanding wines of France are those produced by members of the Rothschild family during the past one hundred years in the beautiful cellars at Château Lafitte-Rothschild and Château Mouton-Rothschild. At the end of the nineteenth century Baron Edmond de Rothschild of Paris established the famous wine cellars in Rishon Letzion, Israel, which now enjoy an international reputation.

Jewish tourists in France inevitably gravitate toward the neighborhood of the former Paris ghetto, now known as The Pletzel, where signs call attention to kosher butcher shops, bakeries, and restaurants. Here typically East European Jewish dishes are served rather than French cuisine. A distinguished American rabbi on a brief visit to Paris was escorted to one of these restaurants by a welcoming committee. At the end of the meal the visitor facetiously remarked to his host, "I do not understand why people rave about French cooking. We have the same dishes at home."

More appreciative of French contributions to civilization was Heinrich Heine, who found refuge in Paris, where he wrote *Hebrew Melodies* and other works. He is buried in Paris and memorialized by the Rue Henri Heine. It was Heine who wrote: "Honor to the French! They have taken good care of the two greatest human needs—good eating and civic equality."

*   *   *

QUICHE LORRAINE

1 cup flour, sifted	3 eggs
⅓ cup shortening	1 cup sour cream
2–3 tablespoons orange juice	½ cup milk
4 tablespoons butter	salt and pepper to taste
2 cups onions, chopped	

Mix the flour and the shortening, cutting in with a pastry blender. Add just enough orange juice to hold the dough together. Roll out on a pastry board to a 10-inch circle. Lift into a 9-inch pie plate. Crimp the edges. To prevent the pie shell from shrinking, put 2 pieces of wax paper (2 × 4 inches each) on opposite sides of the pie shell. Now put another pie plate of same size over the paper. Bake in a 425° oven for 8 minutes. Remove the top pie plate and the wax paper carefully. (This unorthodox way of making a pie shell will probably shock many cooks, but I find it works well for me every time!) Bake the pie shell for a few more minutes but do not brown.

Heat the butter in a frying pan and add the chopped onions. Cook until soft but do not brown (10 to 15 minutes). Allow the onions to cool.

Beat the eggs, and add the cream, milk, and salt and pepper. Add the cooled onions.

Pour the egg mixture into the pie shell, and bake at 350° for 30 minutes or until the center is firm. Serve hot or cold. 6 to 8 servings.

PISSALADIERE (Onion Pie)

2 cups flour
½ teaspoon salt
1 envelope dry yeast
½ cup warm water (105°–115°)
1 egg, beaten
1 tablespoon oil

TOPPING
2 onions, sliced
2 garlic cloves, cut fine
4 tablespoons olive oil
2 tomatoes, chopped
salt and pepper to taste
1 can flat anchovies, drained
Greek black olives, pitted and
    quartered

Mix the flour with the salt. Dissolve the yeast in ¼ cup warm water. Add the egg, oil, and the yeast to the flour. Mix well. Add more warm water, just enough to make a smooth dough. Knead for a few minutes. Put the dough in a well-oiled bowl, turning the dough to bring the oiled side up. Cover and let rise in a warm spot until double in bulk (2 to 3 hours). Roll out the dough to ¼-inch thickness and line a 10-inch pie plate with the dough.

While the dough is rising, prepare the topping.

Cook the onions and garlic in the olive oil until the onions are soft, but not browned. Add the tomatoes and salt and pepper, and cook for 10 more minutes over very low heat. Allow to cool. Cover the dough with the sauce. Arrange the anchovies spoke-fashion on the topping, and decorate between the anchovies with the black olives.

Bake in a 375° oven for 25 to 30 minutes. Serve hot. 8 servings.

*   *   *

ONION SOUP

2 medium onions
2 tablespoons margarine
1 tablespoon flour

4 cups water
4 bouillon cubes
salt and pepper to taste

Slice the onions very thin. Heat the margarine, and cook the onions in it, being careful not to brown them. When the onions are soft, add the flour and cook for a minute. Then add the 4 cups of water with the bouillon cubes. Stir well, and add salt and pepper. Simmer for 30 minutes. Serve with toast or French bread. 4 servings.

POT-AU-FEU

3 pounds lean chuck
bones
3 quarts water or soup stock
1 onion, studded with 3 cloves
1 garlic clove
2 celery stalks with leaves
a few parsley sprigs

2 bay leaves
¼ teaspoon peppercorns
1 medium parsnip
2 teaspoons coarse salt
3 carrots, quartered
3 leeks, white part only
1 medium white turnip

Put the meat and bones in a soup pot and add the water or soup stock. Slowly bring to a boil, skimming frequently. Add the onion, garlic, soup greens (celery, parsley, bay leaves, peppercorns, and parsnip), and salt. Simmer for 2 hours. Add the carrots, leeks, and turnip. Cook for 1 more hour or until meat is tender.

Remove the meat from the soup. Discard the soup greens, but not the carrots, leeks, and turnip. Strain the soup and cool.

When the soup is cold, refrigerate it so that the fat will solidify on top. When ready to serve, remove the fat and bring the soup to a boil. Correct the seasoning. Serve the soup plain or with any soup garnish.

The meat is served as the main course with the vegetables. Reheat the meat in some of the soup. Serve the meat with tomato sauce, mustard, and pickles. Peeled potatoes can also be cooked with the carrots and leeks in the soup and served with the meat. 8 servings.

*   *   *

BOUILLABAISSE

½ pound codfish
½ pound red snapper
½ pound sea bass
½ pound mackerel
½ pound carp
½ pound fillet of flounder
2 cups water
a few parsley sprigs
1 carrot
1 celery stalk
1 onion, sliced
2 tomatoes, sliced

2 garlic cloves, crushed
1 bay leaf
pinch of saffron
pinch of thyme
½ teaspoon fennel seeds
piece of dry orange peel
1 tablespoon tomato paste
1 parsley sprig, chopped
salt and pepper to taste
½ cup white wine
¼ cup olive oil

To make the fish stock, place the fish heads and bones into the water and add parsley sprigs, carrot, and celery. Cook for 20 minutes. Strain and reserve the fish stock.

In a heavy pot put the onion, tomatoes, garlic, bay leaf, saffron, thyme, fennel seeds, orange peel, tomato paste, chopped parsley, salt and pepper, fish stock or water, wine, and olive oil. Put all the fish except the fillets on top of the vegetables. Cover and bring to a boil; boil for 10 minutes over high heat. Add the fillets and cook for 5 minutes. Correct the seasoning.

Serve in soup plates, dividing the assorted fish in each plate. Pour the stock over the fish.

Any fish combination can be used. It is also delicious when reheated the next day. 6 servings.

* * *

FISH FILLETS IN WINE

1 small carrot, chopped
¼ cup onion, chopped
1 bay leaf
½ lemon, sliced thin
1 pound fillet of flounder

salt and pepper to taste
pinch of thyme
½ cup white wine
parsley

Combine the vegetables and bay leaf, and place in a well-greased baking dish. Arrange the sliced lemon over the vegetables and lay the fillets on top. Add salt and pepper, and sprinkle the thyme over all. Pour the wine over the fish. Bake in 400° oven for 20 minutes. Garnish with parsley. 3 servings.

* * *

CARP À LA JUIVE

2 small onions, sliced thin
½ cup olive oil
2 pounds carp, evenly sliced
1 tablespoon flour
1 garlic clove, crushed
¼ cup white wine
fish stock or water

1 celery stalk
1 parsley sprig
1 small carrot, sliced
1 small bay leaf
salt and pepper to taste
pinch of saffron
chopped parsley

Cook the onions in ¼ cup of the oil until soft. Put the sliced carp on top of the onions and add the flour. Add the garlic. Cover the fish with the wine and stock or water. Add the bouquet garni (celery, parsley, carrot, and bay leaf tied together) and salt and pepper, and cook for 20 minutes.

Remove the fish to a serving dish. Discard the bouquet garni. Boil down the fish stock by two-thirds and beat in the rest of the oil drop by drop. Add the saffron. Pour the fish stock over the fish. Sprinkle with parsley. 4 servings.

*   *   *

TROUT IN WINE

2 tablespoons onion, chopped
2 tablespoons parsley, chopped
pinch of thyme
salt and pepper to taste

1 bay leaf
⅓ cup red wine
2 small trout (about 1 pound)
butter or margarine

In a baking dish, put half the onion and half the parsley. Add the thyme, salt and pepper, bay leaf, and wine. Lay the fish over the vegetables. Sprinkle the fish with the rest of the onions and parsley. Dot with butter or margarine. Bake in 375° oven for 30 minutes. 2 servings.

*   *   *

DUCK À L'ORANGE

1 duck (4–5 pounds)
salt and pepper to taste
½ cup white wine
2 oranges
1 tablespoon sugar

1 tablespoon vinegar
juice of ½ lemon
1 cup water
1 bouillon cube
1 orange, sliced for garnish

Roast the duck for 20 minutes in 450° oven. Pour off the fat. Lower the oven heat to 350°. Sprinkle the duck with salt and pepper and baste with the wine. Roast until the duck is tender.

While the duck is roasting, prepare the sauce. Grate the rind of the oranges. Combine the sugar and vinegar, and bring to a boil. Add the juice of the oranges, lemon juice, the water with the bouillon cube, and the grated orange rind. Simmer for 5 minutes.

Disjoint the duck and arrange on a platter. Remove all the fat from the roaster in which the duck was roasted and add all the brown juice left in the roaster to the orange sauce. Pour the sauce over the duck.

Garnish with orange slices. 4 servings.

BOEUF À LA MODE

3 pounds boneless pot roast,
   tied
3 tablespoons brandy (cognac)
veal bones
12 small white onions or 3
   regular onions, cut up
3 carrots, cut in thirds

1 cup white wine
pinch of thyme
2 bay leaves
3 parsley sprigs
1 garlic clove
salt and pepper to taste
1 cup soup stock

Have the butcher put a layer of fat around the meat. Brown the meat on all sides in a heavy saucepan. Pour the brandy over the meat and ignite. Add the bones, onions, carrots, wine, thyme, bay leaves, parsley, garlic, and salt and pepper. Add the stock and bring to a boil.

Lower the heat and cover pot. Allow to simmer for 4 hours or until the meat is tender. Remove the meat and cut against the grain in thin slices. Remove the vegetables and arrange around the meat. Reduce the gravy somewhat and skim the fat. Pour the gravy over the meat. The gravy can be strained and served in a sauce boat. 6 servings.

*   *   *

BLANQUETTE DE VEAU

3 pounds veal (shoulder center
   cut), cut in 12 slices
3 cups water
12 small white onions
2 carrots, cut in large pieces
1 onion, studded with 3 cloves
1 celery stalk with leaves
2 parsley sprigs
2 bay leaves
1 garlic clove

a few peppercorns
salt to taste
dash of white pepper
pinch of thyme
¼ pound mushrooms, sliced
2 tablespoons margarine
2 tablespoons flour
2 egg yolks
1 tablespoon lemon juice
chopped parsley

Cover the veal slices with the water. Bring slowly to a boil, skimming all the time. If there is too much scum, take the meat out of the water and strain the water through cheesecloth. Return the water and meat to the pot. Reduce the heat, and add the small onions, carrots, and onion studded with cloves. On top of the meat and the vegetables, put the celery, parsley, bay leaves, and garlic. Add the peppercorns, salt, white pepper, and thyme. Cook for about 1½ hours or until the meat is tender.

Remove the meat, white onions, and carrots. Discard the parsley, celery, bay leaves, peppercorns, and the onion with cloves.

Sauté the mushrooms in the margarine for 5 minutes. Remove the mushrooms to the meat dish. Add the flour to the margarine left in the pan in which the mushrooms were sautéed and cook for a few minutes but do not brown the flour. Reduce the soup stock to half its original volume by boiling at high heat and slowly add to the flour, stirring constantly. Cook for 10 minutes. Beat the egg yolks and add the lemon juice. Slowly combine the egg yolks with the stock. Heat but do not boil the sauce.

Arrange the meat and vegetables on a platter; cover with the sauce and sprinkle with parsley. 6 to 8 servings.

*   *   *

CASSOULET (Lamb and Bean Casserole)

2 cups dried Great Northern
  beans
2 pounds lamb (shoulder lean)
3 tablespoons margarine
2 large onions, sliced thin
4 tablespoons tomato paste

2 garlic cloves, crushed
salt and pepper to taste
pinch of thyme
½ cup water
1 pound garlic salami

Soak the beans in water overnight. Bring to a boil and simmer beans until they are tender. (Ready-cooked white beans in cans can be used.)

In the meantime, in the margarine brown the lamb on all sides. Remove the meat and place the onions in the margarine. Brown the onions. Add the tomato paste, garlic, salt and pepper, thyme, and water. Add the lamb. Bring to a boil and simmer until meat is tender. Slice the meat.

Layer the meat and beans in a casserole. First put some of the beans, then some of the meat and some of the salami sliced into small chunks. Cover with the onions and the sauce in which the meat was cooked. Add another layer of beans and meat and more beans on top.

Bake in 325° oven for 2 hours. During the baking period stir the top layer down so that the beans will have browned by the time it is ready to serve. Longer baking will not spoil this dish.

The cassoulet can be prepared ahead and refrigerated overnight, then baked the next day. 6 servings.

PEAS À LA FRANÇAISE

8 lettuce leaves, shredded
6 small white onions
½ teaspoon salt
1 teaspoon sugar

parsley sprig
½ cup water
1 package frozen peas
2 tablespoons margarine

In a saucepan put the lettuce, onions, salt, sugar, parsley, and water. Bring to a boil and add the frozen peas. Cook for 20 minutes. Add the margarine and bring to a quick boil. 4 servings.

*   *   *

POTATOES LYONNAISE

4 tablespoons margarine
1 large onion, sliced thin

1 pound cooked potatoes,
   peeled and sliced
salt and pepper to taste

Melt the margarine and add the onion. Sauté until slightly browned. Remove onions and add the potatoes. Cook for 15 minutes, shaking pan a few times. Add the onions and salt and pepper, and cook for 10 more minutes, shaking pan occasionally. 4 servings.

*   *   *

BUTTERED SPINACH

1 package frozen spinach,
   chopped
salt and pepper to taste

2 teaspoons lemon juice
dash of garlic powder
3 tablespoons margarine

Cook the spinach according to directions on the package. Add the salt and pepper and then the lemon juice and garlic powder. Bring to a boil and add the margarine. Mix well and serve. 3 to 4 servings.

*   *   *

RATATOUILLE (Eggplant Stew)

⅓ cup olive oil
1 large onion, sliced thin
1 pound eggplant, peeled
½ green pepper, sliced thin

2 tomatoes, peeled and
   quartered
1 garlic clove, chopped fine
salt and pepper to taste

Heat the oil, and add the onion. Cook for 10 minutes but do not brown. Cut the eggplant into small pieces and add it to the oil. Add the green pepper. Cook covered for 10 minutes. Add the tomatoes, garlic, and salt and pepper, and cook for 10 more minutes. 4 servings.

*   *   *

RICE SALAD

1 cup cooked rice
1 tomato, peeled and cut in small pieces
1 green pepper, cut in small pieces
1 small onion, chopped

1½ tablespoons salad oil
1½ tablespoons wine vinegar
¼ teaspoon dry mustard
dash of white pepper
dash of black pepper
salt to taste

Put all ingredients together in a bowl. Mix well. Chill and serve. 4 servings.

*   *   *

POTATO SALAD NIÇOISE

1 pound potatoes, cooked
1 small onion, sliced thin
¼ cup green pepper, cut fine
parsley sprig, chopped fine
2 tablespoons olive oil
1 tablespoon wine vinegar

salt and pepper to taste
½ teaspoon garlic powder
18 black olives
6 anchovy fillets, cut in pieces
2 tomatoes, sliced

Cut the potatoes in thin slices and add the onion, green pepper, and parsley. Mix the olive oil with the vinegar, salt and pepper, and garlic powder. Pour over the potatoes. Mix lightly. Stir in 12 olives.

Arrange the salad on a plate and garnish with the rest of the olives, the anchovies, and the tomatoes. Chill and serve. 4 servings.

CRÊPES SUZETTE

3 eggs
2 tablespoons sugar
½ cup flour, sifted
1 cup milk
1 tablespoon butter, melted
1 teaspoon orange extract

SAUCE
3 tablespoons butter
5 tablespoons confectioners'
  sugar
peel of 1 orange, grated fine
3 tablespoons orange liqueur
½ cup orange juice
3 tablespoons brandy (cognac)

In a medium bowl, beat the eggs and the sugar. Add the flour with the milk, and beat until well blended. Add the butter and orange extract, and beat the mixture until it is smooth. Let it stand for 2 hours.

Heat a 5- or 6-inch frying pan and grease well. When the pan is hot (a drop of water will "dance" on the bottom), pour 2 tablespoons of the batter into the frying pan, quickly rotate the pan so as to cover the bottom with the batter. Cook for 1 minute, then turn crêpe and cook on the other side for another minute. Remove the crêpe to a plate. Repeat with the rest of the batter, greasing between each crêpe. There will be approximately 24 crêpes.

To make the orange sauce, cream the butter with the confectioners' sugar; add the orange peel and the orange liqueur. Mix well.

On each crêpe spread about ½ teaspoon of the butter and orange sauce, and then fold each in half twice.

Place the rest of the butter and sugar sauce in a chafing dish and add the orange juice. Bring to a boil, lower heat, and place the folded crêpes in the sauce, spooning some of the sauce over them.

To create an interesting effect, bring the dish to the table in a darkened room, pour the cognac over the crêpes, and ignite with a match. When flames die out, serve the crêpes and sauce. 5 servings.

Crêpes and sauce can be prepared in advance and refrigerated till needed.

*   *   *

CHEESE SOUFFLÉ

2 tablespoons butter
2 tablespoons flour
¾ cup hot milk

4 eggs, separated
1 cup grated cheddar cheese
salt and pepper to taste

Melt the butter in a saucepan and then add the flour. Cook for a few minutes, stirring constantly, but do not brown the flour mixture. Remove from heat and slowly add the milk, stirring as you add. Return the pot to the fire and keep stirring until the sauce is smooth. Remove from heat.

Beat the egg yolks, and mix some of the sauce into them. Slowly stir the yolk mixture into the sauce. Add the cheese and salt and pepper, and return to flame. Cook, stirring, until the cheese is melted. Allow to cool.

Beat the egg whites until stiff, and fold them into the sauce. Pour the mixture into a buttered soufflé dish or a casserole. Bake for 25 minutes at 375°. Serve immediately. 4 servings.

*   *   *

MOUSSE AU CHOCOLAT

¼ pound semisweet chocolate   4 eggs, separated
¼ cup sugar   1 teaspoon vanilla
2 tablespoons water or wine

Melt the chocolate in top of a double boiler over hot but not boiling water. Remove the chocolate and add the sugar and water or wine. Mix well until the sugar is dissolved. Beat the egg yolks well with the vanilla, and add to the chocolate mixture. Beat the egg whites until stiff and fold gently into the chocolate mixture. The mixture will thicken when chilled. Pour in individual glasses or small cups. Chill for a few hours or overnight. 4 servings.

The mousse may be poured over canned pears or used as a quick icing for a cake.

*   *   *

PEARS IN WINE

½ cup sugar   1 tablespoon lemon juice
2 cups water   8 medium pears, peeled
4 cloves   1 cup red wine

Mix the sugar with the water, and add the cloves and lemon juice. Poach the pears in this syrup for 30 minutes. Add the wine, and cook for 15 more minutes. Remove the pears from the syrup to a bowl. Reduce the syrup by a third and pour it over the pears. Chill. 4 servings.

BABA AU RHUM

1 envelope dry yeast
½ cup warm water (105°–115°)
2 egg yolks
2 whole eggs
¼ cup sugar

¼ pound margarine, melted
2 cups flour, sifted
½ teaspoon salt
1 teaspoon vanilla
2 tablespoons currants

Dissolve the yeast in ¼ cup of warm water.

With a mixer, beat the egg yolks and the 2 whole eggs with the sugar, and add the margarine and the other ¼ cup of warm water. Beat well. By hand, slowly blend in the flour and salt. Beat well and add the dissolved yeast, mixing with a wooden spoon. Add the vanilla and currants. Beat again. Grease a bowl and put the dough into the bowl. Cover the dough with wax paper and a towel, and let it rise in a warm place until it doubles in bulk (about 2 to 3 hours).

Grease a large ring mold or cake pan and fill it with the dough to two-thirds capacity. Let it rise uncovered in a warm place until the dough reaches the top of the mold. Bake in 350° oven for 30 minutes.

While the cake is baking prepare the rum syrup.

SYRUP

¾ cup apricot nectar
½ cup sugar

1 teaspoon lemon juice
¼ cup rum

Bring the apricot nectar, sugar, and lemon juice to a boil. Simmer for 10 minutes over very low heat. Add the rum.

When the cake is baked, remove from oven and unmold while hot onto a large serving dish. Pour the hot syrup over the hot cake, and then spoon the syrup that collects on the bottom of the dish over the cake. Serve the cake warm or cold.

*   *   *

ECLAIRS

½ cup margarine
1 cup water
1 cup flour, sifted

½ teaspoon salt
4 eggs

Put the margarine and water in a saucepan. Bring to a boil. When the margarine is melted, add the flour and salt all at once, and with a wooden spoon mix well, until the mixture is smooth and does not cling to the sides of the pan. Remove from the fire.

Stir the eggs, one at a time, into the mixture. Beat well until the mixture is smooth.

Shape the dough, or force it through a pastry bag, into 1 × 4-inch oblongs on an ungreased baking sheet, allowing 2 inches between each eclair.

Bake the eclairs for 40 minutes or until lightly browned in a 400° oven. Loosen the eclairs and cool on a rack. Small cream puffs can also be made from the same dough and used with a variety of fillings. Bake them for a shorter period.

Two different fillings are given—one dairy and the other pareve—so that eclairs can be served with dairy or meat meals.

CREAM FILLING

1 package vanilla pudding mix   1 cup whipped cream
1½ cups milk

Mix the pudding with the milk, and slowly bring to a boil, stirring all the time until thick. Cover with wax paper and allow to cool. When cold, add the whipped cream and beat pudding until smooth. Cut the eclairs lengthwise. Fill with the pudding and replace the top. Glaze with chocolate glaze.

LEMON CHIFFON FILLING

¾ cup sugar   *6 tablespoons lemon juice*
4 tablespoons cornstarch   *2 tablespoons margarine*
1½ cups water   *grated peel of 1 lemon*
3 eggs, separated   *confectioners' sugar*

Mix the sugar with the cornstarch and the water, and bring to a boil. Stirring all the time, cook over low heat for about 10 minutes until clear and thick.

Beat the egg yolks and mix with the lemon juice. Slowly stir a little of the cornstarch mixture into the egg yolks. Then pour the egg yolk mixture into the cornstarch mixture. Return to heat and cook for 2 minutes, stirring constantly. Add the margarine and the lemon peel. Cool. Beat the egg whites until stiff. Gently fold the egg whites into the cornstarch and egg yolk mixture. Cool.

Cut the eclairs in half and fill with lemon pudding. Sprinkle with confectioners' sugar.

CHOCOLATE GLAZE

1 cup chocolate chips (6-ounce   2 tablespoons margarine
* package)*

Melt the chocolate pieces and the margarine in the top of a double boiler, over hot water, until smooth. Spread some of the chocolate over each eclair. 12 to 15 eclairs.

*   *   *

BRIOCHES

1 envelope dry yeast
⅓ cup warm water (105°–115°)
1 teaspoon sugar
5 cups flour (approximately)
1 teaspoon salt

1 tablespoon sugar
6 eggs
½ cup margarine
1 egg, beaten

Dissolve the yeast in the warm water and add 1 teaspoon of sugar and 1 cup of flour. Knead into a ball. Put in a bowl. Gash an × on the top of the ball of dough with a knife, and cover with warm water. The ball will rise to the surface in about half an hour.

In a deep bowl put 3 cups of flour, the salt, and 1 tablespoon of sugar. Make a well in the center of the flour, and add 6 eggs and the margarine. Mix together well. The dough will be very soft. Add the ball of the sponge dough to the flour and mix well. It will take a while to mix. Add a little more flour and knead until you have a smooth piece of dough. Put the dough in a greased bowl and cover it with a towel; let it rise in a warm place until double in bulk. Punch down, and knead again for a few minutes. Put the dough in a greased bowl and cover tightly with foil. Refrigerate overnight.

Before using dough, punch down again. Take off a quarter of the dough and set aside. Grease 24 cupcake forms or brioche molds. Into each mold place a small ball of dough. From the quarter of the dough that was set aside, make 24 smaller balls and put them on top of each of the other balls. Set the brioches to rise in a warm place out of drafts. When they double in bulk, brush them with 1 egg beaten with 1 tablespoon of water. Bake in a hot 425° oven until they are brown. The brioches freeze well. 24 brioches.

GERMANY

During the first millennium of the Common Era, Jews in Germany enjoyed fair living conditions, engaging in trade and commerce. With the increasing ecclesiastical authority in the Middle Ages their situation worsened, and social intercourse between Jews and Christians declined. The latter were not permitted to eat or drink with Jews or to purchase food from them. These restrictions applied especially to meat and wine, as they were prepared according to Jewish ritual.

Many Jews who lived in the rural communities of Germany were cattle dealers and peddlers who trudged for miles and miles with heavy packs on their backs. In addition to the normal hardships of the road, the peddlers faced a special problem—the lack of kosher food. For their main sustenance they usually carried a large loaf of bread. Occasionally they would be fortunate enough to enjoy the hospitality of a Jewish family. Some village inns kept a saucepan with the Hebrew word kosher written on the back, reserved exclusively for the use of Jewish peddlers. Undoubtedly these itinerants would have welcomed manna from heaven such as that depicted in a stained-glass window in the Church of St. Jacob in Rothenburg: the scene shows the ancient Israelites, wandering in the desert, being showered with manna in the shape of bread, rolls, and pretzels.

Among the communal institutions maintained by Jews in German ghettos was a bakery, for only the well-to-do could afford the luxury of a fully equipped home kitchen. This was used for the baking of matzah for Passover. On Friday afternoon the cholent or *schalet*—the main course of the Sabbath midday meal—was taken to the bakery, also called the *schalantus,* and left overnight to be kept warm in the large stove. Although each pot of *schalet* was identified with the owner's name—and some of the vessels were even locked—there were, alas, frequent instances of "mistaken identity." Besides *schalet,* the stuffed neck of a goose, sweet and sour fish, and meat were some of the favorite dishes of German Jews. In some parts of Germany the

Sabbath bread was called *tatcher*, and in others, *barches*. Both names are derived from the verse *"Birkhat ha-Shem hi ta'ashir* (The blessing of the Lord, it maketh rich [Proverbs 10:22])."

In Mainz, and probably in other cities, the Jewish community owned a copper caldron which could be used by a family in preparing for a wedding feast. When festive occasions created undue extravagance, the Jewish officials set specific limitations on them. In 1728 the community of Fürth issued an ordinance which stated that guests might not be served tea or coffee with meals and that late arrivals to a repast could be given only soup and those courses that had not yet been served.

Anti-Semitism, which played more than a minor role in Germany for many centuries, reached its peak with the rise of Adolf Hitler. Slow starvation was one of the effective means employed by the Nazis to achieve their goal of mass extermination. The ritual slaughter of animals and the purchase of most basic food items were prohibited, while the food rations doled out to Jews were far below any recommended minimal calorie count. Ironically, the inn in Berchtesgaden, which Hitler built for Nazi leaders and his personal guests, was taken over by the U.S. Army for military personnel on leave and was named the General Walker Hotel. Jewish soldiers and chaplains stationed in Europe who gathered there for religious retreats were served kosher meals.

*   *   *

LINSENSUPPE (Lentil Soup)

soup bones	*1 carrot, chopped*
8 cups water	*2 celery stalks, chopped*
1 cup lentils	*1 pound salami*
1 onion, chopped	*salt to taste*

Place the bones in a soup kettle, cover with the water, and bring to a boil. Add the lentils, vegetables, and salami. Cover and simmer until the lentils are very soft. Take out all the bones and discard. Remove the salami, cut in small pieces, and return them to the soup. Bring to a boil and add the salt. 6 servings.

SAUERBRATEN

4 pounds shoulder steak or
  chuck roast
salt and pepper to taste
½ teaspoon garlic powder
1 carrot, sliced
2 onions, sliced
3 bay leaves
½ teaspoon peppercorns

1 teaspoon sugar
2 cups white vinegar
2 tablespoons margarine
2 onions, chopped
⅓–½ cup brown sugar
½ teaspoon ginger or 8
  gingersnaps
1½ tablespoons flour

Put the meat in a large glass bowl. Add salt and pepper. Sprinkle with
garlic powder. Put in the vegetables, bay leaves, and peppercorns.
Add the sugar to the vinegar, and pour over the meat. Cover tightly
and refrigerate.

Meat can be kept in the marinade a few days. Turn the meat over
in the marinade twice a day. Remove the meat from the marinade and
dry on paper towels.

Heat the margarine in a deep pot, and place the meat in the pot;
brown well on all sides. Add the chopped onions, and sauté for 10
minutes. Pour the strained marinade over the meat. Bring to a boil,
lower heat, and simmer for 2 hours. Add the brown sugar and the
ginger or gingersnaps. Continue cooking until the meat is tender.
Remove the meat and slice. Mix the flour with some of the liquid and
add to the pot. Correct the seasoning. Serve the meat with the gravy.
8 servings.

*   *   *

POTATO PANCAKES

6 large potatoes
1 large onion, grated
5 eggs

salt and pepper to taste
½ cup matzah meal
oil for frying

Peel and grate the potatoes. Squeeze out all the water. Add the onion,
eggs, salt and pepper, and matzah meal, and mix well. Heat some oil
in a frying pan; when oil is hot, drop in the mixture by large spoonfuls.
Fry on each side and then remove to paper towels. Yields 18 to 20
large pancakes.

If desired, the pancakes can be prepared ahead of time. Fry lightly
on both sides and then freeze. Before serving, lay pancakes on a

foil-lined baking sheet in one layer and heat them in a 375° oven for 30 minutes.

*   *   *

GEBRATENE GANS (Roast Goose)

10–12-pound goose
6 apples, quartered
salt and pepper to taste
paprika

onion powder
garlic powder
1 ½ cups orange juice

Remove all the fat from the goose. Stuff the goose with the apples. Salt and pepper it, and sprinkle with the paprika and onion and garlic powders. Put on a rack and roast in a 425° oven for 30 minutes. Remove as much of the fat in the roaster as possible. Baste with a third of the orange juice. Lower the heat to 325° and continue roasting, basting the goose with the balance of the orange juice every 30 minutes. Again remove all the fat accumulated in the roaster. Roast the goose until you are sure it is tender (the time required for roasting depends on the age of the goose). If possible, roast the goose in advance. Cool and carve in serving pieces, reserving the apples. If necessary, roast again until tender. Serve with the apples. 8 servings.

*   *   *

CELERY KNOB SALAD

1 pound celery knob
¼ cup vinegar
1 small onion, chopped

salt and pepper to taste
1 tablespoon sugar

Peel and cut the celery into large pieces. Cover with cold water and bring to a boil. Cook until the celery is tender. Cut into small pieces. Add the vinegar, onion, salt and pepper, and sugar. Mix well. Serve cold. 6 servings.

*   *   *

CHESTNUT, PEAR, AND PRUNE COMPOTE

1 pound chestnuts
6 fresh cooking pears, peeled
1 pound sour prunes

½ cup raisins
½ cup brown sugar
1 cup white wine

Cover the chestnuts with cold water and bring to a boil. Cook for 10 minutes. Peel the chestnuts while still hot, removing the brown skins.

Put the pears in water to cover and cook for 10 minutes. Add the prunes, raisins, and chestnuts, and continue cooking for 10 more minutes over low heat. Add the brown sugar and wine, and cook for 5 minutes. Serve hot or cold. 8 servings.

*   *   *

ALMOND AND APPLE PUDDING

margarine
4 large apples, peeled and
    quartered
¼ cup raisins
6 eggs, separated

½ cup sugar
½ cup almonds, chopped
½ cup bread crumbs
grated peel of 1 lemon

With the margarine grease well a 9 × 9-inch baking dish. Put in the apples and the raisins.

Beat the egg yolks with the sugar until light and lemon-colored. Add the almonds, bread crumbs, and lemon peel to the egg yolks. Beat the egg whites until stiff and add to the egg yolk mixture, folding gently. Pour over the apples and raisins. Bake for 1 hour in a 350° oven. Serve with the lemon sauce. 8 servings.

LEMON SAUCE

1 cup water
1½ tablespoons cornstarch or
    potato flour

⅔ cup sugar
juice of 2 lemons
3 eggs, separated

Mix the water, cornstarch, and sugar in a saucepan. Add the lemon juice and the egg yolks. Bring to a boil, stirring constantly until thick. Remove from fire. Beat the egg whites until stiff; slowly add the egg yolk mixture, and mix well. Serve the sauce cold on the hot pudding.

GREECE

Josephus, the Jewish historian of the first century, established the existence of Jewish contacts with Greece in very early times. It is therefore not surprising that in Jewish folklore there are numerous legends of contests of wit between the residents of Athens and those of Jerusalem. These disputes were intended to demonstrate the sharpness of mind of the Jewish children of Jerusalem. Two examples are appropriate to our subject, food. An Athenian visiting Jerusalem accosted a child and gave him a small coin with the request that he buy something to eat that would sate his hunger and still leave a sufficient amount to eat on his return journey to Athens. The child bought salt for the visitor. Another legend is recorded of an Athenian who asked a Jewish boy of Jerusalem to purchase eggs for him and various kinds of cheese. When the lad did as requested, the Athenian asked him, "Tell me, child, which cheese was made from the milk of a white goat and which cheese from the milk of a black goat?" The lad promptly retorted, "I will gladly reply to your question but, since you are my elder, I would like you to answer my question first: Which egg came from a white hen and which egg from a black hen?"

In the sixteenth century Don Joseph Nasi, a leading Jew, was appointed as duke of Naxos and the Archipelago by Selim II, sultan of Turkey. Naxos was renowned for its vineyards and wines, as well as for its rich groves of olives, oranges, lemons, and pomegranates. The duke also owned the famous vineyards of Chios.

Salonika was a great center of Jewish life for two thousand years. The only organized group of Jewish fishermen in any part of the world existed there for many generations, until World War II. They even had their own synagogue. In recent years a large number of the fishermen migrated en masse, with their boats and fishing gear, to Israel, where they still ply the trade they inherited from their ancestors.

Before World War II, a popular rendezvous, not only for Jews but also for local Greeks in Salonika, was the Jewish restaurant of Almosnino, who may have been a descendant of the sixteenth-century Rabbi Moses Almosnino of Salonika.

The porter of the Jewish school in Salonika, Shalom, would go to the homes of the pupils before noon and bring them hot lunches which their mothers had prepared. A popular dish often found in the lunch baskets was grape leaves stuffed with meat or rice and pignon nuts. When the meals were distributed, the children would barter their deserts—a piece of *pistil* (dried apricot) for baklava or a slice of *halva* for *kourabiedes*. Your children will also enjoy these Greek delicacies.

*   *   *

SPINACH PASTRY

2 packages frozen chopped
   spinach
1 medium onion, chopped
3 tablespoons butter or
   margarine
¼ cup dill, chopped
¼ cup parsley, chopped

2 scallions, chopped
salt and pepper to taste
6 strudel leaves*
4 tablespoons butter or
   margarine, melted
6 ounces cream cheese

Defrost the spinach, and cook without water until soft.

Sauté the onion in 3 tablespoons of butter, but do not brown. Add the dill, parsley, and scallions. Add the spinach and let cool. Season with salt and pepper.

In a 8 × 10-inch well-greased pan lay 1 strudel leaf, folding if necessary. Brush generously with some of the melted butter. Add 2 more leaves, brushing each with melted butter. Put the spinach mixture on the top of the leaves, and scatter the cream cheese over the spinach. Put the other 3 strudel leaves over the cream cheese and spinach. Brush with the rest of the butter. (If desired, the cheese may be omitted.)

Bake for 30 minutes in a 350° oven. Serve hot or cold. 6 servings.

*Available in Greek grocery stores and gourmet food shops.

DOLMADES (Stuffed Grape Leaves)

42 grape leaves*
⅓ cup olive oil
1 cup onions, chopped
¼ cup regular rice
½ cup parsley, chopped
½ cup dill, chopped

¼ cup pine nuts
salt and pepper to taste
2 tablespoons lemon juice
2 tablespoons olive oil
1¼ cups water

Blanch the grape leaves in boiling water. Let stand for 5 minutes. Pour off the water.

To make the filling, heat the olive oil in a frying pan. Add the onions, and sauté for 10 minutes. Add the rice, and cook for 10 minutes. Add the parsley, dill, and pine nuts, and continue cooking for 5 additional minutes. Add the salt and pepper. Cool.

On each leaf, put one teaspoon of the rice mixture. Fold the leaf not too tightly over the rice and then roll it up as you would roll a cigarette. Place the dolmades with the seam down in a flat pot. Add the lemon juice, olive oil, and water. Cover with a plate to keep the dolmades in place and then cover the pot. Bring to a boil, lower the heat to simmering, and simmer for 45 minutes or until the rice is done and all the water is absorbed. Serve cold. 42 small dolmades (number of servings depends on size of portion).

*Available in Greek grocery stores and gourmet food shops.

* * *

DOLMADES STUFFED WITH MEAT

30 grape leaves
1 pound ground meat
1 cup onions, chopped
¼ cup rice
1 teaspoon dry mint, crushed
3 tablespoons parsley, chopped

¼ cup soup stock
1 tablespoon olive oil
salt and pepper to taste
2 tablespoons margarine
2 egg yolks
juice of 1 lemon

Blanch the grape leaves in boiling water. Let stand for 5 minutes. Pour off the water.

Mix the ingredients for the filling: the meat, onions, rice, mint, parsley, soup stock, olive oil, and salt and pepper. Place a little of the filling on each grape leaf and roll up. Arrange them in a pot with the seams down to prevent them from opening. Pour some water or soup stock over them to cover and add the margarine. Cook over a low heat for 1 hour. Remove from heat.

Beat the egg yolks with the lemon juice. Spoon some of the stock from the pan over the yolks, mixing well, and slowly add the egg and lemon sauce to the pan. Return to the fire and, stirring constantly, cook over low heat until it comes to a boil. Remove from heat. Pour the sauce over the dolmades and serve hot. 30 small dolmades.

*   *   *

AVGOLEMONO (Egg-Lemon Soup)

1/3 cup rice	2 egg yolks
6 cups soup stock	juice of 1 lemon
salt and pepper to taste	parsley for garnish

Add the rice to the soup stock and bring to a boil. Cook until the rice is soft. Add the seasoning.

Beat the egg yolks until light and add the lemon juice. Slowly pour some of the hot soup into the egg and lemon mixture, stirring constantly. Add the egg and lemon mixture to the rest of the soup, continuing to stir. Bring the soup almost to a boil (do not boil or it will curdle). Serve garnished with parsley. 4 generous servings.

*   *   *

BEAN SOUP

1 cup dried white beans	salt and pepper to taste
1 cup onions, chopped fine	1/2 teaspoon garlic powder
1 tablespoon oil or margarine, melted	(optional)
	1/4 teaspoon thyme
1 carrot, sliced	3 tablespoons tomato sauce
1/2 cup celery, sliced	water or soup stock
a few parsley sprigs	1 tablespoon wine vinegar

Soak the beans overnight in cold water to cover. The next day cook them in the same water until half done.

Sauté the onions in the oil or margarine until golden. Add the onions to the beans, together with the prepared vegetables. Add salt and pepper, garlic, thyme, and tomato sauce; cover with water or soup stock and simmer for 3 hours. Correct the seasoning. Remove the parsley. Add the wine vinegar. 4 servings.

PSARI PLAKI (Baked Fish)

1 3-pound striped bass, sliced
2 medium onions, chopped
¼ cup parsley, chopped
1 large garlic clove, mashed
salt and pepper to taste

1 cup solid pack tomatoes
½ cup white wine
½ cup tomato juice
⅓ cup olive oil
¼ cup lemon juice

Put the fish in a greased baking dish. Over the fish, sprinkle the onions, parsley, garlic, and salt and pepper. Top with the tomatoes. Pour the wine, tomato juice, olive oil, and lemon juice over the fish. Bake for 1 hour in a 350° oven. 6 servings.

*   *   *

STIFFADO (Beef Stew)

3 tablespoons margarine
3½ pounds shoulder steak,
    sliced
2 pounds small white onions
5 garlic cloves, cut in half
1 can tomato paste

½ cup water
1 cup dry red wine
2 bay leaves
½ stick cinnamon
salt and pepper to taste

Melt the margarine in a heavy frying pan. When the margarine is hot, add the meat and sear on all sides over high heat. Sear a few pieces at a time so that the meat will brown on all sides. Remove the meat to a dish, add the onions and garlic, and brown them quickly. Return the meat to the pan.

Add the tomato paste, water, wine, bay leaves, cinnamon, and salt and pepper. Cover the pot, lower the heat, and simmer the meat for 4 to 5 hours. Skim the fat from the gravy. 10 servings.

This dish can be prepared the day before serving. In fact, the flavor will improve if it stands overnight. Reheat before serving.

MOUSAKA

1 pound eggplant, peeled
oil or margarine
1 pound ground meat
1 cup onions, chopped
2 tablespoons tomato paste
3 tablespoons red wine or
    tomato juice

2 tablespoons parsley, chopped
dash of cinnamon
1 large garlic clove, mashed
salt and pepper to taste
3 eggs
2 tomatoes, sliced
bread crumbs

Peel and cut the eggplant in ¼-inch slices. Lay the slices on foil and sprinkle with salt. Let stand for 1 hour. The salt will remove the water from the eggplant. Rinse the slices in water, and pat them dry with paper toweling.

Sauté the slices in oil or margarine on both sides until golden brown.

In a large frying pan, heat 2 tablespoons of oil or margarine, and sauté the meat and onions until brown. Add the tomato paste, wine or tomato juice, parsley, cinnamon, garlic, and salt and pepper; simmer over moderate heat, stirring frequently until all the juice has been absorbed.

In a greased 9 × 9-inch baking dish arrange the eggplant slices. Cover with a layer of meat, and then cover with the rest of the eggplant.

Beat the eggs, and pour them over the meat and eggplant. Arrange the tomatoes on top, and sprinkle with a layer of bread crumbs. Bake in a 375° oven for 35 minutes. 4 servings.

This dish will improve if kept standing one day. Reheat before serving.

*   *   *

KOTOPOULO ME LEMONO (Chicken with Lemon Sauce)

1 3-pound chicken
2 quarts water
1 carrot
3 celery stalks
1 onion
a few parsley sprigs
salt to taste
2 tablespoons margarine or oil
1 cup rice
1½ cups chicken stock

SAUCE
¼ cup margarine
¼ cup flour
2 cups chicken stock
3 egg yolks
3 tablespoons lemon juice
salt and pepper to taste

Place the chicken in a soup pot with the water. Bring to a boil and skim. Lower the heat, and add the vegetables and salt. Cook the chicken until tender. Take the chicken out of the pot, and carve into portions. Strain the soup and reserve 1½ cups for the rice and 2 cups for the sauce.

Heat the margarine or oil, add the rice, and cook for 5 minutes, stirring occasionally. Add 1½ cups boiling chicken stock and bring to a boil. Lower the heat, and cover the pot. Cook the rice for about 20 to 25 minutes or until the rice is tender.

To make the lemon sauce, melt the margarine and blend in the flour; gradually stir in the chicken stock, and then bring it to a boil. Cook until smooth, stirring constantly. Beat the egg yolks with the lemon juice and salt and pepper. Add some of the sauce to the egg yolk mixture, stirring constantly. Add this to the rest of the sauce. Add the chicken, and heat slowly but do not boil.

Arrange the rice in the middle of a platter with the chicken and sauce around it. 4 servings.

Cooked leftover chicken can be used, as well as canned chicken soup and instant rice.

*   *   *

REVIDIA YAHNI (Chick-peas)

½ pound chick-peas
1 onion, sliced
1 cup solid pack tomatoes

a few parsley sprigs
4 garlic cloves
salt and pepper to taste

Soak the chick-peas overnight with water to cover. In the same water, bring the chick-peas to a boil, lower the heat, and simmer until soft. Add the onion, tomatoes, parsley, and garlic; season with salt and pepper. Cook for 30 more minutes. Remove the parsley. Serve hot. 6 servings.

*   *   *

BAMIES (Okra with Tomatoes)

1 small onion, chopped
¼ cup oil
¼ cup stewed tomatoes or 2
   tomatoes, peeled and
   chopped

1 tablespoon parsley, chopped
1 tablespoon lemon juice
salt and pepper to taste
½ pound okra

Cook the onion in the oil until soft. Add the tomatoes, and cook for 10 minutes. Add the parsley, lemon juice, salt and pepper, and okra, and cook over low heat for 30 to 40 minutes. Shake the pan occasionally. 4 servings.

Frozen okra may be used. Follow directions on package for cooking.

*   *   *

EGGPLANT WITH YOGURT

1 pound eggplant
2 tablespoons olive oil
1 large garlic clove, mashed
½ teaspoon oregano

½ teaspoon onion powder
salt and pepper to taste
1 cup yogurt

Peel the eggplant and cut in small pieces. Sprinkle with salt, and let stand for 1 hour. Wash and dry the pieces. Heat the oil in a frying pan; add the eggplant and stir-fry until soft. Add the garlic, oregano, and onion powder; season with salt and pepper to taste. Just before serving, add the yogurt. Serve hot or cold. 4 servings.

*   *   *

SALATA (Mixed Greens)

2 tomatoes, quartered
1 cucumber, sliced thin
2 scallions, sliced
2 tablespoons parsley, chopped
½ green pepper, sliced thin

1 head of romaine or escarole,
  shredded
2 celery stalks, sliced thin
2 tablespoons dill, chopped
1 head of lettuce, shredded

Chill all the vegetables and mix in a large bowl. Before serving, pour the dressing over the greens, and toss lightly.

DRESSING

½ cup olive oil
¼ cup wine vinegar
dash of dry mustard

1 small garlic clove, mashed
salt and pepper to taste

Mix all the ingredients in a jar, and shake well. 8 servings.

*   *   *

PEPPER SALAD

8 fresh green peppers
6 tablespoons olive oil

6 tablespoons wine vinegar
salt and pepper to taste

Place the peppers on a piece of foil. Broil the peppers in a 400° oven, turning them over every few minutes until skin cracks.

Remove them to a plate. Hold each under water and remove the skin. Remove the seeds and membranes. Slice thin.

Put in a bowl, and pour the oil and vinegar over them. Add salt and pepper. Chill. Prepare the peppers a day before serving. 8 servings.

*   *   *

KOURABIEDES (Butter Cookies)

½ pound butter or margarine   2 tablespoons brandy
⅓ cup confectioners' sugar   2½ cups flour, sifted

Cream the butter or margarine for 10 minutes with an electric mixer. Add the sugar and continue beating for 10 more minutes. Add the brandy. Add the flour and mix well. Dough will be soft. Chill in refrigerator for 1 hour or more.

Shape the dough into little oblong cakes, about 2½ inches long. Place on an ungreased baking sheet, and bake in a 350° oven for 15 minutes. Do not brown them. When cooled, sift confectioners' sugar over the cookies. Store in an airtight container. Approximately 36 cookies.

*   *   *

KARETHOPETA (Nut Cake)

¼ cup margarine
½ cup sugar
4 eggs, separated
1 cup flour, sifted
1 teaspoon baking powder
1 teaspoon cinnamon
2 cups walnuts, chopped

SYRUP
½ cup sugar
¼ cup water
½ cup honey
½ teaspoon cinnamon
2 tablespoons rum

Cream the margarine, add the sugar, and beat until fluffy. Add the egg yolks one at a time. Beat the egg whites until stiff. Fold the beaten egg whites into the egg yolk mixture. Combine the flour with the baking powder and cinnamon, and add to the mixture. Add the nuts, mixing well. Pour into a 9 × 9-inch greased pan and bake in a 350° oven for 30 minutes.

While cake is baking, make the syrup. Boil together the sugar and water. Lower heat, and simmer for 10 minutes until syrupy. Stir in the honey and cinnamon. Cook for 5 more minutes, and then add the rum.

Pour the hot syrup over the hot cake. Let the cake stand overnight before serving.

*   *   *

YOGURT CAKE

3 cups flour, sifted
2 teaspoons baking powder
¼ teaspoon salt
5 eggs, separated

1 cup margarine or butter
2 cups sugar
½ pint yogurt
1 teaspoon vanilla

Sift the flour with the baking powder and salt. Beat the egg whites until stiff. With the same beater, cream the margarine or butter with the sugar until fluffy. Add the egg yolks, one at a time. Add the flour mixture alternately with the yogurt, starting with the flour and ending with the flour. Add the vanilla. Mix well. Add the beaten egg whites, folding gently. Pour the batter into a 9 × 12-inch greased and floured pan. Bake in a 350° oven for 1 hour. Remove from oven and allow to cool.

*   *   *

HALVA (Farina Cake)

¼ pound margarine
½ cup sugar
3 eggs, separated
1 cup semolina* (farina)
1 teaspoon baking powder
1 cup ground almonds
¼ cup pine nuts
½ teaspoon cinnamon
1 tablespoon vanilla or brandy
    extract

SYRUP
¾ cup sugar
¾ cup water
1 stick cinnamon
4 cloves
¼ cup honey
1 tablespoon brandy extract

Cream the margarine and the sugar. Add the egg yolks, one at a time, and beat until fluffy. Mix the semolina with the baking powder, almonds, pine nuts, and cinnamon; add to the margarine mixture. Add the flavoring. Fold in the beaten egg whites. Pour the mixture into a well-greased 9 × 9-inch pan. Bake in a 375° oven for 30 minutes.

While cake is baking, make the syrup. Cook the sugar with the water, cinnamon, and cloves for 15 minutes. Add the honey. Remove the cinnamon and cloves. Add the brandy extract. Cool and pour over the cooled cake.

Available in Greek grocery stores and gourmet food shops.

*   *   *

BAKLAVA

3 cups walnuts, chopped
1 cup sugar
1½ teaspoons cinnamon
1 teaspoon allspice
1 pound strudel leaves
1 pound margarine, melted
whole cloves

SYRUP
1 cup water
1 cup sugar
1½ cups honey
1 teaspoon vanilla
1 teaspoon cinnamon

Grease a 9 × 12½-inch baking pan.

Mix the walnuts with the sugar, cinnamon, and allspice.

Place 4 strudel leaves in the pan, brushing each leaf with the margarine. On top of the leaves put a sprinkling of the walnut mixture. Place another leaf on top, and cover with a layer of walnut mixture. Continue this procedure, making sure to brush each leaf with the margarine, until there are 4 to 6 leaves remaining which are to be placed on top.

For easier slicing, dip a knife in melted margarine. Cut the pastry into 2-inch strips and then cut these strips to make diamond-shaped pieces. With a teaspoon pour some of the melted margarine between the cut strips, and pour the rest over the entire surface. Stud each piece with a whole clove.

For the syrup, mix the water and sugar in a saucepan, and simmer over low heat for 12 minutes. Then add the honey, vanilla, and cinnamon, and simmer for 5 more minutes.

Bake the baklava in a 300° oven for 30 minutes, and then slowly pour half of the hot syrup on top. Increase the oven temperature to 400° and continue baking until the syrup has been absorbed.

Remove from oven and pour the rest of the syrup on top. The baklava should be made the day before serving so that all the syrup will be absorbed. Cut into 2¼ × 3-inch pieces. 16 large servings.

INDIA

India was described as "the land of pepper, cinnamon, and ginger" by Benjamin of Tudela, the famous twelfth-century Jewish world traveler. Among the colorful Jewish communities of India are the Bene-Israel, who claim a long history in that country yet were practically unknown to European Jews until the nineteenth century. According to their tradition (which has been challenged), David Rahabi, a Cochin Jew, visited them in the tenth century and, to test their Jewishness, offered to the Bene-Israel women fish, some of which had no fins or scales. The women promptly separated the finless and scaleless fish from the others, maintaining they did not eat such fish. In this manner they convinced their visitor that they were Jews.

One of the harvest festivals observed by the Bene-Israel, on the evening of the fourth of Tishri, is called Khiricha San (Pudding Holiday) and is celebrated by the eating of *khir*, a pudding made of new corn mixed with coconut juice and sweets. Before this dish was eaten, the *Shema* was recited.

The Ninth of Av was called Birdiacha Roja (Fast of Curry) since the break-the-fast meal consisted solely of rice with curry of *birda*, made of *wal* or pulse that was sprinkled with water until it sprouted and then husked and cooked with spice. Prior to the fast, food was served on plantain leaves, symbolizing that "the Israelites had no household utensils from which to partake their food at the time of the loss of their dominion and power," according to H. S. Kehimkar in his *History of the Bene-Israel of India*. In more modern times the fast was broken by eating beans or cereal soaked in water to make it sprout. The beans coming to life by absorbing water symbolized the revival of the Jewish nation.

Kehimkar noted that on the eve of Yom Kippur the main meal included "gharies (cakes of rice flour fried in oil); some pieces of puries (tarts) made of wheat flour and sugar or coconut kernel scrapings and jaggery; and some pieces of liver and gizzards, fried in oil; different kinds of fruit; subja; and a cup of wine, etc."

The diet of the Bene-Israel was generally simple and frugal, with unleavened bread, rice bread, and rice as their main staples.

*   *   *

DHALL CURRY (Lentil Curry)

1 cup dried lentils	*2 dried chilis, seeded and*
water to cover	*crushed*
2 onions, chopped	*1 green pepper, chopped*
1 large garlic clove, chopped	*1 teaspoon curry*
2 tablespoons margarine	*salt and pepper to taste*

Cook the lentils in water to cover until soft but not mushy.

Sauté the onions and garlic in the margarine for 10 minutes. Add the chilis and green pepper, and cook for a few minutes.

Add the cooked lentils to the onion mixture. Add the curry and salt and pepper. Serve with rice. 6 servings.

*   *   *

CHOWL (Rice)

1 cup regular rice	*water to cover*
salt	

Wash the rice in cold water. Put the rice and salt in a pot, and add boiling water to cover. Bring to a boil, lower heat, and cook the rice for 15 minutes. Put the rice in a strainer and pour cold water over the rice to separate the grains of rice. Return to pot and keep warm. 6 servings.

*   *   *

VEGETABLE STEW

3 tablespoons oil	*3 tomatoes, cubed*
1 onion, chopped	*water*
1 garlic clove, chopped	*¼ teaspoon powdered cloves*
2 tablespoons coconut, grated	*½ teaspoon whole mustard*
1 tablespoon curry powder	*seed*
1 large eggplant, cubed	*salt and pepper to taste*
1 green squash, cubed	

Heat the oil in a pot. Add the onion and garlic, and sauté for 10 minutes. Add the coconut and the curry, and sauté for 1 minute. Add the eggplant, squash, and tomatoes. Add water to cover, and stew the vegetables until tender. Add the cloves, mustard seed, and salt and pepper. Stew may be served cold as a salad. 6 servings.

*   *   *

MACHLI WITH DAHI (Fish and Yogurt)

1 large onion, chopped
1 garlic clove, chopped
1 teaspoon salt
pepper to taste
1 teaspoon turmeric
1 teaspoon coriander
dash of cloves

1 cup yogurt
2 pounds halibut, sliced
4 tablespoons margarine or
  butter
2 cups cooked rice
2 tomatoes, cut in eighths

Mix the onion, garlic, salt, pepper, turmeric, coriander, and cloves with the yogurt, and pour over the fish. Let stand for 1 hour.

Remove the fish from the yogurt and reserve mixture.

Heat 2 tablespoons of the margarine or butter in a casserole or frying pan. Sauté the fish on both sides until slightly brown.

Heat oven to 350°.

When fish is browned, cover it with half the yogurt, and then with the rice and tomatoes. Add the rest of the yogurt and spread over the fish. Melt the remaining margarine or butter and spread on top. Cover the casserole or frying pan tightly and bake for 30 minutes. 6 servings.

*   *   *

MURGHI CURRY (Chicken Curry)

4 tablespoons margarine
1 3-pound chicken (or 2
  pounds beef or lamb), cut in
  pieces
4 medium onions, sliced
2 garlic cloves, chopped
1 teaspoon turmeric
1 teaspoon cumin
3 teaspoons curry

1 teaspoon coriander
1 teaspoon powdered ginger
1 chili, seeded and crushed
salt and pepper to taste
2 cups coconut milk*
1 cup chicken soup
3 tablespoons lime or lemon
  juice

Melt the margarine in a fryer, and fry the chicken pieces on all sides. Remove the chicken. Add the onions and garlic, and cook for 10 minutes. Add all the spices, and fry for a few minutes. Return the chicken pieces to the pan. Add the coconut milk, chicken soup, and lime or lemon juice. Cover pot and cook until chicken is very tender. Serve with rice, green peas, and chutney. 6 servings.

*To make coconut milk, grate or grind fresh coconut meat or put in blender and blend. To every cup of grated coconut, add 2 cups of boiling water. Let stand for 1 hour. Strain the liquid through a double layer of cheesecloth. Squeeze the coconut meat until it is dry.

*   *   *

PILAU

3 tablespoons margarine
2 onions, chopped
1 cup rice, washed in cold water
¼ cup raisins
¼ cup almonds, blanched and sliced
½ teaspoon cardamom,* ground

6 coriander seeds
1 stick cinnamon
3 bay leaves
3 cloves
a few strands of saffron, soaked in 2 tablespoons hot water
salt to taste

Melt the margarine, and add the onions. Sauté for 10 minutes, but do not brown. Add the rice, and continue to sauté for 5 minutes. Add the raisins and almonds, and cook for a few minutes. Add the rest of the ingredients. Cover with boiling water and cook until rice is soft. Do not overcook. 6 servings.

*Available in gourmet food shops.

*   *   *

CHUTNEY

2 pounds apples
½ cup raisins
½ cup dried apricots, sliced
1 cup pitted prunes, sliced
¼ cup candied ginger, sliced
1 cup vinegar
1 cup brown sugar

½ teaspoon chili powder
¼ teaspoon powdered cloves
½ teaspoon garlic powder
½ teaspoon cinnamon
¼ teaspoon black pepper
¼ teaspoon coriander
½ teaspoon salt

Peel, core, and slice the apples. Add the raisins, apricots, prunes, and ginger.

In a pot, bring to a boil the vinegar and the brown sugar. Add the fruits and all the spices. Bring to a boil, lower heat, and cook for 1 hour. Serve with curry.

*   *   *

PHIRINI (Rice Pudding)

2 cups milk
2 tablespoons Cream of Rice
½ cup sugar
½ teaspoon rose water*
1 tablespoon butter

2 tablespoons blanched
*   almonds, chopped*
2 tablespoons pistachio nuts,
*   chopped*
2 tablespoons raisins

Bring the milk to a boil, and add the Cream of Rice and the sugar. Cook slowly, stirring all the time, until thick. Add the rose water. Pour into individual dessert dishes. Chill and serve with the topping.

For the topping, melt the butter and sauté the almonds, pistachio nuts, and raisins until nuts are browned. Garnish the pudding with the topping mixture. 6 servings.

*Available in gourmet food shops.

*   *   *

CARROT PUDDING

1 bunch carrots
milk to cover
½ cup sugar
¼ cup water
2 tablespoons butter

1 cup blanched almonds,
*   chopped*
¼ teaspoon powdered
*   cardamom*

Scrape the carrots, and grate on a fine grater. Put the carrots in a pot, cover with milk, and bring to a boil. Lower heat, and cook the carrots until they are soft and all the milk is evaporated.

Boil the sugar with the water for 5 minutes to make a syrup.

Melt the butter, and sauté the carrots in the butter until all the butter is absorbed. Add the syrup, and cook for 10 minutes. Remove from heat, and add the chopped almonds and cardamom. Serve hot or cold with cream. 6 servings.

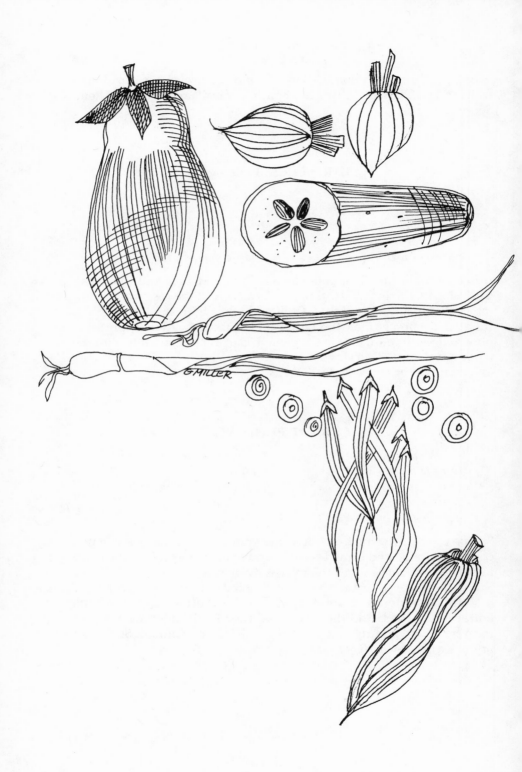

ISRAEL

The Bible repeatedly speaks of Eretz Israel as a "land flowing with milk and honey" where the children of Israel can feed on the rich produce of the soil. Yet when the Jewish state was proclaimed in 1948, the country was lacking basic food staples. Jerusalem had been under siege for months, and the shortage of food was critical. At the sacrifice of many lives, convoys from Tel Aviv to Jerusalem ran the gantlet of Arab attackers and brought thousands of tons of food to the beleaguered city. Rationing was the order of the day during the first years of the state.

At present food products in abundance are seen in the local supermarkets, and Israel has a substantial international trade in a wide variety of fresh and processed foods of high quality. Even before the establishment of the state, the popular Jaffa oranges (in Hebrew *tapuhe zahav*, "golden apples"), lemons, and grapefruit were exported to Europe. Many Israeli products are now available in the United States.

Carp, grown in ponds, is probably the most popular fish in Israel and raising carp has become a big business.

The ingathering in Israel of the exiles from Europe, Asia, and Africa brought with it a wide divergence of culinary habits. The cuisine of the Ashkenazic Jews was naturally quite different from that of the Sephardim. However, the early European Jewish settlers soon recognized the necessity of utilizing the available local agricultural produce and of suiting their diets to the Israeli climate. These were among the factors which led them to change their cuisine, and they soon learned to eat and enjoy many of the oriental dishes prevalent among the Sephardic Jews. Eggplant prepared in a variety of ways, squash, salted olives, and other vegetables virtually unknown in Europe have become staples in most households. Many, although not all, of the traditional "dishes of mother" are disappearing from the menu.

Oriental delicacies which have become widely accepted as Israeli dishes are *tehinah,* a sesame dressing; *humus,* ground chick-peas with *tehinah*, which is eaten with bread as a dip; and *falafel*, a chick-peas mixture made into small fried croquettes and served with a chopped vegetable salad in *pitta* (flat round bread). *Falafel* is sold in street kiosks, as is the "national drink"—*gazoz*, soda water with syrup.

Israelis generally eat a hearty breakfast. The main meal is in the early afternoon, and a light supper is served in the evening.

Kashrut is observed in government-owned and public and semipublic establishments, such as the Israeli airline, El Al. The army, known as the "pressure cooker" as it seems to blend all elements of the population, likewise maintains the dietary laws under the supervision of the chief of chaplains.

Israeli gastronomy is still in a formative stage and as yet no national diet has emerged, although there is a marked tendency, particularly among the young, toward oriental cuisine. To encourage the creation of an indigenous culinary art in Israel by utilizing the rich produce of the land, a "Queen of the Kitchen" contest has been conducted for a number of years, which has attracted hundreds and hundreds of entrants who submit and demonstrate favorite recipes. This, too, is an ingredient of Israel's "pressure cooker" for the integration of Jews from many lands.

*   *   *

TEHINAH DIP

½ cup tehinah *	*1 garlic clove, crushed*
⅓ cup water	*juice of 1 lemon*
salt to taste	*parsley, chopped*

In a bowl, mix the *tehinah* with the water, and stir well. It will become thick. Add the salt, garlic, and lemon juice, stirring until it becomes pale in color and thinned to a consistency of heavy cream. Scatter the parsley on top.

Serve with raw carrot, cucumber, and celery sticks, or with French bread or *pitta*.

Available in Greek grocery stores and gourmet food shops.

CHEESE SPREAD

½ pound cream cheese
¼ pound butter
paprika
½ teaspoon caraway seeds

2 teaspoons prepared mustard
2 tablespoons anchovy paste
½ cup onion, chopped fine
¼ cup beer

Mix all the ingredients, using enough paprika to color the mixture a pastel orange. Serve with thin black bread or rye bread.

*   *   *

SALAT (Salad)

1 cucumber, diced
2 tomatoes, diced
1 green pepper, diced
2 green scallions, diced

a few sprigs Italian parsley,
   chopped
salt and pepper to taste
2 tablespoons oil
juice of 1 lemon

Mix all the vegetables in a bowl. Season with salt and pepper. Add the oil and lemon juice, and mix. 4 servings.

*   *   *

FALAFEL

½ pound dry chick-peas
3 cloves garlic
½ cup bread crumbs
½ teaspoon cumin
½ teaspoon coriander

½ teaspoon turmeric
1 egg
salt and pepper to taste
dash of cayenne pepper

Soak the dry chick-peas in water to cover for 24 hours. Drain and put them through a grinder with the garlic. Grind the chick-peas a second time.

Mix the bread crumbs, cumin, coriander, turmeric, egg, salt and pepper, and cayenne. Form into balls the size of a small walnut (will make about 40).

Heat 1 inch of oil in a frying pan. When the oil is hot, drop the *falafel* balls, one by one, into the oil. Fry on all sides until lightly browned. Serve hot.

Serve in *pitta* together with *tehinah* sauce and a salad of mixed vegetables. Hot peppers and pickles are a must!

HUMUS

2 cups chick-peas, cooked
2 garlic cloves
1 teaspoon salt
½ teaspoon pepper
1 teaspoon cumin
3 tablespoons tehinah

2 tablespoons water
juice of 1 lemon
olive oil
parsley, chopped
dash of paprika or cayenne
    pepper

The chick-peas must be very soft. Put the chick-peas with the garlic through a grinder or blend in a blender. Add the salt, pepper, and cumin.

Make *tehinah* sauce by mixing the *tehinah*, water, and lemon juice. Combine the dressing with the chick-peas, mixing well. Correct the seasoning.

On individual flat plates, put a layer of the chick-pea mixture. Sprinkle with olive oil and parsley, and add a dash of paprika or cayenne pepper. Serve with green olives and *pitta*. 6 servings.

*   *   *

COLD TOMATO SOUP

1-pound 12-ounce can of
    tomatoes
2 cups water
½ teaspoon onion powder
½ teaspoon salt

3 tablespoons sugar
2 eggs, beaten
6 tablespoons sour cream or
    yogurt
parsley, chopped

Put the tomatoes with the juice from the can in a blender, and blend for a few minutes, liquifying the tomatoes; or put through a sieve. Measure 4 cups of the liquid into a saucepan. Add the water. Bring to a boil. Lower heat and add the onion powder, salt, and sugar. Remove from heat.

Beat the eggs well, then slowly add one cup of the hot tomato soup to the eggs, beating all the time. Slowly add the rest of the soup, continuing to beat. Soup will thicken somewhat. Taste for seasoning, and add more sugar if needed.

Refrigerate the soup for a few hours. Serve with a tablespoon of sour cream or yogurt, sprinkled with parsley. 6 servings.

This soup can be made with fresh ripe tomatoes. Cook the tomatoes in water, and when they are soft proceed as above.

FRIED EGGPLANT WITH TOMATO SAUCE

1 ½ pounds eggplant
salt
2 eggs, beaten
½ cup flour
salt and pepper to taste
oil for frying

SAUCE
1 small onion, chopped
2 garlic cloves, crushed
2 cups fresh tomatoes, skinned
  and chopped, or solid pack
  tomatoes
¼ cup parsley, chopped
2 tablespoons lemon juice
1 tablespoon sugar
½ teaspoon paprika
a dash of cayenne (optional)
salt to taste

Peel and cut the eggplant into ¼-inch slices. Lay the slices on foil and sprinkle with salt. Let stand for 1 hour. The salt will remove the water from the eggplant. Rinse the slices in water, and pat dry with paper toweling.

Place the beaten eggs in a flat bowl. Put the flour seasoned with salt and pepper in another flat plate. Dip the eggplant slices in the flour and then in the eggs.

Heat the oil in a large frying pan. The oil should be 1 inch deep. When the oil is hot but not smoking, add the coated slices of eggplant to the oil, and fry until the slices are lightly browned and the eggplant is soft. Remove the slices and lay them on paper toweling.

While the eggplant slices are being fried, make the sauce. In a saucepan, put the onion, garlic, and tomatoes, and bring to a boil. Lower the heat, and add the parsley, lemon juice, sugar, paprika, cayenne, and salt. Simmer the sauce for 30 minutes.

Add the fried eggplant slices to the tomato sauce and continue to simmer for another 30 minutes. Correct the seasoning. Serve hot or cold. 6 servings.

MEAT AND NOODLE BAKE

½ pound medium noodles
½ cup margarine
3 eggs
salt and pepper to taste
½ cup pine nuts
2 onions, chopped

2 garlic cloves, minced
1 pound ground lamb or beef
1 teaspoon mild curry
½ teaspoon thyme
½ teaspoon oregano
1 tablespoon parsley, chopped

Cook the noodles in salted water for 10 minutes. Drain and rinse with cold water. Add 2 tablespoons of margarine. Beat 2 eggs, and add to the noodles. Season with salt and pepper.

In a frying pan, melt 2 tablespoons of margarine. Sauté the pine nuts until lightly browned. Remove the pine nuts to a dish. Add 2 more tablespoons of margarine to the frying pan, and sauté the chopped onions and garlic for 10 minutes. Break up the meat. Push the onions to one side, and add the meat to the pan to brown. When all the meat is brown, mix with the onions, and cook for 5 more minutes. Add the pine nuts, curry, thyme, oregano, and parsley. Add salt and pepper, and then 1 beaten egg. Mix well.

In a casserole, melt the rest of the margarine. Place a layer of noodles on the bottom and then the meat mixture. Put the rest of the noodles on top. Bake the casserole in a 350° oven for 45 minutes. If the top dries out too soon, cover with a piece of foil. 6 servings.

*   *   *

BAKED CARP

1 3-pound carp
salt and pepper to taste
paprika

onion powder
garlic powder

Have the fish sliced. Salt the fish and refrigerate overnight.

Oil well a foil-lined baking sheet. Lay the sliced fish on the foil. Add salt and pepper, and sprinkle with paprika, onion powder, and garlic powder.

Bake the fish in a 375° oven for 1 hour. Serve hot or cold. 8 servings.

WAX BEANS AND SOUR CREAM

2 cups cooked French-style wax   ¼ cup dill, chopped
  beans   salt to taste
1 tablespoon white vinegar   1 cup sour cream
1 teaspoon sugar

Drain the wax beans well. Add the vinegar, sugar, dill, salt, and sour cream. Mix well and refrigerate. Serve cold. 6 servings.

*   *   *

SESAME COOKIES

6 tablespoons sugar   6 tablespoons flour
6 tablespoons oil   2 cups sesame seeds*
2 eggs, well beaten

Toast the sesame seeds in a 350° oven until lightly browned, being careful not to burn them. Allow to cool. Mix well the sugar, oil, and eggs. Add the flour and sesame seeds. Spread the mixture in a 9 × 12½-inch pan.

Bake in a 350° oven for 15 minutes. Then remove the pan. Leaving the partly baked dough in the pan, cut into 1½ × 2¼-inch cookies.

Return the pan to oven, and bake until light brown. While warm, cut the cookies again along the lines made previously. 32 cookies.

*Available in gourmet food shops.

*   *   *

SUMSUM BEIGELACH (Sesame Cookies)

½ cup margarine   2 teaspoons baking powder
¼ cup oil   1 teaspoon mahleb,* crushed
2 eggs, beaten   (optional)
1 tablespoon sugar   ¼ cup warm water
1 teaspoon salt   ½ egg, beaten
3 cups flour, sifted   sesame seeds

Mix the margarine, oil, 2 eggs, sugar, and salt. Add the flour, baking powder, mahleb, and water, and form into a dough. Knead the dough a few minutes, until soft but not sticky.

Put the ½ egg in a saucer and the sesame seeds in another saucer.

Take small pieces of the dough, the size of a walnut, and shape like small doughnuts. Dip sparingly in the egg and then in the sesame seeds.

Lay the *beigelach* on a greased cookie sheet. Bake in a 375° oven until lightly browned.

*Mahleb *is a spice sold in many Greek stores.*

*   *   *

ORANGE CAKE

4 eggs	1 cup flour, sifted
1 cup sugar	1 teaspoon baking powder
3 tablespoons orange juice	grated peel of 1 orange

Beat the eggs with the sugar until sugar is dissolved and the mixture is pale yellow. Add the orange juice, and continue beating. Sift the flour with the baking powder, and fold it gently into the egg mixture. Add the orange peel and mix lightly.

Pour the batter into a 9-inch springform pan, the bottom lined with oiled paper. Bake the cake in a 350° oven for 30 minutes, or until the top of the cake will spring back when touched. Remove from oven and allow the cake to cool before removing from pan.

ORANGE CREAM FILLING

1½ cups orange juice	3 egg yolks
⅓ cup lemon juice	grated peel of 1 orange
¾ cup sugar	1½ tablespoons margarine
4 tablespoons cornstarch	

Mix the orange juice, lemon juice, sugar, and cornstarch in a heavy saucepan. Bring to a boil, stirring constantly with a wooden spoon. Lower heat and continue to cook for 10 minutes, stirring frequently.

Beat the egg yolks. Take some of the hot cornstarch mixture and pour over the egg yolks, stirring constantly. Add the egg yolk mixture to the rest of the orange and cornstarch mixture, stirring constantly until smooth. Return to heat and slowly bring to a boil, stirring the mixture for 1 minute. Remove from the heat, and add the grated orange peel and margarine. Allow to cool.

Slice the cake in half. Place the bottom half on a serving plate and cover with half the filling. Put the top part of cake over the filling, and cover the top and sides with the rest of the filling. Chill the cake before serving.

ORANGE DELIGHT

4 large Jaffa oranges   *½ cup corn syrup*
½ cup water   *3 tablespoons orange liqueur*
½ cup sugar

With a vegetable peeler or a sharp knife remove the peel from the oranges in long strips, being careful to remove only the orange part (zest).

Remove all the white part from the oranges, section the oranges, and reserve.

Put the strips of orange peel in a saucepan, cover with water, and bring to a boil. Pour off the water. Cover again with water and bring to a boil. Drain the peels.

In a saucepan, bring to a boil the ½ cup water, sugar, and corn syrup. Lower the heat and simmer for 10 minutes. Add the drained orange peels, and cook over very low heat for 20 minutes. Add the liqueur.

Pour the hot syrup over the reserved orange sections. Refrigerate overnight.

Use the peel and sections to decorate the top of an orange cake or use as an accompaniment to any cake. The oranges are also good as a dessert mixed with other fruits.

ITALY

When the Maccabees sent ambassadors to Rome to form an alliance in the second century B.C.E., they were welcomed by Jews who had already established themselves in Italy. Since then the lot of Italian Jews has weathered various vicissitudes. Sometimes they enjoyed complete freedom, but more often than not they were confined to ghettos and exiled from various Italian cities. During the Renaissance the Jews and Christians of Italy had frequent social contacts, and it was only natural that Italian dishes, insofar as they did not violate Jewish dietary laws, became part of the cuisine of Jewish households. The Italian practice of serving many courses at a meal was also adopted by Jews.

Kalonymus ben Kalonymus, the Jewish parodist who lived in the fourteenth century, listed twenty-four meat and pastry dishes that "were told to Moses on Mount Sinai, all of which one must prepare on Purim." Among them were such delicacies as *mostacciuoli* (pastries), *anatre* (ducks), *fasani* (pheasants), *culaccio* (paunch of a stuffed fowl), *tocchetto* (ragout), and *maccheroni* (macaroni).

It is not surprising, therefore, that at the beginning of the fifteenth century the leaders of the Jewish communities of northern Italy, recognizing that some Jews were extravagant with food and that they spent on banquets "more than they could afford and more than the wealthy Christians among whom we live," enacted regulations to limit such expenditures.

Cecil Roth, the historian of Italian Jewry, points out that while there was much similarity between the social life of the Jews and that of their neighbors, there were definite distinctions, including preferences for different foods: "Certain ghetto delicacies, for example, artichokes *alla giudea*, in Rome, were famous; certain vegetables, such as the beet and eggplant, were little eaten except among the Jews; and their fondness for goose, especially in Piedmont, was proverbial."

ANTIPASTO (Appetizer)

Arrange a colorful platter of such items as hard-cooked eggs, anchovy fillets, finocchio (Italian celery), artichoke hearts, black olives, green olives, green and red (roasted) peppers, and other fresh vegetables. Serve with breadsticks.

*   *   *

PIZZA

1 envelope dry yeast
1 cup warm water (105°–115°)
2 cups flour

1 teaspoon salt
2 tablespoons oil

TOPPING

olive oil
salt and pepper to taste
oregano to taste
2 garlic cloves, mashed
7-ounce can tomato paste

½ pound Münster cheese, sliced
¾ cup shredded or grated cheddar cheese

Dissolve the yeast in the warm water and let stand for 5 minutes. Put the flour, salt, and oil into a large bowl; gradually add the water and yeast mixture, and mix well with your hands. Dough will be soft. Knead dough on a well-floured board for 10 to 15 minutes, until dough is elastic and does not stick to hands. Put the dough in a floured bowl, cover with a towel, and let the dough rise in a warm place for about 2 hours until double in bulk. Spread the dough in a greased baking tin 10 × 16 inches, and with fingers stretch the dough out until it has a thickness of ½ inch or less.

Spread olive oil over the dough, then sprinkle with salt and pepper, oregano, and garlic. Spread the tomato paste on top. Cover with Münster cheese. Sprinkle the cheddar cheese over the Münster cheese.

Bake in a 400° oven for 30 minutes or until crust is a delicate brown. Serve hot. 6 to 8 servings.

MINESTRONE

4 tablespoons olive oil
1 medium onion, chopped
1 garlic clove, minced
1 carrot, diced
2 celery stalks, diced
1 cup lettuce, shredded
2 cups cabbage, shredded
1 cup canned tomatoes

8 cups soup stock
salt and pepper to taste
1 cup cooked red beans
½ package frozen mixed
  vegetables
½ cup small macaroni
2 tablespoons instant rice

Heat the olive oil in a large soup pot. Add the onion, garlic, carrot, celery, lettuce, and cabbage. Cook for 10 minutes, but do not brown the vegetables. Add the tomatoes, soup stock, and salt and pepper, and cook for 1 hour. Add the beans and frozen vegetables. Cook for 30 minutes. Then add the macaroni and rice. Cook for 10 more minutes. Correct seasoning and serve hot. 8 servings.

*　　*　　*

CHESTNUT SOUP

1 pound chestnuts
4 cups soup stock
1 bay leaf

2 cloves
2 tablespoons margarine

Score the chestnuts with a sharp knife and bake in a 400° oven for 10 minutes. Peel and skin the chestnuts. Bring the stock to a boil (4 cups of water and 4 bouillon cubes can be used). Add the chestnuts, bay leaf, cloves, and margarine, and cook for 45 minutes. Strain the chestnuts, reserving the broth. Put in a blender with a little of the broth and blend, covered, for a few seconds. Return the puréed chestnuts to the broth, and bring to a boil. Serve hot. 4 servings.

*　　*　　*

BAKED FILLET OF FISH

½ cup bread crumbs
salt and pepper to taste
1 teaspoon oregano
2 teaspoons parsley flakes
1 pound fillet of fish

3 tablespoons margarine or
  butter
1 cup tomato sauce
1 lemon, sliced

Mix the bread crumbs with the salt and pepper, oregano, and parsley flakes. Dip the fish in the mixture, coating it well. Cover a cookie tin with foil, and melt the margarine or butter in it. Place the fish in the tin. Cover each slice with some of the tomato sauce, and bake for 10 minutes in a 400° oven. Serve garnished with lemon slices. 3 servings.

*   *   *

VEAL SCALLOPINI

*1½ pounds veal (from
    shoulder cut), sliced thin
½ cup flour
1 garlic clove, minced*

*salt and pepper to taste
4 tablespoons margarine
½ cup sherry
1 lemon for garnish*

Dredge the veal in a mixture of flour, garlic, and salt and pepper.

Heat the margarine in a frying pan, and brown the veal slices for about 15 minutes. Turn the veal over and cook on the other side for about 10 minutes. (Cooking time depends on the thickness of the slices.) Add the sherry, and cover the pan; cook for 10 more minutes over very low heat. Serve garnished with lemon quarters. 4 servings.

*   *   *

CHICKEN CACCIATORE

*½ cup flour
salt and pepper to taste
½ teaspoon oregano
4-pound chicken, cut in
    eighths
4 tablespoons olive oil*

*4 small onions, sliced
1 garlic clove, minced
1 cup canned tomatoes
1 green pepper, sliced
1 cup mushrooms, sliced*

Mix the flour, salt and pepper, and oregano. Roll the chicken in the mixture.

Heat the oil in a large frying pan and add the chicken. Brown well on all sides for about 20 minutes. Add the onions, garlic, tomatoes, and green pepper. Cover and simmer for 45 minutes. Add the mushrooms, and continue to cook until the chicken is tender. 4 servings.

CHICKEN BROILED WITH OREGANO

¼ cup lemon juice   *2 garlic cloves, minced*
⅓ cup olive oil   *salt and pepper to taste*
2 teaspoons oregano   *4-pound broiler, cut in quarters*
1 teaspoon parsley flakes

Mix the lemon juice, olive oil, oregano, parsley flakes, and garlic; add salt and pepper. Marinate the chicken in the mixture for 1 hour.

Place the chicken in a flat pan. Broil in a hot oven, about 5 inches from the flame, for 30 minutes on one side until brown, basting with the marinade; turn over the chicken and broil on the other side, basting the pieces with the rest of the marinade, for 20 additional minutes or until chicken is tender. Pour the liquid from the pan over the chicken and serve hot. 4 servings.

*   *   *

BOEUF À L'ITALIENNE (Beef in Wine)

½ teaspoon thyme   *2 onions, sliced*
½ teaspoon rosemary   *1 cup tomato purée*
1 garlic clove, mashed   *peel of ½ lemon, shredded*
salt and pepper to taste   *peel of ½ orange, shredded*
3 pounds breast of beef   *1 cup dry red wine*
2 carrots, sliced

Mix the thyme, rosemary, garlic, and salt and pepper, and rub into the meat. Braise the meat in its own fat on both sides. Add the carrots, onions, tomato purée, lemon peel, orange peel, and wine. Simmer for 4 to 6 hours. Meat should be very tender. Slice and serve with the vegetables and the sauce. 8 servings.

LASAGNE

4 tablespoons olive oil
1 onion, chopped
1 garlic clove, mashed
1 can tomato sauce
1 cup canned solid pack
    tomatoes
½ teaspoon oregano

salt and pepper to taste
½ package lasagne
½ pound sliced Münster cheese
1 pound cottage cheese
½ cup cheddar cheese,
    shredded

Heat 3 tablespoons of olive oil; add the onion and garlic. Sauté until light yellow. Add the tomato sauce, tomatoes, oregano, and salt and pepper. Simmer over low heat for 45 minutes.

While sauce is cooking, prepare the lasagne. Bring 5 quarts of water to a boil. Add 1 tablespoon of olive oil, to prevent the noodles from sticking together. Cook for 15 minutes, then strain. Cover the bottom of a casserole with some of the cooked sauce. Place 3 lasagne over the sauce; then add a layer of half the Münster cheese and half the cottage cheese. Spread some tomato sauce over the cottage cheese. Cover with 3 more lasagne, the balance of the Münster cheese and of the cottage cheese and more sauce. Add the rest of the lasagne and top with the balance of the sauce. Over this sprinkle the cheddar cheese. Bake in 375° oven for 30 minutes. Serve hot. 6 servings.

*   *   *

RISOTTO

4 tablespoons margarine
1 medium onion, chopped
1 cup rice

2 cups broth, or 2 cups water
    and 2 bouillon cubes
a few strands of saffron
salt and pepper to taste

Melt the margarine and add the onion. Cook for 10 minutes, but do not brown the onion. Add the rice and stir well. Cook for 5 minutes. Add the broth or water with bouillon cubes, saffron, and salt and pepper. Cover and cook for 20 minutes over low heat. Turn off the heat and let the rice stand for 5 minutes. Fluff up before serving. 4 servings.

EGGPLANT PARMIGIANA

1½ pounds eggplant
2 eggs, well beaten
¾ cup bread crumbs
salt and pepper to taste

oil for frying
tomato sauce (see below)
½ pound Münster cheese,
  sliced

Peel the eggplant and cut in ¼-inch slices. Sprinkle with salt, and let stand for 1 hour. Rinse with cold water. Dry the slices well with paper toweling. Dip the slices in the eggs and then in the bread crumbs mixed with the salt and pepper. Fry in hot oil until soft and brown on both sides.

In a casserole or a square pan, put some of the tomato sauce, a layer of eggplant, a layer of Münster cheese, more tomato sauce, the rest of the eggplant, and the rest of the sauce. Bake for 30 minutes in a 375° oven. Serve hot. 8 servings.

TOMATO SAUCE

1-pound can plum tomatoes
¾ cup tomato purée
1 teaspoon basil, crushed
½ teaspoon oregano, crushed

½ cup onion, chopped
1 teaspoon sugar
1 garlic clove, mashed
salt and pepper to taste

Mix all the ingredients, and simmer for 1 hour over very low heat.

* * *

TOMATO SALAD WITH OREGANO

4 large tomatoes
salt and pepper to taste
2 teaspoons oregano, crushed

1 teaspoon parsley flakes
3 tablespoons olive oil

Slice the tomatoes and arrange on four individual plates. Sprinkle with salt and pepper, oregano, and parsley flakes. Drizzle the olive oil over the tomatoes. Chill. 4 servings.

MARINATED ARTICHOKES

1 package frozen artichoke
  hearts
1 tablespoon lemon juice
½ teaspoon salt
¼ cup wine vinegar
¼ cup olive oil

2 garlic cloves, mashed
¼ teaspoon oregano
¼ teaspoon onion powder
¼ teaspoon parsley flakes
1 bay leaf, crushed

Cook the frozen artichokes with the lemon juice and salt in ½ cup of water until tender. Drain.

Make a marinade with the vinegar, oil, and spices. Pour over the artichokes. Chill well. 6 servings.

*   *   *

BAKED POTATOES ITALIAN STYLE

5 medium potatoes
1¼ cups milk
1 egg, beaten

1¼ teaspoons salt
dash of pepper

Peel the potatoes, slice very thin, and place in a well-buttered baking dish. Mix the milk with the egg, salt, and pepper, and pour over the potatoes. Bake in a 400° oven for 1¼ hours. Serve hot. 4 servings.

*   *   *

SWEET AND SOUR ZUCCHINI

1 pound zucchini (green
  squash)
oil
salt to taste

1 tablespoon sugar
2 tablespoons wine vinegar
1½ teaspoons basil, crushed

Scrape the squash and cut into 3-inch slices. Heat the oil, and add the squash. Sauté on all sides until soft and brown in color. Remove the squash from the frying pan.

Mix the salt, sugar, vinegar, and basil in a small pan; add the squash and bring to a boil. Serve hot or cold. 4 servings.

CARCIOFI ALLA GIUDEA (Artichokes Jewish Style)

4 artichokes	salt and pepper to taste
juice of 1 lemon	1½ cups oil

Remove the outer green leaves of the artichokes. Cut the tips of the other leaves with scissors. Spread the remaining leaves open by pressing down the artichokes, while holding the stems. Scoop out the choke from the middle with a knife or a teaspoon. Trim the stalks. Wash the artichokes in water with the lemon juice to prevent discoloration. Dry well. Sprinkle with salt and pepper.

Heat the oil in a deep saucepan. When the oil is hot, carefully put in the artichokes, allowing sufficient space for each one. Fry on all sides for about 10 minutes until light brown. Remove the artichokes from the oil to a plate covered with paper toweling. Allow the artichokes to stand 1 to 2 hours. Then reheat the oil. Holding the stalks of each artichoke with a fork, dip into the hot oil and cook for a few minutes until the artichoke leaves open up and turn brown. Remove again to toweling and allow to drain. Serve hot, sprinkled with salt and pepper. 2 servings.

*   *   *

ITALIAN CHEESE PIE

CRUST	FILLING
2 cups flour	4 eggs
1 teaspoon baking powder	¾ cup sugar
½ teaspoon salt	1½ pounds cottage cheese
⅔ cup butter or margarine	1 tablespoon flour
2 tablespoons cognac	1 teaspoon vanilla
	2 tablespoons almonds, chopped
	2 tablespoons citron, chopped

Sift together the dry ingredients (flour, baking powder, salt). Mix the flour mixture, butter, and cognac to form a soft dough; if necessary, add 1 or 2 tablespoons of water. Chill the dough. Roll out to ⅛-inch thickness. Place in a greased 9-inch pie plate, reserving leftover dough.

To prepare the filling, beat the eggs with the sugar. Add the cottage cheese, flour, and vanilla, and beat well. Stir in the almonds and citron.

Pour the prepared cheese filling into the shell. Roll out the leftover dough and cut in long strips. Place the strips over pie filling in lattice fashion. Pinch the edges all around. Bake in a 350° oven for 50 minutes. Cool. Before serving, dust with confectioners' sugar.

*   *   *

ZABAGLIONE

3 egg yolks   6 tablespoons sherry
1 tablespoon sugar

Beat the egg yolks with the sugar until lemon-colored. Add the wine and beat again. Pour the mixture into the top of a double boiler, and place it over hot but not boiling water. Cook the mixture over very low heat, stirring constantly, until it starts to thicken. Do not cook it too long. Remove immediately from the fire, and beat it until it is almost cold and smooth. Cool and serve in sherbet glasses. 2 servings.

This can also be used as a wine sauce and is nice served warm over fruit or cake.

*   *   *

CHESTNUT TORTA

½ pound chestnuts or ¾ cup   ½ cup sugar
  purée of chestnuts   3 eggs, separated
¾ cup flour   5 tablespoons apricot jam
3 teaspoons baking powder   ¼ cup chopped almonds
⅓ cup margarine   2 tablespoons rum extract

Boil the chestnuts for 30 minutes in water to cover. While still warm, shell them and remove the skins. Put through a chopper or a blender to make ¾ cup of purée.

Sift the flour with the baking powder.

Cream the margarine until light and fluffy. Then add the sugar. Beat until sugar is dissolved. Add the egg yolks, one by one. Add the apricot jam, together with the chestnuts, the almonds, and the rum flavoring. Mix in the flour. Beat the egg whites until stiff and fold into the mixture. Pour into 2 9-inch cake pans which have been slightly greased. Bake for 30 minutes in a 350° oven. Allow to cool before icing.

ICING

⅓ cup margarine or butter   3 cups confectioners' sugar,
3 teaspoons instant coffee   sifted
4 tablespoons hot water   1 tablespoon rum extract

Cream the margarine or butter. Dissolve the coffee in the hot water. Add the coffee, sugar, and rum extract and beat until very smooth. Put ⅓ of the icing between the layers of the cooled cake. Then swirl the rest of the icing on top and sides of the cake.

* * *

BISCUIT TORTONI

2 eggs, separated
1 cup heavy sweet cream or
   nondairy topping
1½ tablespoons brandy extract

¼ cup sugar
¾ cup almonds, chopped
¾ cup cookie crumbs
maraschino cherries

In a small bowl beat the egg whites until stiff. In a second bowl, with the same beater, beat the cream or topping until thick, and add the brandy flavoring. In a large bowl beat the egg yolks with the sugar until lemon-colored. Then fold the egg whites and the cream into the egg yolk mixture. Mix the almonds with the cookie crumbs. Line a cupcake tin with 8 paper cupcake liners. Into each cup put some of the cookie and almond mixture, then some of the whipped cream mixture, another layer of cookie and almond mixture, and more of the cream. Finish off with the rest of the cookie and almond mixture. Garnish with maraschino cherries. Chill at least 3 hours or more. 8 servings.

This biscuit tortoni freezes well and will keep for some time. If frozen, let it stand at room temperature for 15 minutes before serving.

* * *

MERINGUE NUTS

1 egg white
dash of salt
½ cup sugar

1 teaspoon cinnamon
2 cups shelled pecan halves

Beat the egg white, adding the salt and the sugar. Beat until it stands in peaks. Add the cinnamon and pecans. Drop the meringues on a greased foil-lined baking sheet, using two pecan halves to a cookie.

Bake in a slow 300° oven for 45 minutes. Cool and remove from baking sheet. Store in an airtight container.

G. MILLER

NORTH AFRICA

James Riley, an Ohio sea captain, visited the Jewish ghetto of Morocco (called mellah, meaning place of salt or marsh) in 1815 and described his observations in a book known as *Riley's Narrative*. Therein is found this account of the Sabbath meal: "The Jews' Sunday [Sabbath] begins on Friday evening at sunset . . . so that they heat their ovens on Friday, put in their provisions before night for their next day's meal and let it stand in the ovens until Saturday noon, when it is taken out and set on the table, or on the floor, by Moors, whom they contrive to hire for that purpose. . . . Their principal and standing Sunday [Sabbath] dinner is called *skanah;* it is made of peas [in a later account he called them beans] baked in an oven . . . with a quantity of beef marrow bones (which contain very little meat) broken to pieces over them: it is a very luscious and fattening dish, and by no means a bad one: this, with a few vegetables, and sometimes a plum-pudding, good bread and Jew's brandy, distilled from figs and aniseed, and bittered with wormwood, makes up the repast of the Jews who call themselves rich. The poor can only afford *skanah* and barley-bread."

Moroccan Jews likewise enjoy a dish called *adefina,* a cholent with meat, chick-peas, and eggs.

A popular North African delicacy for the Sabbath was kuskus (steamed semolina granules) and soup of chick-peas and vegetables with meat or chicken. It was also made with fruits and nuts and served as a dessert.

Bazin, the national dish of the Sahara, was also a favorite of Jews. It is a thick soup made of maize or barley with oil and red peppers. A welcome treat of Egyptian Jews was *mamoul*—a pastry filled with nuts and rose water.

Figs, olives, and peppers were among the staples of the masses of North African Jewry, and arak—date or fig brandy—was their favorite drink.

One of the Jewish congregations of Tunis, known as Tunsi, had its own peculiar way of baking matzot for Passover: the unleavened dough was fashioned into sticks and the ends joined to form rings.

At the turn of the century one of the sources of revenue of Jewish communities in North Africa was a tax on matzot and kosher meat.

*   *   *

TCHAK-TCHOUKA (Eggs and Vegetables)

¼ cup olive or other oil
1 large onion, chopped
1 garlic clove, mashed
2 green peppers, cut thin

3 large tomatoes, peeled and
   chopped
salt and pepper to taste
dash of cayenne or Tabasco
6 eggs

Heat the oil in a frying pan. Add the onion and garlic and then the green peppers and tomatoes. Simmer the vegetables over very low heat for an hour. Add salt and pepper and cayenne or Tabasco. Break the eggs one at a time into a saucer or cup and slip into the stewed vegetables. Cover the pan, and continue to cook for about 10 minutes, until the eggs are set. 6 servings.

*   *   *

RED LENTIL SOUP

2 onions, chopped
1 tablespoon olive oil
6 cups water
soup bones

½ pound red lentils*
2 carrots, sliced
a few parsley sprigs
salt and pepper to taste

Sauté the onions in the olive oil in a soup kettle for 5 minutes. Add the water, soup bones, lentils, carrots, and parsley. Bring to a boil. Lower the heat, remove the scum, cover the pot, and simmer the soup for 2 hours. Add the salt and pepper. Remove the bones and parsley. 6 servings.

Available in Greek grocery stores and gourmet food shops.

EGGPLANT SALAD

1 pound eggplant	*2 tablespoons olive oil*
juice of ½ lemon	*1 tablespoon parsley, chopped*
1 garlic clove, crushed	*1 tablespoon wine vinegar*
salt and pepper to taste	*1 tomato, peeled and cubed*
1 onion, chopped	*olives*

Wash the eggplant and prick all over with a fork. Put the eggplant on a piece of foil, and broil on all sides until very soft and the skin is charred. Remove from the stove. Drain the eggplant. Make a slit in the eggplant and with a wooden spoon scrape the insides into a bowl. Add the lemon juice and mash the eggplant. Add the garlic and salt and pepper.

Brown the onion in the olive oil and add to the eggplant, with the parsley, vinegar, tomato, and olives. Serve cold as a salad. 4 to 6 servings.

* * *

HUT MAMAR (Cooked Fish)

a few parsley sprigs	*¾ teaspoon cumin*
6 slices of striped bass	*¼ teaspoon powdered saffron*
1 onion, chopped fine	*¼ cup olive oil*
salt to taste	*¼ cup water*
dash of cayenne pepper	*juice of 1 lemon*

Put the parsley sprigs in a pan, and arrange the fish slices over them. Mix the onion, salt, cayenne, cumin, and saffron with the olive oil. Add the water and the lemon juice, and pour over the fish. Cover the pot, and cook over low heat for 20 minutes.

Heat the oven to 350°. Put the fish in the oven and bake, basting with the sauce, for 20 minutes. Serve hot or cold. 6 servings.

* * *

MISSAA (Ground Meat and Eggplant Casserole)

¼ cup pine nuts	*1 15-ounce can tomato sauce*
3 tablespoons margarine or oil	*½ teaspoon cumin*
2 large onions, chopped	*salt and pepper to taste*
1 pound ground meat (beef or	*1 eggplant, sliced and*
* lamb)*	* unpeeled*

Sauté the pine nuts in the margarine or oil for a few minutes, being careful not to burn them. Then remove the pine nuts.

Sauté the onions in the margarine or oil for 10 minutes. Add the ground meat, and sauté until the meat is browned. Add the tomato sauce, and bring to a boil. Remove the meat and onion mixture, and add to it the pine nuts, along with the cumin and salt and pepper.

In the same frying pan, add oil as needed, and fry the eggplant on both sides. Layer the eggplant and the meat mixture in a casserole, starting with the eggplant. Pour the rest of the mixture on top. Bake in a 350° oven for 30 minutes. 6 servings.

*   *   *

ADEFINA (Meat and Chick-Peas Cholent)

1½ pounds chuck	1 calf's foot, cut up
½ pound dry chick-peas	2 onions, chopped
3 garlic cloves, chopped	1 teaspoon chili powder
salt and pepper to taste	6 eggs

Place all the ingredients except the eggs in a large casserole or heavy pot. Wash the eggs, leaving on the shells, and place them carefully on the other ingredients. Cover with water to the top. Cover the casserole or pot tightly, first with a piece of foil and then with the pot cover. Bake overnight or all day in a 250° oven. Eggs will be browned but not hard. 6 servings.

*   *   *

KUSKUS

6 tablespoons margarine	2 green or yellow squash,
3 pounds lean lamb, cubed	cubed
2 large onions, chopped	2 tomatoes, cubed
1 green pepper, sliced	1 teaspoon powdered ginger
1 can cooked chick-peas	salt and pepper to taste
2 carrots, sliced	2 cups chicken broth
	1 cup kuskus*

Melt 4 tablespoons of margarine in a heavy pot. Brown the lamb on all sides and then remove. Add the onions to the margarine, and sauté for 10 minutes. Add the green pepper, and sauté for a few minutes. Add the chick-peas, carrots, squash, and tomatoes, and sprinkle with the ginger and salt and pepper. Return the meat to the pot. Cover and stew gently until the lamb is done. Taste for seasoning.

Bring the chicken broth to a boil. Place the kuskus in a pot. Pour the boiling broth over the kuskus, stirring constantly. Cover the pot, and let it stand for 10 minutes. Add to the kuskus 2 tablespoons of margarine, and salt if needed. Put the kuskus in a strainer, and place the strainer with the kuskus over the stew. Cover the pot, and keep warm until serving time. Serve the lamb stew over the kuskus. 6 servings.

Semolina granules, available in Greek, Near Eastern, and gourmet food stores.

* * *

MAMOUL

1½ cups semolina
1 cup unsalted margarine
¾ cup boiling water
¼ cup flour

1 cup confectioners' sugar
¾ cup chopped nuts
1 tablespoon rose water

Mix the semolina with the margarine, and add the boiling water. Knead together. Add the flour and knead again. Cover tightly and refrigerate overnight.

Mix the sugar and nuts with the rose water to make the filling.

Break off small pieces of the dough, the size of a small walnut, and shape into balls. Then make depressions in the balls.

Put some of the filling in the depressions and then cover over with dough, making sure the filling is entirely covered. Elongate into small fingers. Put on a greased, foil-lined baking sheet. Bake in a 350° oven until light brown. While still hot, sift confectioners' sugar over the cookies. When cookies are cool, sift more sugar over them. Keep in a covered box.

PERSIA

Jewish settlement in Persia (Iran) dates back to ancient times. The early history is recounted in the biblical Book of Esther. Jews have lived in that land under varying conditions from the reign of Ahasuerus through the Mohammedan conquest of Persia up to the present, very often compelled to inhabit ghettos and to suffer various other disabilities. Beset with the typical persecutions faced by so many other Jewish communities, they also fell prey to the exhortations of several false messiahs.

At times many Jews were forced to become Muslims, but they devised ingenious methods to maintain at least some Jewish traditions clandestinely. For example, in Meshed during the nineteenth century converted Jews (known as "Jadid al-Islam") bought meat from a Muslim butcher to publicly demonstrate their adherence to Islamic law— and then they fed it to Muslim beggars or to dogs. They themselves ate only meat that was secretly slaughtered by a shohet.

The type of dishes prevalent among Persian Jews for many generations reveals their poverty. Their regular fare consisted primarily of cereals of one kind or another. One of their most popular dishes was *gipa*, stomach filled with rice, similar to the stuffed *kishke* of East European Jews. Indeed, a song was composed in honor of this dish, which was generally reserved for festive occasions. Other favorites were *bardasah*, intestines filled with rice, and *petcha*, calves' feet cooked with beans. Among the Persian dishes that were eaten were "*hala* and *bebe*," referring to "aunt and grandmother," who supposedly converse on the ingredients of a stew, which generally consisted of vegetables and pulses, highly seasoned with garlic and pepper. Other dishes were *kailak*, peppered potatoes and onions in oil; *kefta brinji*, meat dumplings with finely ground rice and a mixture of herbs; and the poor man's meal, *tilltak*, onion soup, radishes, olives, and dry bread.

The Sabbath meal menus, the weekly highlights of the poverty-

stricken Persian Jews, are detailed by Devorah and Menahem Hacohen in *One People: The Story of the Eastern Jews* (Sabra Books, 1969):
the Friday evening meal "began with a fresh citrus fruit, a benediction
over a twig of myrtle or some other aromatic plant, and back to the
fruit. Washing of the hands followed, then the *hamotzi* benediction as
the father passed the round, flat bread to members of the family,
according to age, and blessed each one." The menu featured "fried
fish, rice pudding and dumplings made of chopped sour grass and bits
of meat." The Sabbath day meal included fruit, hard-boiled eggs,
cooked vegetables, fish, and "the omnipresent and eagerly awaited
cholent, the universal trademark of Jewish gastronomy. The copper
pot containing the stew was kept hot with coals underneath and blan-
kets above."

*   *   *

ONION SOUP

2 onions, chopped
1½ tablespoons margarine
2 tablespoons flour
2 cups broth or water
salt and pepper to taste
¼ teaspoon turmeric

juice of 1 lemon
3 tablespoons sugar
½ teaspoon dried mint,
    crushed
1 egg, beaten

Sauté the onions in the margarine for 10 minutes but do not brown
them. Blend in the flour. Slowly add 1 cup of the broth, stirring constantly. Add the second cup of broth and then the salt and pepper and
turmeric. Cover the pot, and simmer the soup for 30 minutes.

Add the lemon juice, sugar, and mint. Simmer for 10 minutes more.
Beat the egg and slowly add some of the hot soup to the egg, beating
all the time. Pour the mixture back into the rest of the soup. Serve with
a sprinkling of mint over each portion. 4 servings.

JONDEE OF CHOPPED LAMB (Lamb Meatballs)

1 onion
½ cup cooked rice
½ cup cooked chick-peas
1 pound ground lamb
1 egg
salt and pepper to taste
½ teaspoon cardamom
¼ teaspoon cinnamon
¼ teaspoon turmeric

SAUCE
1 onion, chopped
1 tablespoon margarine
1 carrot, diced
½ cup tomatoes, chopped
¼ cup parsley, chopped
½ cup soup stock
salt and pepper to taste
mint leaves, crushed
radishes, sliced

Put the onion, rice, and chick-peas through a food grinder. Mix in the lamb, egg, salt and pepper, cardamom, cinnamon, and turmeric.

To make the sauce, sauté the onion in the margarine for 5 minutes. Add the carrot, tomatoes, parsley, and soup stock. Cook for 10 minutes. Add salt and pepper.

Form the meat mixture into small balls and add to the sauce. Lower the heat, and simmer the meatballs for 45 minutes. Serve with a sprinkling of crushed mint and sliced radishes. 4 servings.

*   *   *

CHIRIN POLO (Sweet Chicken Pilau)

1 4-pound chicken, cut in
    serving pieces
salt and pepper to taste
½ teaspoon turmeric
8 tablespoons margarine
4 carrots, grated coarsely

⅓ cup almonds, blanched and
    sliced
¼ cup sugar
grated peel of 1 orange
½ pound rice
½ tablespoon coarse salt
a few strands of saffron

Rub the chicken pieces with a mixture of salt and pepper and turmeric. Melt 4 tablespoons of margarine, and fry the chicken on all sides until browned and tender. Remove the chicken. Add the carrots and almonds to the pan, and sauté until carrots are browned. Add the sugar, orange peel, and ¼ cup water. Cook until carrots are soft.

Soak the rice for 1 hour in cold water, and then rinse it in cold water. Bring 3 quarts of water to a boil with the coarse salt. When the water is boiling, add the rice and cook for 10 minutes. While the rice is cooking, stir twice. Drain the rice and rinse with warm water.

In a casserole, melt 2 tablespoons of the margarine and add 1 table-spoon of water. Swish it around the pan. Put in a layer of rice, then the carrot mixture, another layer of rice, then the chicken parts, and cover with the rest of the rice. Cover the pot and bake in a 350° oven for 30 minutes.

Mix the saffron with 1 tablespoon of hot water, and pour over the rice. Melt the remaining 2 tablespoons of margarine and pour over the rice. Serve hot on a large serving plate. 6 servings.

*　　　*　　　*

CUCUMBER AND YOGURT SALAD

2 cucumbers
1 cup yogurt
salt and pepper to taste

¼ teaspoon mint, crushed
1½ tablespoons fresh dill,
  chopped

Peel the cucumbers and slice thin. Pour the yogurt over them. Add the salt and pepper, mint, and dill. Chill a few hours. 4 servings.

*　　　*　　　*

STUFFED DATES

10-ounce container pitted dates
walnut quarters
4 tablespoons honey

1 cup coconut, shredded or
  flaked

Stuff each date with a quarter of a walnut. Put the honey in a dish. Dip each date in the honey and then roll in the coconut. Put on a foil-lined dish, cover with plastic wrap, and refrigerate until served.

*　　　*　　　*

ROSE WATER FRUIT COMPOTE

4 cups water
½ cup sugar
1 cup dried prunes

1 cup dried apricots
1 cup dried apples
2 tablespoons rose water

Bring the water and sugar to a boil. Add the prunes, apricots, and apples. Cook for 30 minutes over very low heat. Add the rose water. Cool and keep refrigerated. Prepare a few days in advance to let the flavor develop. 8 servings.

HALVAH

½ cup water
¾ cup sugar
½ cup margarine
1 cup flour

6 strands of saffron, dissolved
    in 2 tablespoons of hot water
½ teaspoon powdered
    cardamom

Mix the water and the sugar, and simmer for 10 minutes until syrupy.

Melt the margarine in a heavy pan over medium heat. Add the flour, and stir constantly until mixture is light brown. Remove from the heat. Add ½ cup of the sugar and water syrup, and mix well. The mixture should resemble a thick cake batter. Add the saffron with the rest of the sugar and water syrup and the cardamom.

Pour the mixture into a 9 × 9-inch pan and, while still warm, cut into small pieces. This will resemble fudge. The taste improves if left standing a few days.

SCANDINAVIA

The oldest Jewish settlement in the Scandinavian countries is that of Denmark, which began in 1622. Jews did not settle in Sweden until the last quarter of the eighteenth century. At that time, ordinances were enforced which prohibited Jews from selling victuals and liquor but allowed them to sell among themselves foods that required special preparation according to the Jewish dietary laws, such as wine, meat, and matzot.

Jews migrated to Finland and Norway starting in 1830 and 1852, respectively. Although anti-Semitism was practically unknown in Norway until 1938, the ritual slaughtering of cattle was banned by the parliament in 1929. A similar law was proposed but defeated in Finland in 1934.

Kosher meat must be imported to Norway, generally from Denmark. It is interesting to note that the second Danish rabbi, Israel ben Issachar Berendt of Copenhagen, wrote a book on the ritual slaughtering of animals which was quite popular in the eighteenth century.

The heroic defense of Jews by the Danes during the Nazi occupation of Denmark came to a climax in October 1943, when the SS and Gestapo sought to round up the Jews for shipment to concentration camps. The Danish underground hid them until they were able to escape in fishing boats to Sweden. A key member of the underground was David Sompolinsky, a young Orthodox Jew who hardly slept during that month and fasted for extended periods because he would not eat food that was not kosher. Finally, Mrs. Aage Bertelsen, whose underground exploits are recorded in her husband's book *October '43*, prepared a special kosher concoction of egg yolks and claret, upon which Sompolinsky subsisted. When the Jews returned from Sweden in 1945 they were greeted with flowers, candy, chocolate, and bottles of milk. Many of them found their homes cleaned and their refrigerators stocked with food by their neighbors.

In recent years the outstanding social event of all the Jewish communities in the Scandinavian countries has become the annual banquet of the Scandinavian Jewish Youth Federation.

*   *   *

HERRING SALAD

2 herrings	1 tablespoon sugar
2 cups cooked beets, diced	pepper to taste
3 cups cooked potatoes, diced	salad greens
2 apples, diced	3 hard-cooked eggs
½ cup onions, chopped	tomatoes
2 pickles, diced	parsley
5 tablespoons vinegar	black olives

Soak the herrings for 24 hours in cold water, changing the water a few times. Keep refrigerated while soaking.

Cut the herrings in small pieces. Add the beets, potatoes, apples, onions, and pickles. Mix the vinegar, sugar, and pepper, and pour over the herring mixture. Chill well in a greased mold. Unmold onto salad greens. Mash the egg whites and yolks separately, and use to decorate the mold. Garnish with tomatoes, parsley, and olives. 8 generous servings.

*   *   *

PICKLED HERRING

2 herrings	1 tablespoon pickling spices
2 onions	sugar to taste
½ cup vinegar	

Soak the herrings for 24 hours in cold water, changing the water a few times. Keep refrigerated while soaking.

Cut the herrings and the onions in slices. Layer the herrings and onions in a jar.

Bring the vinegar and spices to a boil, and add the sugar. Let cool. When cold, pour over the herring and onions. If the vinegar does not cover the herring to the top, add more vinegar. Cover and refrigerate for a few days before serving. The pickled herring will keep for 2 weeks or more. 6 servings.

PICKLED FRIED FISH

½ cup bread crumbs
salt to taste
2 pounds smelt
1 egg, beaten
3 tablespoons margarine
1 cup vinegar

¼ cup water
½ cup sugar
a few peppercorns
1 large onion, sliced thin
fresh dill

Mix the bread crumbs with the salt. Dip the fish in the egg and then in the bread crumbs. Sauté in the margarine on both sides until golden brown. Place the fish in a deep serving dish.

Mix the vinegar, water, and sugar, and add the peppercorns. Cover the fish with the onion and pour the vinegar mixture over it. Refrigerate overnight. Garnish with fresh dill. Serve in same dish. 6 servings.

* * *

LOX (Fresh Salmon)

2-pound piece of fresh salmon
¼ cup salt
¼ cup sugar
black pepper to taste
bunch of fresh dill

DRESSING
¼ cup salad oil
2 teaspoons vinegar
1 teaspoon dry mustard
dash of sugar
dash of salt

Buy a middle cut of salmon. Have the fish boned and cut in half.

Mix the salt, sugar, and black pepper. In a deep bowl put a thick layer of dill. On top of the dill lay one piece of salmon, skin side down. Cover with some of the salt and sugar mixture, and more dill. Put the second piece of salmon, skin side up, on top of this. Cover with the rest of the salt and sugar mixture, and more dill.

Put a board on top of the fish, and weigh it down with a heavy weight. Refrigerate overnight. Slice very thin for serving.

For the dressing, combine all ingredients and serve with the salmon. 8 to 10 servings.

The salmon will keep well for a few days, but will become more salty with standing. Any leftover salmon can be used in the Salmon Pudding.

SALMON PUDDING

4 cups potatoes, sliced thin	pepper to taste
2 cups onions, sliced thin	3 eggs
½ pound "marinated" salmon (lox), cut up	2 cups milk

In a well-buttered baking dish, layer the potato slices, onion slices, and the salmon. Sprinkle each layer with pepper. Top layer should be potatoes.

Beat the eggs with the milk, and pour over the potatoes and onions. Cover with foil, and bake for 30 minutes in a 350° oven. Remove foil, and bake for 15 more minutes or until potatoes are soft. 6 servings.

*   *   *

FISH PUDDING

1 pound flounder fillet	½ cup margarine, melted
1 pound haddock fillet	1 tablespoon dry mustard
2 medium onions	salt to taste
6 eggs	½ teaspoon white pepper
1½ cups bread crumbs	parsley for garnish

Grind the fish fillets with the onions twice. Add the eggs to the fish together with the bread crumbs, margarine, mustard, salt, and pepper.

As an alternative for a smoother pudding, grind once, and then blend for a few minutes in a blender, mixing some of the fish with one of the eggs. Repeat with the rest. Add the bread crumbs, margarine, mustard, salt, and pepper.

Pour the pudding into a greased mold or glass casserole; cover tightly with foil. Place the mold in a large pan or kettle two-thirds filled with hot water.

Bake in a 325° oven for 1 hour or until a knife inserted in the middle of the pudding comes out clean. Unmold carefully on a hot serving plate. Garnish with parsley and serve with mushroom sauce. The pudding can be prepared in advance and reheated in the oven. 6 servings.

MUSHROOM SAUCE

1 small onion, chopped
2 tablespoons butter or
  margarine
½ pound fresh mushrooms or
  2 cans mushrooms

1 can mushroom soup or celery
  soup
½ cup milk

Sauté the onion in the butter for a few minutes, but do not brown. Add the mushrooms, and cook for 5 minutes. Add the soup and the milk, bring to a boil, and serve with the fish pudding.

* * *

FRUIT SOUP

½ cup dried apricots
1 cup dried prunes
¼ cup currants
¼ cup white raisins
2 apples, peeled and diced
6 cups water

salt to taste
grated peel of 1 lemon
¼ cup sugar
2 tablespoons cornstarch
1 package frozen raspberries
sour cream

Prepare the dried fruits by cutting them in small pieces.

Put the dried fruits and the apples in the water in a saucepan. Bring to a boil, lower heat, and simmer for 15 minutes. Add the salt, lemon peel, and sugar.

Dissolve the cornstarch in a little cold water, and add a little of the hot soup. Slowly add the soup and cornstarch mixture to the rest of the soup, stirring constantly. Simmer for 10 minutes.

Add the raspberries and mix well. Chill and serve with sour cream for a dairy meal. 6 servings.

Fresh fruits such as plums, apricots, currants, grapes, and peaches can be used instead of the dried fruits, using double the amount of the dried fruit.

* * *

YELLOW PEA SOUP

1 cup dried yellow peas
4 cups water
a few soup bones
1 carrot, diced

2 celery stalks, diced
1 leek or onion, sliced
½ pound smoked beef*
dash of ginger

To the yellow peas, add the water and the soup bones. Bring to a boil. Add the prepared vegetables, beef, and ginger. Cover the pot and lower the heat. Simmer for 2 to 3 hours or until peas are very soft. Slice the beef, and serve the soup with the beef. 6 servings.

*Available in kosher German Jewish butcher shops or delicatessen stores.

* * *

BIKSEMAD (Danish Hash)

1 cup onion, chopped	1½ cups cooked potatoes, diced
5 tablespoons margarine	salt and pepper to taste
1½ cups cooked meat, diced	3 fried eggs

Sauté the onions in the margarine until light brown. Remove to a plate. Add the meat to the frying pan and sauté the meat until brown; remove it to a plate. Sauté the potatoes until brown. Mix the meat with the onions and potatoes, and return to the frying pan. Add salt and pepper. Serve the hash topped with a fried sunny-side-up egg. 3 servings.

* * *

VEAL WITH DILL SAUCE

2 pounds veal, shoulder cut	SAUCE
4 cups boiling water	2 tablespoons margarine
a few peppercorns	2 tablespoons flour
1 bay leaf	2 cups stock
a few dill sprigs	2 tablespoons dill, chopped
salt to taste	1½ tablespoons vinegar
	1½ teaspoons sugar
	1 egg yolk

Put the veal in a soup pot, and pour the water over it. Bring to a boil again and skim. Add the peppercorns, bay leaf, dill, and salt. Cover and simmer for 2 hours or until meat is tender.

Remove meat and cut in thin slices. Strain the stock and reserve.

To make the sauce, melt the margarine, blend in the flour well, and add the stock, stirring constantly. Cook for 10 minutes. Add the dill, vinegar, and sugar. Remove from heat and mix the egg yolk with a little of the sauce, and then add the rest of the sauce. Correct the seasoning. Serve the veal with the sauce. 4 servings.

BEEF LINDSTROM

1 pound ground beef
½ cup mashed potatoes
½ cup pickled beets, chopped
1 small onion, chopped

2 egg yolks
¼ cup water
salt and pepper to taste
margarine

Mix all the ingredients except the margarine. Form into 8 cakes. Melt the margarine in a frying pan; when it is very hot, sauté the meat cakes on both sides. 4 servings.

*   *   *

SAILORS STEW

3 tablespoons margarine
4 onions, chopped
3 pounds chuck, cut up
8 medium potatoes
salt and pepper to taste

1 bay leaf
a few peppercorns
2 bouillon cubes
1 cup water

Melt the margarine in a pan, and sauté the onions. Remove the onions, and add the meat a few pieces at a time. Brown on all sides. Add the potatoes, onions, salt and pepper, bay leaf, and peppercorns. Dissolve the bouillon cubes in the water, and add to the meat. Bring to a boil. Lower heat, and simmer until meat is very tender. (The best potatoes for this dish are the mealy ones, as they should be almost the consistency of mashed potatoes by the time the stew is ready.) 8 servings.

*   *   *

SPINACH PUDDING

1 tablespoon margarine
1 tablespoon flour
dash of black pepper
½ teaspoon onion powder

¼ cup water
1 cup chopped spinach, frozen
2 eggs, separated

Melt the margarine; add the flour, and blend well. Add the pepper, onion powder, and water, mixing well. Bring to a boil, stirring constantly. Remove from heat. Thaw and add the spinach. Beat in the egg yolks. Beat the egg whites until stiff, and add to the spinach, folding gently.

Grease a square serving dish and pour in the mixture. Set the dish in a baking pan half filled with hot water, and place in a 375° oven. Bake for 25 minutes. Serve from the dish. 4 servings.

*   *   *

CREAMED VEGETABLES

1 package frozen mixed vegetables	1½ tablespoons margarine
	1½ tablespoons flour
1 bouillon cube	1 cup water or vegetable stock

Cook the vegetables according to directions on package, adding the bouillon cube.

Melt the margarine and add the flour, mixing well, and cook over low heat for a few minutes. Remove from the fire, and slowly add the water or vegetable stock, stirring constantly. Continue cooking for 10 minutes. Add the cooked vegetables, and bring to a boil. Serve hot. 4 servings.

Milk instead of water may be used for a dairy meal.

*   *   *

PICKLED BEETS

2 1-pound cans sliced beets	½ cup sugar
¾ cup vinegar	1 teaspoon pickling spices
½ cup beet juice	½ teaspoon salt

Drain the beets, reserving ½ cup of the beet juice.

Mix the vinegar, beet juice, sugar, spices, and salt. Add the beets. Prepare a few days before serving. Keep in refrigerator.

A few thinly sliced onions can be added.

*   *   *

CUCUMBER SALAD

¼ cup water	dash of pepper
¼ cup vinegar	1 large cucumber, sliced thin
1 tablespoon sugar	chopped dill
salt to taste	

In a bowl mix the water, vinegar, sugar, salt, and pepper. Add the sliced cucumber. Mix well. Add the dill. Chill for a few hours. 3 servings.

RHUBARB

1 cup sugar	1 pound rhubarb, cut in small
1 cup water	pieces
	2 tablespoons cornstarch

Bring the sugar and water to a boil. Add the rhubarb, and cook until soft. Mix the cornstarch with a little cold water, and add to the rhubarb. Cook for 5 minutes. Pour into a bowl and chill. 4 servings.

*　　*　　*

DANISH PASTRY

4⅓ cups sifted flour	1 cup warm milk
1½ cups butter	⅓ cup sugar
1½ packages dry yeast	1 egg, beaten
¼ cup warm water (105°–115°)	¼ teaspoon ground cardamom

Mix ⅓ cup flour and the butter with a pastry blender. Pat out the butter mixture on a piece of wax paper to measure approximately 8 × 8 inches, ¼ inch thick. Refrigerate.

Sprinkle the yeast over the warm water, and let stand for 5 minutes.

In a large bowl, mix the milk, sugar, and the egg. Add the dissolved yeast and cardamom. Mix well. Add 4 cups flour, and mix until dough is smooth and elastic.

Roll out the dough on a floured board into a 16 × 20-inch rectangle. Place the cold butter and flour mixture on half the dough. Fold dough over it, sealing edges all around.

Roll out the dough and fold both ends to make 3 layers. Repeat this process 3 times. If butter starts to soften, put the dough in refrigerator for half an hour before rolling and folding the dough again.

Roll out the dough on a floured board to a 16 × 20-inch rectangle. Cut into 4 × 4-inch squares. Spread with filling, and shape into envelopes. Put the pastry on a greased baking sheet, cover with a towel, and let it rise in a warm place until double in bulk. Brush with an additional beaten egg, and sprinkle sugar over the tops.

Bake in a 400° oven for about 20 minutes or until brown. 20 pastries.

ALMOND FILLING

½ cup blanched almonds,	½ cup sugar
chopped	1 egg

Mix all the ingredients together.

CHEESE FILLING

1 cup cottage cheese
1 egg yolk
¼ cup sugar

1 tablespoon butter
½ teaspoon vanilla

Mix all the ingredients together until smooth.

PRUNE FILLING

½ cup prune butter (lekvar)   dash of cinnamon

Mix the ingredients together.

*   *   *

CHOCOLATE ROLL

6 eggs, separated
½ teaspoon cream of tartar
1 cup sugar
4 tablespoons flour, sifted
4 tablespoons cocoa
confectioners' sugar

FILLING
1 cup heavy sweet cream
3 tablespoons confectioners'
    sugar
1 teaspoon vanilla

Beat the egg whites with the cream of tartar and ½ cup of sugar until stiff. Beat the egg yolks with the other ½ cup of sugar until lemon-colored. Add the flour and cocoa to the egg yolk mixture, and then carefully fold in the egg white mixture.

Spread in a 10½ × 15½-inch pan or cookie sheet, greased and lined with wax paper. Bake in a 325° oven for 25 minutes. Cake will spring back when touched lightly with finger.

Have ready a towel which is heavily sprinkled with confectioners' sugar. When the cake is baked, immediately turn it upside down on the towel and remove the wax paper. Roll up the cake with the towel and let the roll cool.

To make the filling, whip the cream with the 3 tablespoons confectioners' sugar and vanilla until thick. Unroll the cooled cake and spread the cream over the surface. Reroll the cake without the towel. Wrap in foil and refrigerate until serving time. Cut in 10 or 12 slices.

CARDAMOM BARS

¾ *cup butter or margarine*
¾ *cup sugar*
2¼ *cups flour, sifted*
2 *egg yolks*
2 *tablespoons water or white*
  wine

ALMOND FILLING
2 *cups ground unblanched*
  almonds
1¼ *cups confectioners' sugar*
¾ *teaspoon ground cardamom*
2 *egg whites*
4 *tablespoons water*
½ *teaspoon cinnamon*

Cream the butter or the margarine with the sugar, and add the flour. Mix the egg yolks and water or wine, and add to the flour mixture. Mix well. Press two-thirds of the dough into a 9 × 12½-inch baking pan. Spread with the filling.

Roll the remaining dough to ⅛-inch thickness and cut into long strips with a pastry wheel. Place the strips crisscross fashion on the filling and bake in a 350° oven for 45 minutes. Cool and cut into 32 bars.

For the filling, mix all the ingredients well.

If whole cardamom is used, remove outer shell, and crush the black cardamom seeds between wax paper.

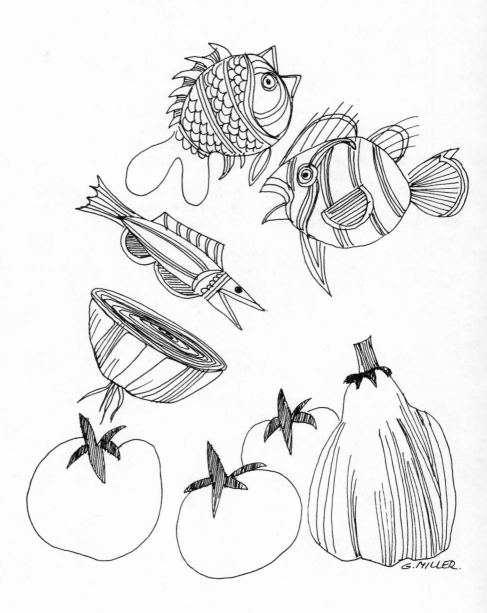

G. MILLER.

SPAIN

Until the expulsion of the Jews from Spain in 1492, they were often subjected to forced conversions. In the seventh century "converted Jews" were obligated to take an oath that "we shall not keep to our old habit of discriminating in matters of food." The Marranos—Jews of Spain who, though forced to become converts to Christianity, secretly tried to remain loyal to Judaism—had a difficult time in observing the dietary laws. While the Marranos made every effort to avoid eating such forbidden foods as pork, rabbit, and scaleless fish, the Inquisition was on a constant watch for people who habitually refrained from purchasing those items. Though frequently compelled to eat forbidden foods, Marranos refrained from doing so on the Sabbath, on the day prior to Passover and the Day of Atonement, and on several other occasions. There are instances of a shohet (ritual slaughterer) who practiced even though he was baptized. Sometimes the crypto-Jews obtained meat and matzot from Jews. Many would eat the unleavened bread throughout the entire year so that they would not arouse the suspicions of the Inquisition during Passover.

During the Middle Ages, Jews played a significant role in the economy of Spain as agrarian merchants. They were granted licenses to export foodstuffs by James I. However, the church disliked having Jews sell milk, meats, wine, and other foods to Christians. It discouraged Christians from buying food from Jews on the pretext that the latter sold products which, because they did not conform to the Jewish dietary laws, the Jews themselves refrained from eating.

In some Spanish Jewish communities where Jews enjoyed a degree of autonomy, taxes imposed on wine and meat were used to support the Jewish school and other communal needs.

In Spain, Jews learned to fry fish and other food in oil and cultivated a taste for olives.

HUEVOS EN SALSA AGRIA (Eggs in Sweet and Sour Sauce)

4 eggs	1 tablespoon sugar
1 onion, chopped fine	1 cup vegetable broth
1 tablespoon margarine	juice of 1 lemon
1 tablespoon flour	1 bay leaf
salt and pepper to taste	¼ cup white wine

Put the eggs in cold water and bring to a boil. Lower the heat, and simmer the eggs for 8 minutes. Remove from heat, and cover with cold water. Peel.

Sauté the onion in the margarine for 10 minutes, but do not brown the onion. Mix the flour, salt and pepper, and sugar with the vegetable broth and lemon juice, and add to the onion, stirring until thick. Add the bay leaf, and cook for 15 minutes. Add the wine and the eggs, and simmer for 5 minutes or until eggs are heated. 4 servings.

*   *   *

GAZPACHO (Cold Fresh Vegetable Soup)

1 garlic clove	salt and pepper to taste
1 medium onion, sliced	pinch of dry tarragon
1 cucumber, sliced	dash of cayenne pepper
1 green pepper, sliced	1 teaspoon paprika
3 tomatoes, peeled	juice of 1 lemon
2 parsley sprigs	1½ cups tomato juice
¼ cup olive oil	garlic croutons
¼ cup wine vinegar	

In a blender, put the garlic, onion, cucumber, pepper, tomatoes, parsley, olive oil, vinegar, salt and pepper, tarragon, cayenne pepper, and paprika. Blend until all the vegetables are mixed. Add the lemon juice and tomato juice. Correct the seasoning. Chill and serve in soup bowls with garlic croutons. Chopped onions, tomatoes, pepper, and cucumber may be added. 6 servings.

BACALAO A LA VICCAINA (Dried Codfish)

1½ pounds dried codfish,
  sliced
½ cup olive oil
1 large onion, chopped
2 cups canned tomatoes

2 garlic cloves, crushed
1 large green pepper, chopped
black pepper to taste
¼ teaspoon dried basil
a few parsley sprigs

Soak the codfish for 24 hours in cold water to cover, changing the water a few times.

Heat the olive oil in a large pot, and add the onion. Sauté for 10 minutes. Add the tomatoes, garlic, green pepper, black pepper, basil, and parsley. Bring to a boil, and add the sliced fish. Lower the heat and simmer for 1½ hours. 4 servings.

*   *   *

MONTANESA STEW

¼ cup flour
salt and pepper to taste
2 pounds chuck, cubed
4 tablespoons margarine
2 cups onions, chopped

1 cup carrots, diced
1 bay leaf
beef broth
1 teaspoon dry mustard
2 tablespoons cocoa

Mix the flour with salt and pepper. Dredge the meat in the flour. Melt 2 tablespoons of margarine, and brown the meat on all sides. Remove the meat. Add the chopped onions with 2 more tablespoons of margarine, and sauté the onions for 10 minutes. Add the meat, carrots, bay leaf, and broth to cover. Bring to a boil, lower the heat, and simmer for 30 minutes. Add the mustard. Continue cooking for about 1½ hours or until meat is very tender.

Remove ½ cup of broth and add to it the cocoa, mixing well. Add to the meat. Cook a few minutes longer. Serve with rice. 4 servings.

*   *   *

CALABACINES (Green Squash)

½ cup onion, chopped fine
2 tablespoons oil
1 garlic clove, crushed

2 cups green squash, sliced
salt and pepper to taste

Sauté the onion in the oil for 10 minutes. Add the garlic, squash, and salt and pepper. Stew for 30 minutes over low heat. 4 servings.

CHURROS (Fried Batter)

½ cup water
¼ cup margarine
1 tablespoon sugar
dash of salt

1 cup flour
3 eggs
oil for frying
confectioners' sugar

Place the water, margarine, sugar, and salt in a saucepan. Bring to a boil, and immediately dump in the flour, stirring with a wooden spoon until the batter is smooth. Remove from heat and cool for a few minutes. Then add the eggs, one at a time, until the batter is glossy and smooth. Heat the oil. Take small pieces of the dough, and roll into long sticks, about 4 inches each. Drop the pieces into the hot oil, and fry until golden. Drain on paper towels. Sprinkle with confectioners' sugar. Serve hot or cold. 4 to 6 servings.

*   *   *

POSTRE DE NARANJA (Orange Dessert)

4 oranges
orange juice
1 tablespoon cornstarch
3 egg yolks

½ cup sugar
whipped cream or nondairy
   topping
chopped almonds

Cut the top off the oranges and with a teaspoon take out all the pulp and juice from each orange, leaving only the orange peel cups. Measure the juice and pulp. If there are not 2 full cups of the pulp and juice, add more orange juice. In the top of a double boiler, mix the 2 cups of pulp and juice, cornstarch, egg yolks, and sugar. Place over hot water, and cook the pudding, stirring until thickened. Chill the pudding and the orange peel cups in refrigerator. Before serving, pour the pudding into each orange peel cup. Decorate with whipped cream or topping and chopped almonds. 4 servings.

THE HOLIDAYS

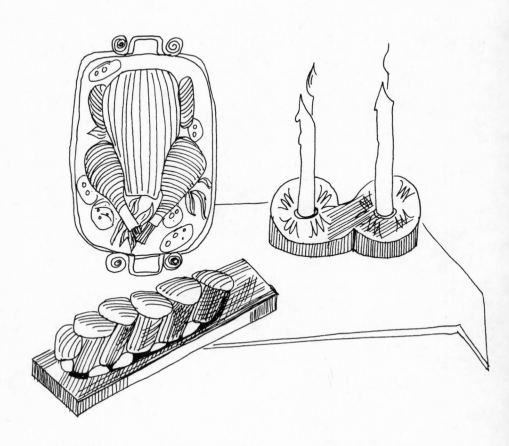

SABBATH

In all generations the Sabbath brought the Jew respite from his earthly toil and drudgery and was eagerly awaited as an oasis of joy in a desert of endless burdens and sorrows. The prophet proclaimed: "And [you shall] call the Sabbath a delight" (Isaiah 58:13). The joy of a day of rest, bringing relief and renewal of spirit after the humdrum weekday routine, promised richer living and a brighter future to the Jew.

"He who took the pains to prepare on the eve of the Sabbath will enjoy the Sabbath" (Avodah Zarah 3a) has been a guiding principle in Jewish life. Jacob Molin, "Maharil," a leading rabbi of German Jewry (c. 1360–1427), connected the legend of the two angels, who escort the Jew from the synagogue to his home on Friday evening, to the preparations for the Sabbath meals. If the proper food was prepared, the angels blessed him, according to the Maharil. A Yiddish folk proverb claims: "If for the Sabbath there is no food/On weekdays there will be nothing good."

Maimonides taught that one is obligated to prepare the best food and drink for the enjoyment of the Sabbath, each according to his means. If one is wealthy and always eats well, he should vary the Sabbath dishes so that they will be different from those of the weekdays. If this is not feasible, he should at least change the accustomed hours of the meal. However, if one does not have the means, he need not impoverish himself or borrow to provide for the Sabbath. Nevertheless, many poor people skimped throughout the week and were satisfied to eat a bare minimum so that they could have the necessities for enjoying the holy Sabbath. In the Talmud it is said of Shammai the Elder that all his days he would eat in honor of the Sabbath. When he found a fine animal, he would say, "Let this be for the Sabbath." If he found a better animal later on, he would reserve it for the Sabbath and eat the first one (Betzah 16a). The Talmud also relates that the rabbis of old set an example by doing manual labor in preparation for ushering in the Sabbath: one cut the vegetables for the Sabbath, another chopped wood for cooking, and a third lit the fire (Shabbat 119a).

The Jewish "woman of valor" always shopped well in advance of the Sabbath and rose early on Friday to prepare the traditional meals, at which the choicest dishes were served. Rashi, commenting on the passage in the Talmud that states that a woman should rise early to bake bread (Baba Kamma 82a), explains that she does so in order to have the bread ready for the poor when they come to the door. The spirit of generous hospitality is especially evident on the Sabbath, when householders anxiously seek strangers and poor persons to invite as table companions. "The reception of guests is as important as the reception of the Sabbath," Rabbi Nahman of Bratzlav once said.

Three meals are prescribed for the Sabbath—Friday evening and Saturday midday, which are the main ones, and Saturday in the late afternoon, usually a light repast. The Talmud (Shabbat 117b) deduces this practice from the repetition three times of the word today, once for each of the Sabbath meals, in the following verse: "Then Moses said, 'Eat it today, for today is a sabbath of the Lord; you will not find it today on the plain' " (Exodus 16:25). These meals are a significant element in the Sabbath commemoration.

The Sabbath is greeted with prayer, candlelight, songs, wine, and the festive meal. Before the candles are kindled, the table is set with the finest linen, cutlery, and dishes available. At the head of the table are placed a wine goblet and decanter and two covered hallot. Before the family sits down to enjoy the Friday evening meal, a selection from Proverbs (31:10–31) is sung in praise of the Jewish wife who "looketh well to the ways of her household and eateth not the bread of idleness" and then the greeting to the Sabbath, "Sholom Aleichem," is chanted. The Kiddush (Sanctification) of the Sabbath is pronounced over a cup of wine. The blessing for bread is said over the two hallot. Zemirot appropriate to the Sabbath are sung between courses. The singing of these table hymns of praise to God while dining is the distinguishing characteristic of the Sabbath meals. The evening meal is generally lengthy and, at least among the Jews of Baghdad, often extended to midnight.

A typical menu included gefilte fish, "golden soup" with yellow pieces of chicken fat floating on the surface and noodles or mandlen, chicken or meat, tzimmes, and compote. In the Middle Ages Jews in Arabian countries would start the Sabbath meal with the Kiddush. Then they ate fruits and drank a second glass of wine with the toast "To health and life." This procedure was repeated several times until the main dish of meat was served.

The pièce de résistance of the Sabbath midday meal is the cholent.

Chopped eggs and onions or chopped liver was often the entrée. Besides the kugel, another choice morsel was *petsha,* a concoction of calves' feet and other ingredients.

The third meal—*seudah shelishit*—is considered by Hasidim to be the most important, for then they gather with their leader and listen to his words of Torah and join in singing. In honor of the departure of Queen Sabbath they also eat a fourth meal after dark, called *melaveh malkah* (escorting the queen).

While there are common threads woven in the pattern of Jewish life through the world, traditions and customs vary from place to place. The distinctive culinary practices observed by Yemenite Jews on the Sabbath are described by Devora and Menahem Hacohen: "*Kiddush* was followed with *geala*—a trayful of fruits and roasted beans, the standard appetizer preceding every festive meal, washed down with wine or *arak* and accompanied with *zemirot* or special mealtime chants and Torah talk. Next, a tray laden with *shoiya*, roast meat, was placed in front of the head of the household, which he would proceed to divide among the others, each in turn according to his age. All but the young quaffed wine in varying amounts; for the young, wine was held to be unhealthful. Everyone joined in the singing on the Sabbath; on weekdays, one person would lead and the others respond. And only at this point did the formal meal commence, with the father and his male progeny washing their hands in the *majassal,* a water basin used only for this purpose. Each had his pair of *hallot,* which he dipped in the bowls of *hilbeh* [a spice mixture] and soup. In conclusion, following the grace, the assemblage partook of sweets, coffee and dates" (*One People: The Story of the Eastern Jews,* Sabra Books, 1969).

In Morocco, as in so many other countries, cholent was the indispensable Sabbath dish. The ingredients were usually meat, eggs, potatoes, rice, and *humus. Humus* was also cooked with the Sabbath fish. Tunisian Jewry likewise enjoyed a cholent on the Sabbath; they disdained fish as too cheap to be eaten in honor of the seventh day. On Friday evening the main dish was a stew of steamed kuskus, meat, and vegetables. The special Sabbath dishes of Libyan Jews were *harimi* (fish cooked with tomato sauce, garlic, peppers, and onions) and *mafrum* (ground meat with eggs, onion, and different spices, cooked between slices of eggplant).

A more detailed picture of the role of Sabbath foods can be gained by a closer examination of several specific dishes, such as the hallah, fish, cholent, and kugel.

The two twisted loaves of bread, called hallot, covered with a special decorative napkin, are set at the head of the table. The twin loaves are symbolic of the double portion of manna ("bread from heaven") that the children of Israel collected on Friday during their sojourn in the desert so that they would not desecrate the Sabbath by gathering manna (Exodus 16). The cover recalls the dew which fell on the manna. It was generally made of linen or silk embroidered with wool, silk, or beadwork, with an inscription such as "Remember the sabbath day and keep it holy" (Exodus 20:8). Hallah originally meant the portion of the dough given as a thanksgiving offering to the priests during the days of the Temple. Hence when the pious Jewish housewife bakes hallah she separates a small piece of the dough (about the size of an olive) when it is kneaded, recites an appropriate benediction, and casts the piece into the fire. The enriched bread is often flavored with saffron, painted with egg yolk, and sprinkled with poppy seeds or sesame seeds.

From time immemorial fish has been a favorite Sabbath dish. In response to the question, "With what does one enjoy the Sabbath," one of the rabbis of the Talmud said (Shabbat 118b), "With a dish of beets, large fish, and garlic heads." Another responded that even a trifle is a delight provided it is prepared in honor of the Sabbath. And what is a trifle? "A pie of fish-hash." These may be the first references to eating fish on the Sabbath. Some pious Jews refrain from partaking of fish throughout the week so they may relish it on the Sabbath. One reason for the exalted place that fish occupies on the Sabbath table is derived from the legend that the manna had the taste of many foods but not that of fish. Therefore fish is eaten on the Sabbath to complete the joy of the day with all manner of savor. Another explanation was devised by ingenious epicures. As the Hebrew word for fish, *dag*, is numerically equivalent to seven, it is fitting that fish be a main dish for the seventh day. The head of the fish is customarily served to the head of the family. Frankfurt Jews had a folk saying: "Carp is no shame, pike is all right, but salmon is best of all." Among East European Jews gefilte (stuffed) fish was most beloved and they would say: "Well-known is the Sabbath pleasure of stuffed fish / And even during the week it's no mean dish."

The prohibition against cooking on the Sabbath made it difficult to provide hot dishes in the winter months. So Jewish ingenuity created such delectable eatables as cholent and kugel (pudding), which were prepared ahead, placed in a heated oven before the Sabbath, and kept there overnight until served steaming hot at the noon meal. In many communities public ovens were available for this purpose. The word cholent stems from *chauld*, an Old French word meaning warm. Germans call it *schalet*, possibly a corruption of the French. One lexicographer claims that cholent came to Yiddish from the Latin *calens* (hot), through the French. By whatever name it is called, this Sabbath dish has received glowing homage. Heinrich Heine extolled the virtues of *schalet* that he gulped down at a Sabbath noon meal "with appetite, enthusiasm, fervor and conviction." In his poem "Princess Sabbath," Israel Zangwill sings of "Schalet, ray of light immortal! Schalet, daughter of Elysium!" and calls it "food of heaven," "pure ambrosia," and "paradisal bread of rapture."

The cholent ingredients, which vary from community to community, may include potatoes, beans, groats, barley, and meat. Some added *helzel,* the skin of the neck of a fowl stuffed with flour and matzah meal.

"A Sabbath without kugel is like a bird without wings," a folk proverb reminds us. Indeed, a kugel, whether made with rice, raisins, and cinnamon or (preferably) with noodles and a stuffed *helzel,* was considered indispensable. The name may be derived from the German *Kugel,* which means ball or bullet, referring to its round shape, or from the Hebrew *ke-igul,* "as a circle."

That the special Sabbath dishes have enhanced the joyousness and spirituality of the seventh day is evident to all those who share in the observance of the day of rest. The Talmud (Shabbat 119a) records a conversation between an emperor and Rabbi Joshua ben Hananiah. The emperor asked: "What gives your Sabbath dishes such an appetizing aroma?" The rabbi replied, "We have a spice called Sabbath and this makes the pleasing aroma." "Give us some of this seasoning," the emperor ordered. The rabbi replied, "The spice is effective only for those who observe the Sabbath."

* * *

HALLAH*

1 package (¼ ounce) active dry yeast	1 egg, beaten
1 cup warm water (105°–115°)	3¼–3½ cups flour, sifted
¼ cup sugar	⅓ cup raisins (optional)
1 teaspoon salt	1 egg yolk
2 tablespoons margarine, softened	poppy or sesame seeds

In a mixing bowl, dissolve the yeast in the warm water. Stir in the sugar, salt, margarine, egg, and 2 cups of flour. Beat with a wooden

---

This recipe was given to me by Mrs. Solomon Grayzel.

spoon or by hand until smooth. Add the raisins. With spoon or hand, work in the remaining flour until dough is easy to handle and is not sticky. Knead the dough for 5 minutes.

Grease a bowl and place the dough in it. Turn the dough over so that the greased part is on top to prevent it from drying. Cover tightly with foil and refrigerate overnight, or up to 5 days.

Divide the dough in half. Then divide each half into 3 pieces.

On a floured board, roll each piece of dough into a strand, tapering the ends. Braid three strands together, pinching the ends to hold them together.

Lay the braided hallah on a greased pan. Repeat the same procedure with the other three strands.

Cover the shaped hallot with a clean towel and allow to rise in a warm place (85°) for 2 hours or until double in bulk.

Beat the egg yolk with a teaspoon of water. Brush the tops of the hallot with the egg yolk mixture, and sprinkle with poppy or sesame seeds.

Bake for 25 to 30 minutes in a 375° oven or until the hallah sounds hollow when tapped on the bottom. Remove from oven and allow to cool away from drafts. 2 medium hallot.

The hallah dough can be used to make rolls of any shape desired.

According to Jewish law, if a substantial amount of dough is being used (approximately 3½ or more pounds), then a piece of dough the size of an olive is separated from the bulk and is burnt in the oven while the hallah is baking. Before the separation a special blessing is recited.

*   *   *

SWEET AND SOUR SALMON

2 pounds salmon, sliced	⅓ cup blanched almonds
1½ cups water	juice of 1 lemon
1 lemon, sliced	2 bay leaves
½ cup vinegar	¼ cup crystallized ginger,
1 teaspoon onion powder	sliced
½ cup brown sugar	

Clean and salt the salmon. Refrigerate overnight.

Bring the water, lemon, vinegar, onion powder, brown sugar, almonds, lemon juice, and bay leaves to a boil. Lower the heat, and simmer for 15 minutes. Add the ginger. Correct the seasoning by adding more sugar or lemon to taste.

Add the salmon, and cook for 20 minutes. Allow to cool.

Remove the salmon to a glass dish, and pour the sauce over the fish. Refrigerate. The fish will keep for 10 days. 6 servings.

*   *   *

CHOPPED CHICKEN LIVERS

1 pound chicken livers
4 tablespoons margarine,
* chicken fat, or oil*

2 medium onions, sliced
salt and pepper to taste

Broil the livers and rinse in cold water.

Melt the margarine, and add the onions. Sauté for 15 minutes, until the onions are soft and lightly browned. Remove the onions to a plate.

Add the livers to the same pot. Cover the pot and cook the livers for 8 minutes over very low heat.

Put the livers and the onions through a grinder. Add salt and pepper and more margarine or chicken fat if it seems dry.

For a finer texture, put the liver mixture through the grinder a second time. This is especially important when calves' liver or beef liver is used instead of the chicken livers.

Serve with radishes and pickles. Decorate with a sprig of fresh dill. 6 servings.

Two hard-cooked eggs may be added when grinding the livers. This will make 8 servings.

*   *   *

PETSHA

1 calf foot, cut up
4 cups water
1 onion
salt and pepper to taste
a few peppercorns
1 bay leaf

2 eggs, hard-cooked and sliced
2 garlic cloves, crushed
4 tablespoons vinegar
lettuce leaves
lemon slices
1 hard-cooked egg, chopped

Pour boiling water over the calf foot. Scrape off all the hair. Wash again and put into a pot with the water. Add the onion, salt and pepper, peppercorns, and bay leaf. Bring to a boil; lower heat, and simmer for 3 hours until the meat falls off the bones.

Strain the *petsha*. Reserve the meat from the calf foot, and cut into very small pieces. Return the meat to the *petsha*.

To the sliced eggs, add the garlic, salt and pepper, and vinegar. Pour into the *petsha*.

Pour into a square dish and chill overnight. To serve, cut in squares and set on plates covered with lettuce leaves. Garnish with lemon slices and a sprinkling of chopped egg. The *petsha* can also be served hot as a soup. 6 servings.

*   *   *

EGGS AND ONIONS

6 eggs, hard-cooked
1 onion, chopped
2 scallions, chopped
6 tablespoons chicken fat or oil
½ pound liver, broiled and
  sliced (optional)

salt and pepper to taste
lettuce leaves
radishes
sliced tomatoes

Cut up the eggs; add the onion, scallions, and the fat or oil. (If the liver is used, more oil will be required.) Season with salt and pepper. Serve on lettuce leaves with radishes and sliced tomatoes. 6 servings.

*   *   *

CHICKEN SOUP

4 pounds chicken and giblets
6 cups water
salt and white pepper to taste
2 medium onions
2 carrots
1 sweet potato
1 small green or yellow squash

2 celery stalks with leaves
4 parsley sprigs
4 dill sprigs
1 parsley root
small piece of fresh ginger or
  ½ teaspoon powdered ginger
5 peppercorns

In a soup pot, bring the chicken and the giblets to boil in the water. As soon as the water boils, lower the heat to simmering. Add the salt and pepper, onions, carrots, sweet potato, and squash. Tie the celery, parsley, dill, and parsley root together with a string, and add to the pot. Add the ginger and peppercorns.

Simmer the soup until the chicken is tender. Remove the chicken, and continue to simmer the soup for 30 minutes.

Strain the soup of all the vegetables. Then pour through a strainer lined with paper towels. The scum and fat will remain on the paper, and the soup will be clear.

Correct the seasoning. Reheat the soup before serving. 6 servings. The chicken soup may be served with the semolina *kugelach*.

SEMOLINA KUGELACH

1 large egg
5 tablespoons semolina
1 tablespoon parsley, chopped

1 teaspoon salt
¼ teaspoon pepper
oil for frying

Beat the egg well. Add the semolina together with the parsley, salt, and pepper. Let the mixture stand for 1 hour.

Heat ½ inch of oil in a frying pan and, when the oil is hot, drop the semolina mixture by teaspoons into the oil. Fry on both sides until lightly golden. Remove the *kugelach*, and drain them on paper toweling.

When the soup is boiling, drop the *kugelach* into the soup. Cover the pot, reduce the heat, and simmer the *kugelach* for 20 minutes.

*   *   *

ROAST CHICKEN

4 pounds roasting chicken
salt to taste
½ teaspoon pepper
1 teaspoon paprika

½ teaspoon garlic powder
½ teaspoon onion powder
½ teaspoon thyme
½ teaspoon powdered ginger

Clean and truss the chicken. Salt and pepper it well, and sprinkle with the other spices.

Lay the chicken in a roaster or pot that is not too large (chicken or any meat will dry out if the utensil used is too large). Roast the chicken in a 325° oven for about 2 hours, depending on the tenderness of the chicken, or until nicely browned and tender. 6 servings.

*   *   *

STUFFED HELZEL

1 tablespoon matzah meal
2 tablespoons flour
salt and pepper to taste
1 small onion, grated

1½ tablespoons cut-up chicken
fat or margarine
1 chicken neck (helzel)

Mix all the ingredients for the stuffing.

With white thread, sew up the wide side of the chicken neck first. Stuff the neck with the stuffing mixture, and finish sewing up the neck. Do not stuff too full, as room should be allowed for expansion while it is being cooked.

Cook the *helzel* in soup or water for 1 hour, and then add it to the juices in the pan of the roast chicken. Before serving, remove the threads from both sides and slice into desired portions. 4 servings.

*   *   *

POTATO KUGEL

5 *large potatoes, peeled*	2 *teaspoons salt*
1 *medium onion*	½ *teaspoon black pepper*
3 *eggs*	6 *tablespoons margarine or oil*
3 *tablespoons matzah meal*	

Peel and grate the potatoes and onion. Squeeze as much water out of the potatoes as possible. Add the eggs, matzah meal, salt, and pepper. Mix well. Do not allow the mixture to stand too long, as it will turn brown.

Heat 4 tablespoons of margarine in a 9 × 9-inch baking dish. Pour the potato mixture into the dish.

Melt the 2 remaining tablespoons of margarine, and pour over the top of the kugel. Bake in a 375° oven for 1 hour. Serve hot. 6 large servings.

*   *   *

CHOLENT

a *few bones*	*salt and pepper to taste*
2 *large onions, sliced*	½ *pound large pearl barley,*
12 *medium potatoes, peeled*	*washed*
1 *pound large lima beans,*	1 *medium onion, chopped*
washed	3 *tablespoons margarine or*
2 *bay leaves*	*chicken fat*
½ *teaspoon peppercorns*	3 *pounds flank (flanken) meat*
2 *garlic cloves*	3 *pounds brisket*
½ *tablespoon paprika*	*water to cover*

In a very large roaster, place the bones and onions. At one end of the roaster put the potatoes, and at the other end, the beans. Scatter the spices all around; salt and pepper the potatoes and beans. Take a piece of foil, and on it put the barley, onion, salt and pepper, and margarine or chicken fat. Close all sides of the foil like an envelope, leaving enough room for expansion. Place the foil envelope in the middle of the roaster. Lay the flanken and brisket over the beans and potatoes. Salt and pepper the meat.

Cover with water, making sure that the water is above the meat but leave enough room so that the cholent does not boil over.

Cover with foil, securing it all around the pot, and then put on the cover of the roaster.

A few hours before the Sabbath, place the cholent in an oven set at 200°. Bake overnight until lunchtime.

Before serving, remove the foil, and skim off the fat that has accumulated on top. 12 servings.

Landjaeger, a sausage bought in German Jewish butcher stores, adds a lot of flavor when put into the cholent together with the meat.

Serve sour pickles and pickled beets with the cholent and a citrus fruit for dessert.

*   *   *

CHOLENT KUGEL

1 pound medium noodles	3 eggs
½ cup margarine or oil	1 teaspoon cinnamon
⅓ cup sugar	½ teaspoon nutmeg
⅓ cup flour	1 cup water
salt and pepper to taste	

Boil the noodles in salt water for 10 minutes. Strain and rinse with cold water.

Heat the margarine or oil; add the sugar and caramelize it, being careful not to burn the caramel. Add this to the noodles. Mix in the flour, salt and pepper, eggs, cinnamon, and nutmeg.

Pour the pudding into a very well greased pot, and bake in a 375° oven until browned all over. When the kugel is done, pour the water over it and allow to simmer overnight as for cholent. 12 servings.

*   *   *

NOODLE KUGEL

½ pound medium noodles	1 teaspoon cinnamon
6 tablespoons margarine or butter	¼ teaspoon nutmeg
	1 teaspoon vanilla
salt to taste	½ cup raisins
3 eggs	½ cup apricots, diced
½ cup sugar	

Cook the noodles in salted water for 10 minutes. Drain well.

Put the noodles in a bowl and add 4 tablespoons of margarine. Add salt. Beat the eggs with the sugar, cinnamon, nutmeg, and vanilla. Add the egg mixture to the noodles. Add the raisins and apricots.

Melt the 2 remaining tablespoons of margarine in a 9 × 9-inch baking dish, and pour the noodle mixture into the dish.

Bake the kugel for 45 minutes in a 350° oven. Serve hot. 6 servings.

*   *   *

EIER KICHEL (Egg Cookies)

3 eggs	*½ teaspoon salt*
¼ cup oil	*2–2½ cups flour*
¼ cup sugar	*1 teaspoon baking powder*

Beat the eggs with the oil, sugar, and salt. Add 2 cups of flour with the baking powder, and mix well. Dough will be sticky. Knead for a few minutes until dough is soft and smooth. If the dough is sticky, add more flour.

On a floured piece of wax paper measuring 12 × 24 inches, roll out the dough to cover the surface.

Brush the dough lightly with oil and sprinkle with sugar.

Cut into squares or diamonds and put the kichel on a greased foil-lined cookie sheet. To make bow ties, cut the dough into 1½ × 6-inch pieces and twist each piece into a tie shape.

Bake in a 350° oven for 15 minutes or until light brown in color. 32 cookies.

*   *   *

APPLE STRUDEL

1 can apples for pie, drained	*margarine or butter, melted*
¾ cup sugar	*1 cup cornflake crumbs or*
1 teaspoon cinnamon	*bread crumbs*
grated peel of 1 lemon	*1 cup almonds, chopped*
6 strudel leaves	

Mix the apples with the sugar, cinnamon, and lemon peel for the filling.

Remove 3 strudel leaves, and spread some melted margarine or butter over the top leaf. Sprinkle with half the crumbs and almonds.

Spread half the apple filling across one end of the strudel, a few inches from the edge. Fold the dough over the filling, and roll up the strudel.

Place the filled strudel on a greased cookie sheet, brush with more melted margarine or butter, and sprinkle with some sugar. Cut the strudel in portions, but do not cut all the way through.

Repeat with the other 3 strudel leaves.

Bake the strudel in a 375° oven until browned. Cool and cut in portions. 12 servings.

*   *   *

CHERRY CAKE

2 eggs
1 cup sugar
½ cup margarine
2 cups flour, sifted
2 teaspoons baking powder

1 teaspoon vanilla
1 can cherry pie filling
1 can pitted sour cherries,
    drained

Beat the eggs with the sugar and margarine until fluffy. Stir in the flour, baking powder, and vanilla.

Mix the cherry pie filling with the sour cherries.

Spread half the batter in a greased 9 × 9-inch cake pan. Cover with the cherry mixture. Drop the rest of the batter by teaspoons all over the top of the cherry mixture. Sprinkle sugar over the top. Bake the cake in a 375° oven for 45 minutes.

HIGH HOLY DAYS

A number of symbolic customs enhance the significance of Rosh Hashanah meals. According to some writers, originally they may have been motivated by a belief that these customs would be omens of "good luck," a concept many rabbis condemned as an exercise in superstition. As they evolved, however, they serve to induce a festive atmosphere appropriate to the holiday, and to inspire faith and confidence that God's mercy would be ever present in the new year.

The biblical source for the custom of feasting on Rosh Hashanah is adumbrated in the Book of Nehemiah (8:10). After Ezra the scribe had read from the book of the Law to the assembled people on the first day of the seventh month (Tishri), they burst into weeping. Whereupon Nehemiah said to them: "Go your way, eat the fat, and drink the sweet, and send portions unto him for whom nothing is prepared; for this day is holy unto our Lord." This passage also reminds the Jew of his obligations to provide food for the poor. Thus it is customary to invite the needy for the Rosh Hashanah meals.

The hallot (loaves of bread) for the New Year meals are usually baked in different shapes, each with a symbolic meaning. Some are made in the shape of a ladder or topped with a ladder, in keeping with the midrashic assertion that on Rosh Hashanah, "The Holy One, blessed be He, sits and erects ladders; on them He lowers one person and elevates another . . . that is to say, God judges those who will descend and those who will ascend." The interpretation is clear: He decrees who will rise on the ladder of prosperity and who will be reduced to poverty.

Bread is also baked in the form of a bird, which is tender imagery for God's protection suggested in Isaiah 31:5: "As birds hovering [over their fledglings], so will the Lord of hosts protect Jerusalem." Lithuanian Jews bake hallot topped with a crown, in accordance with the piyyut by Eleazar Kalir, "And thus let all crown God." To signify the desire for a long span of life, circular loaves of bread are usually served.

At the evening meal, after the Kiddush over wine is chanted and the benediction for bread is pronounced, a piece of hallah is dipped in a dish of honey and eaten. The blessing for fruit is then said over a slice of apple dipped in honey, and the following formula is recited: "May it be Thy will to renew unto us a good and sweet year." Some continue eating apples with honey until the conclusion of Sukkot. Rabbi Jacob Molin, "Maharil" (c. 1360–1427), cites this custom of eating an apple dipped in honey as a long-established tradition based on Nehemiah 8:10, and indicates that special meaning is ascribed in Jewish mysticism.

The Maharil also points out that the head of a lamb is eaten at the evening meal in remembrance of the ram sacrificed by Abraham as a substitute for his son Isaac. Eating a head was believed to presage that one will become a head, a leader, rather than a tail, a follower. In modern practice the head of a fish is served, and he who eats it says: "May it be Thy will that we become like a head [le-rosh] and not a tail." Some hold that fish are eaten because they are so prolific, wherefore they recite the following: "May it be Thy will that we will be fruitful and multiply like fish." Others avidly sought a certain fish called *kerat*, meaning "destroy," which they ate to signify the hoped-for destruction of their enemies.

Many Sephardic Jewish families eat a series of special foods preceding the meal, in observance of the talmudic tradition: "Abaye said, If you maintain that symbols are meaningful, every man should acquire the habit of eating pumpkin, fenugreek, leek, beet and dates on Rosh Hashanah" (Keritot 6a). As these foods grow rapidly, they are considered symbolic of fertility, abundance, and prosperity.

It appears that the attempt to find symbolic meanings for foods was always popular. According to *Mahzor Vitry,* on Rosh Hashanah in France in the twelfth century "the custom was to eat red apples; in Provence they ate white grapes, white figs, and a calf's head, or any new food easily digestible and tasty, as an omen of good luck to all Israel."

A favorite Ashkenazic dish is carrot tzimmes; the Yiddish for carrot is *mehren,* which also means "increase." Eating the carrot tzimmes is accompanied by the expression: "May it be Thy will that our merits will be increased." Carrots were also cooked whole and then sliced into circles, resembling coins in color and shape. This patently alluded to a yearning for a prosperous year.

Sweet cakes have long been considered appropriate fare for Rosh Hashanah. This custom is said to be traceable to King David. The Bible relates: "So David and all the house of Israel brought up the ark of the Lord with shouting, and with the sound of the horn [shofar]. . . . And he dealt among all the people . . . to every one a cake of bread, and a cake made in a pan, and a sweet cake" (2 Samuel 6:15, 19). The "sweet cake" is identified as a raisin cake (Hosea 3:1).

Honey cake and teiglach have long been popular among many Jews.

Sour or bitter foods are not eaten on Rosh Hashanah. It is customary not to eat nuts because the numerical equivalent of the Hebrew letters for "nut" *(egoz)* is 17, the same as for "sin" *(het)* when the silent vowel is dropped. To avoid the possibility of suggesting sin, eating nuts is frowned upon.

Notwithstanding the general avoidance of sour foods, in France and in Jerusalem bitter pickled olives were distributed to the worshipers as they departed from the synagogue on the night of Rosh Hashanah. This was a reminder to have faith in God, as asserted in the Talmud: "Let my sustenance be as bitter as the olive in Thy Divine charge, rather than sweet as honey in the charge of flesh and blood" (Sanhedrin 108b).

An innovation is introduced on the second night of Rosh Hashanah. Since the two days of Rosh Hashanah are regarded as a single "long day," doubt arises about the necessity of pronouncing the Sheheheyanu blessing on the second night. In order to avoid the possibility of reciting a *berakhah le-vatalah* (a blessing in vain), a new seasonal fruit is placed on the table or a new garment is worn when the Kiddush is recited. Thus, the Sheheheyanu will be on the fruit or on the garment, both of which require this benediction.

The festive pre-Yom Kippur meal goes back many centuries. In Galilee and Babylonia elaborate banquets were held on the eve of the Day of Atonement. The Talmud states: "If a man eats and drinks on the ninth [day of Tishri], Scripture considers it as if he fasted on both the ninth and tenth [Yom Kippur] days" (Yoma 81b). The feasting symbolizes rejoicing and spiritual exaltation evoked by the imminent approach of the day on which atonement is attained. The heart of the Jew glories in the knowledge that the following day will provide an opportunity for genuine repentance, thereby leading to self-regeneration and to removing whatever chasm may intervene between him and his Maker. In light of this anticipated spiritual boon that will be showered upon him on Yom Kippur, eating and drinking on the eve of its arrival is considered a mitzvah.

There is yet another consideration. On all other festivals it is customary to partake of a *seudat mitzvah* (a meal in fulfillment of a commandment). But Yom Kippur, being a fast day, does not come within the purview of this practice; therefore, the festive meal was introduced on

the eve of the Day of Atonement. Indubitably, humanitarian considerations also prompted the institution of special meals. The welfare of
the individual was always a precious component in Jewish law; he
must be provided with vitality to endure the fast and to concentrate
on the day-long prayers and communion with God. In their zeal to
approach the Day of Awe adequately prepared, Persian Jews established the custom of eating seven meals before the eve of Yom Kippur.

It is regarded as meritorious to offer hospitality to the poor when
preparing for the Day of Atonement. In the days of the Temple in
Jerusalem the sacrifice on the altar made atonement for man's sins; at
present "a man's table makes atonement for him," according to the
Talmud (Hagigah 27a). Rashi interprets "table" as "hospitality," implying that one should invite the needy to partake of the pre-Yom
Kippur meal.

In Eastern Europe the sexton or the gabbai of the synagogue would
distribute candy or slices of honey cake to all the worshipers after the
morning services on the eve of the Day of Atonement. Before eating,
each would say, "If, God forbid, it will be the celestial decree that in
the coming year I will be condemned to accept charity, may I fulfill
the decree with this morsel I took from you."

The hallot for the eve of Yom Kippur are usually round and braided.
Hallot were also baked in the shape of wings, in keeping with the
tradition that on the Day of Atonement Jews are considered pure as
angels.

The favorite dish on this day is kreplach, dough filled with meat. The
meat symbolizes inflexible justice, the soft dough which covers it
denotes compassion. Like the hallot, the kreplach metaphorically sug-
gest that the attribute of God's strict justice will be mellowed on the
side of mercy. Kreplach are eaten three times a year: Yom Kippur eve,
Hoshana Rabbah, and Purim—days reckoned as festivals with regard
to eating and drinking, but not as regards forbidding work.

The main dish of the meal is generally poultry. In communities like
those in North Africa, chicken was "such a luxury that it was almost
never eaten by any but the very rich except once a year at the last
meal before the annual fast day of Yom Kippur." Fish and spicy foods
which may create thirst are generally avoided.

After the final meal, a white cloth is spread over the dining table,
on which a Bible, *Siddur,* and other sacred books are placed in lieu
of the traditional Sabbath and festival loaves. The books are covered
with a cloth until the break-the-fast meal as symbolic testimony that
this holy day is being honored not with food and drink but with study
and prayer.

One is expected to eat and rejoice on the night following Yom

Kippur, which is considered to be somewhat of a festival. According to Midrash Ecclesiastes Rabbah, at the conclusion of the long day of fasting a heavenly voice proclaims: "Go thy way, eat thy bread with joy/And drink thy wine with a merry heart;/For God hath already accepted thy works."

In the Sephardic Day of Atonement rite, this verse from Ecclesiastes is quoted immediately following the shofar blast which concludes the Neilah service.

*   *   *

ROUND HALLAH

For the list of ingredients and instructions for making the dough, see the recipe for hallah in the Sabbath chapter.

Divide the dough in half and, on a floured board, roll the dough out in a rope 16 inches in length, tapering the ends. Coil the rope tightly, tucking the end under. Lay the hallah on a greased pan.

Repeat this procedure with the second piece of dough.

To decorate a hallah with the traditional symbol of a ladder, reserve a piece of dough. Half of the reserved dough is to be used for each hallah. For each ladder, form dough into 2 pencil-thin 4-inch strips for the 2 sides and 4 pencil-thin 2-inch strips for the rungs. Beat the egg yolk with 1 teaspoon of water. Brush the strips with egg yolk mixture, and place on the hallah in the form of a ladder. Small pieces of dough may be shaped into little birds or wings to symbolize angels.

Cover the shaped hallot with a clean towel and allow to rise in a warm place (85°) for 2 hours or until double in bulk.

Brush the tops of the hallot with the rest of the egg yolk mixture, and sprinkle with the poppy or sesame seeds.

Bake for 25 to 30 minutes in a 375° oven or until the hallah sounds hollow when tapped on the bottom. 2 medium hallot.

*   *   *

GEFILTE FISH

3 pounds fish fillets (white,
  pike, and carp)
fish heads
fish bones
salt
4½ cups water

5 onions
3 carrots
2 teaspoons sugar
salt and white pepper to taste
4 eggs, beaten
⅓ cup matzah meal

When buying the fish, request all the bones and heads of the fish purchased.

Wash and dry the fish fillets, heads, and bones, and put into a bowl. Sprinkle with salt and refrigerate overnight or for a few hours. Do not wash off the salt.

To make the broth, put all the bones (but not the fish heads) into a pot and cover with 4 cups of cold water. Bring to a boil, lower the heat, and simmer for 30 minutes. Strain the broth, discarding the bones. Return the broth to the pot. Add 3 sliced onions, the carrots, sugar, and salt and pepper.

While the broth is cooking, make the stuffing. Put the fish fillets and 2 onions through the grinder twice. Add the eggs, matzah meal, salt and pepper, and ½ cup of water. Mix well. Correct the seasoning, if necessary.

Wet your hands with cold water, then take some of the fish mixture and form into a ball. Stuff the reserved fish heads with the ball, and put on top of the onions and carrots in the pot with the broth. Continue to form balls with the rest of the fish mixture, wetting hands with water, and placing the balls in the pot.

Cover the pot, bring to a boil, lower the heat, and cook for 1 hour. Shake the pot occasionally so the fish will not stick to the bottom of the pot. Lift the cover, taste the broth for seasoning, and, if needed, add more water. Continue to cook the fish covered for another hour. Let the fish cool in the pot before removing the fish balls. When cold, remove the fish to a bowl. Remove the carrots and slice. Strain the broth into another bowl or, if preferred, pour over the fish. Refrigerate the fish and the broth. Serve the fish with a slice of carrot and some of the jellied broth. The stuffed fish head is served to the head of the family. 12 servings.

*   *   *

CARROT TZIMMES WITH MEAT

2 pounds carrots	½ cup honey
3 pounds brisket	1 teaspoon cinnamon
1 onion, chopped	2 tablespoons lemon juice
salt to taste	1½ tablespoons flour

Scrape the carrots, and slice into rounds.

Put the meat, carrots, onion, and salt in a pot. Cover with water and bring to a boil. Lower the heat, and cook until the meat is tender. Add the honey, cinnamon, and lemon juice. Correct the seasoning, if necessary.

Mix the flour with some of the broth from the pot, and slowly add to the rest of the ingredients. Continue to cook for 20 more minutes. The tzimmes can also be baked in a 325° oven. 6 servings.

* * *

CARROT TZIMMES

1 pound carrots
¼ cup margarine
½ cup brown sugar

salt to taste
1 teaspoon powdered ginger
orange juice

Scrape the carrots, and slice into rounds. Place the carrots in a pot with the margarine, brown sugar, salt, and ginger. Add orange juice to cover, and bring to a boil. Lower the heat, and continue to cook until the carrots are soft and glazed. 4 servings.

* * *

LEEK PANCAKES

2 large leeks
1 egg
¼ cup bread crumbs

salt and pepper to taste
oil

Wash the leeks thoroughly in cold water to remove all sand from the leaves. Cut off the discolored parts and discard. Cut the clean leeks into small pieces and place in a pot. Cover with water, and cook for 10 minutes. Remove the leeks from the water, and drain well.

Chop up the leeks. Mix the chopped leeks with the rest of the ingredients, except the oil.

Heat the oil in a frying pan, and drop the leek mixture by table-spoons into the hot oil. Cook on both sides until light brown. Serve hot. 4 servings.

* * *

PUMPKIN WITH DUMPLINGS

3 pounds pumpkin
1 teaspoon salt
1 cup brown sugar
4 tablespoons margarine

½ teaspoon cinnamon
¼ teaspoon nutmeg
¼ teaspoon allspice
¼ teaspoon powdered ginger

Peel the pumpkin, and scrape out the seeds. Wash and cut in 2-inch pieces. Place the pumpkin in a pot, and add the salt, brown sugar, and margarine. Sauté over very low heat until the pumpkin is soft. Add the spices and ½ cup of water. Transfer to a casserole, and bake the pumpkin in a 350° oven for 30 minutes. Add the cooked dumplings (recipe follows), and continue to bake for 15 minutes. Serve hot. 6 servings.

DUMPLINGS

½ cup farina	2 eggs
¼ cup matzah meal	4 tablespoons margarine,
1 teaspoon salt	melted

Mix the farina with the matzah meal and salt.

Beat the eggs, and add the margarine. Beat in the dry ingredients, and mix well. Cover and refrigerate overnight or for a few hours.

In a big pot with a cover, bring 2 quarts of water to a boil. Add a little salt to the water. Wet hands, and form dumplings the size of a walnut. Drop the dumplings into the boiling water. Cover the pot, and cook the dumplings for 45 minutes. Do not remove the cover, but shake the pot so dumplings will not stick to the bottom of the pot.

Drain the dumplings, and add to the pumpkin casserole, placing them in the syrup. Bake for 15 minutes.

*   *   *

PINEAPPLE PUDDING

1-pound 14-ounce can crushed pineapple	1½ tablespoons margarine
3 tablespoons flour	½ teaspoon salt
4 eggs	juice of 1 lemon

Mix the flour with some of the pineapple juice, and stir the flour into the crushed pineapple. Beat the eggs well, and add to the crushed pineapple. Add the margarine, salt, and lemon juice, and mix well. Pour into a greased baking dish, and bake for 45 minutes in a 350° oven. Serve as a pudding or as a side dish with chicken or meat. 6 servings.

RAISIN CAKE

1 cup raisins
1 cup water
1 cup brown sugar
½ cup margarine
2 cups flour, sifted
2 teaspoons baking powder

½ teaspoon baking soda
1 teaspoon cinnamon
1 egg, beaten
grated peel of 1 lemon
juice of 1 lemon
confectioners' sugar

Put the raisins, water, brown sugar, and margarine in a saucepan, and bring to a boil. Lower the heat, and simmer for 5 minutes. Allow to cool.

Sift the flour together with the baking powder, baking soda, and cinnamon. Add the dry ingredients to the cooled raisin mixture together with the egg, lemon peel, and lemon juice, and mix well.

Pour the batter into a 9 × 9-inch greased pan. Bake in a 350° oven for 1 hour.

Sift confectioners' sugar over the top of the cake when cooled.

*　　　*　　　*

HONEY CAKE

4 cups flour, sifted
1 teaspoon baking soda
2½ teaspoons baking powder
1 teaspoon cinnamon
½ teaspoon powdered ginger
½ teaspoon allspice
½ teaspoon nutmeg

1½ cups sugar
2 tablespoons brown sugar
½ cup margarine
4 eggs
1 pound honey
¾ cup strong coffee

Sift the flour together with the baking soda, baking powder, and the spices.

Cream the sugars with the margarine until fluffy. Add the eggs, one at a time, mixing well. Add the honey.

Stir the flour and spices together with the coffee into the sugar, margarine, and honey mixture. Mix well.

Pour the batter into a greased and floured 9 × 12-inch pan.

Bake the cake in a 350° oven for 15 minutes. Reduce the oven to 325°, and continue to bake for 45 minutes longer or until done.

TEIGLACH

3 eggs
1 tablespoon sugar
3 tablespoons margarine
2 cups flour
2 teaspoons powdered ginger
1 cup broken walnuts

SYRUP
1 cup honey
1 cup sugar

Cream the eggs with the sugar and margarine. Add the flour, and mix together to form a soft but not sticky dough. If the dough is too sticky, use a little more flour.

Divide the dough into several batches. On a floured board, roll out each batch of the dough into a long rope. Cut into ½-inch pieces.

To make the syrup, bring the honey and sugar to a boil in a deep pot.

Drop the pieces of dough into the syrup. Cover the pot, lower the heat, and cook for 30 minutes. Shake the pot a few times while cooking so that the teiglach will not stick to the bottom of the pot. After cooking for 30 minutes, remove the cover and stir the teiglach with a wooden spoon to move the top pieces down into the syrup and bring the bottom ones to the top. Stir gently in order not to break the teiglach. Add the ginger and walnuts. (Those who adhere to the custom of not eating nuts on Rosh Hashanah can omit the walnuts.) Cover and continue to cook until all the pieces are browned. The teiglach are done when they are dry inside and not doughy.

Pour the teiglach on a flat wet board, and with wet hands flatten them out. Sprinkle with more ginger if ginger flavor is desired. When cold, cut in squares. Teiglach are best made on a dry, not humid, day.

*   *   *

APPLE AND HONEY COMPOTE

2 pounds baking apples
1 cup honey
2 tablespoons lemon juice

¼ teaspoon nutmeg
¼ cup white wine or orange
  juice

Peel and cut the apples into quarters, and place them in a baking dish. Mix the honey, lemon juice, nutmeg, and the wine or orange juice, and pour the mixture over the apples.

Bake uncovered in a 375° oven for 45 minutes, basting the apples a few times during the baking. 6 servings.

SUKKOT AND SIMHAT TORAH

Sukkot (Booths), also known as the Festival of Ingathering, when the grain and the fruits have been harvested, was always celebrated as the most joyful of the three festivals. The festival, including Shemini Atzeret, the Eighth Day of Solemn Assembly, is designated in the liturgy as "the season of our rejoicing," and this period is concluded with Simhat Torah, the Festival of the Rejoicing in the Law. It is a season of thanksgiving for the bounties of the Lord. The biblical injunction "You shall rejoice in your festival" (Deuteronomy 16:14) implies an obligation to enjoy festive meals. However, we are also reminded that good fortune and gladness should be shared with the unfortunate and the stranger. In this spirit guests are always welcome in the sukkah where the meals are served during the festival. Indeed, the cabbalists instituted a special prayer, Ushpizin, to be recited as one enters the sukkah. This prayer extends a hospitable invitation to the sainted guests: Abraham, Isaac, Jacob, Joseph, Moses, Aaron, and David—one of whom, according to a mystical tradition, comes to the sukkah each day. As these holy persons would undoubtedly refuse to enter a sukkah where the indigent are not welcome, it is customary to invite poor persons to dine and enjoy the holiday. The mystics assert, furthermore, that if one thinks that the invitation to the ancestors is merely a formality (since the host knows they will not come to eat at his table), he should understand that they expect their portions to be given to the poor. The poor are to be regaled with the kind of banquet that one would give in honor of distinguished guests.

According to Jewish tradition, it is obligatory to eat one's meals in a sukkah throughout the festival, especially on the first night. The Talmud states: "Rabbi Eliezer said: 'A man is dutibound to partake of fourteen meals in the *sukkah*, one every day and one every night.' But the Sages say: 'There is no fixed number [of meals], except [that he must eat in the sukkah] on the first night of the festival'" (Sukkah 2:6).

Observant Jews generally eat two full meals in the sukkah on each day of Sukkot. It is forbidden to fast throughout Sukkot, and the festival offers many opportunities for the epicure to enjoy delicacies.

The sukkah is decorated with an abundance of fruits and vegetables which hang from the roof, and some also display the seven spices that grow in Israel—"a land of wheat and barley, of vines, figs, and pomegranates, a land of olive trees and honey" (Deuteronomy 8:8)—as a reminder that Sukkot is the Festival of Ingathering. A favorite sukkah ornament is a bird made with an eggshell or an onion on which feathers or colored paper are glued. The source of this practice is shrouded in mystery, although some claim that it alludes to the words of Isaiah 31:5: "As birds hovering, so will the Lord of hosts protect Jerusalem."

During the intermediary days of Sukkot some conduct a Simhat Bet ha-Shoevah (Joy at the House of the Water Drawing), commemorating the joyful water libation in Temple times, at which prayers and psalms are read and refreshments are served.

Hoshana Rabbah, the seventh day of the festival, is considered the last day of the new year season on which the divine judgment is finally sealed. As on Rosh Hashanah, round hallot and honey are eaten on Hoshana Rabbah. Hallah and cake are baked in various symbolic shapes: a ladder for the ascent of prayers to heaven, a key for the opening of the heavenly gates, and a hand for receiving the divine decree for the new year. Pious Jews devote the entire night preceding Hoshana Rabbah to study at the synagogue, where coffee and cake are served.

Marking the completion and commencement of the yearly cycle of Torah reading in the synagogue, Simhat Torah is a day of merrymaking and feasting. Some even maintain that it is permissible to imbibe more strong drink than usual, although the rabbis frowned upon any excesses. The men carrying the Scrolls of the Law make hakkafot (circuits) around the synagogue, to the accompaniment of gay singing and dancing. The children join the merry procession, bearing Simhat Torah flags topped with apples in which lit candles are set. In German congregations candy is given to the children as they march, and many come prepared with large bags to hold their loot. At the services in some communities, cake, fruit, wine, and other refreshments are available to enhance the festivity for both young and old.

In many lands the *hatan Torah* (bridegroom of the Torah) and *hatan Bereshit* (bridegroom of Genesis), who are called to the reading of the last and first portions of the Torah, respectively, are hosts to the congregation at a meal, often quite elaborate, to show their appreciation of the signal honor bestowed on them. It was a widespread practice for the women in the synagogue gallery to toss nuts, raisins, and candy on the bridegrooms as they stood at the reading desk, as was done with a bridegroom on the Sabbath prior to his wedding. Even in staid England, it was reported, the women would throw sugarplums down from the balcony, which the children in the men's synagogue would eagerly gather up, until this breach of decorum was prohibited. In other places, women threw small paper bags filled with raisins and nuts. In Salonika the bridegrooms distributed candy to the children.

In his codification of laws Maimonides states that on a festival children should be given roasted ears (popcorn?), nuts, and sweetmeats.

Culinary customs for Sukkot have varied from country to country. In Yemen a number of families would join in purchasing a sheep or an ox to be assured of having sufficient meat for the lengthy festival. In the south of Russia a favorite dish was cabbage leaves stuffed with chopped meat. In Berlin it was the custom to eat a type of cabbage called *vasser kal* on Hoshana Rabbah, because on this day the liturgical hymn *Kol mevasser* is recited as one strikes the willows. Elsewhere cabbage is eaten on Simhat Torah, for its Hebrew translation is *cherub*, which alludes to the cherubim that were on the ark of the covenant (Exodus 25:18–22).

Kreplach are a traditional dish for Hoshana Rabbah, one of the three days of the year on which they are the pièce de résistance (see the chapter on Purim). In some communities the etrog was eaten on Simhat Torah and in others jam was made from this citrus fruit. Teiglach, honey balls, are the most typical of the Sukkot delicacies, and the bread of each meal's benediction is dipped in honey throughout the festival as an omen for a sweet year to come.

* * *

STUFFED CABBAGE

1 large cabbage (4 pounds)	*2 onions, sliced*
2 onions, grated	*28-ounce can solid pack*
¼ cup bread crumbs	*tomatoes*
2 eggs	*bones*
salt and pepper to taste	*½ cup light brown sugar*
½ teaspoon garlic powder	*2 bay leaves*
1½ pounds ground meat	*juice of 1 lemon*

With a sharp knife core the cabbage, removing as much as possible of the center.

Bring a big pot of water to a boil. Immerse the cabbage in the water with the core down. Take off each leaf with a fork. When all the leaves are removed, put them back into the water and turn off the heat. Let stand until the filling is prepared and then drain the water.

To make the filling, add the grated onions, bread crumbs, eggs, salt and pepper, and garlic powder to the meat, and mix well.

Lay each cabbage leaf flat on a plate. Cut off the hard part of the cabbage leaf. Put some of the filling on each leaf. Cover the filling by folding two sides of the leaf over it, and roll up like blintzes.

In a large roaster or pot, put the sliced onions, tomatoes, and bones. If any cabbage leaves remain, shred and place them in the roaster. Lay the stuffed cabbage leaves seam down on top. Cover the pot, and bring to a boil. Lower the heat, and cook for 1 hour. Add the sugar, bay leaves, and lemon juice, and continue to cook for 1 hour longer. Taste for seasoning, and add more sugar or lemon juice if required. The cabbage can also be baked in the oven at 325°. 8 servings as main dish or more for entrée.

The stuffed cabbage improves in taste if left standing for a day. If this is done, reheat slowly. It may be served with rice as a main dish.

If small stuffed cabbage portions are preferred, use a small head of cabbage, or cut big leaves in half.

*   *   *

MARINATED FISH

3 pounds white fish, sliced
1 cup vinegar
2 cups water
2 onions, sliced
3 bay leaves

1 cup sugar
⅓ cup white raisins
1 tablespoon kosher unflavored
   gelatin

Clean the fish and salt it. Refrigerate overnight.

Bring to a boil the vinegar, water, onions, bay leaves, sugar, and raisins, and cook for 15 minutes.

Add the fish to the pot. Bring to a boil; cover the pot, lower the heat, and cook for 10 minutes.

Mix the unflavored gelatin with a little cold water, and add to the fish. Cook for 5 more minutes. Remove from heat and let cool.

Remove the fish to a glass dish, and pour the sauce over it. Refrigerate. The fish will keep for 10 days. 8 servings.

GRUENKERN SOUP

1 pound soup meat
bones
8 cups water
½ package Gruenkern* (green
   wheat kernels)
1 onion
1 carrot
soup greens
salt to taste

MEATBALLS
½ pound ground meat
1 small onion, grated
1 tablespoon bread crumbs
1 egg
salt and pepper to taste

In a soup pot, place the meat, bones, and water. Add the *Gruenkern*, onion, and carrot. Tie the soup greens together, and add to the pot. Add salt, and bring to a boil. Lower the heat, cover the pot, and cook the soup for 2½ hours. Remove the bones and vegetables.

Mix the ground meat, grated onion, bread crumbs, egg, and salt and pepper, and shape into tiny meatballs. Drop the meatballs into the soup and continue to cook the soup for 30 minutes.

Remove the meat, cut into serving slices, and return to pot; or serve the slices of meat as a main dish. 8 servings.

Available in German Jewish butcher stores.

*   *   *

STUFFED BREAST OF VEAL

4 pounds breast of veal
½ pound ground meat
2 onions, chopped
1 cup celery, sliced
¼ cup parsley, chopped
3 cups matzah or crackers,
   broken
2 eggs

salt and pepper to taste
½ teaspoon powdered ginger
1 teaspoon thyme
2 tomatoes, sliced
2 tablespoons margarine
2 teaspoons paprika
1 teaspoon garlic powder

Have the butcher cut a deep pocket in the veal in which to place the stuffing.

Mix the ground meat with 1 onion, celery, and parsley. Dip the matzah or crackers in water for a few seconds, just to soften them, and add to the ground meat. Add the eggs, salt and pepper, ginger, and ½ teaspoon of thyme. Stuff the pocket, and sew it up with white thread.

In a roaster, put the other onion and the tomatoes. Lay the veal on the vegetables. Mix the margarine with the paprika, salt and pepper, garlic powder, and ½ teaspoon of thyme, and rub this mixture into the veal.

Roast the veal in a 325° oven for 3 hours. Baste with the juice in the roaster. If too dry, add ½ cup of water or white wine. 8 servings.

*   *   *

FRUITED MEATBALLS

1 apple, cored	1 cup cornflake crumbs
1 pear, cored	1 teaspoon salt
1 large onion	¼ teaspoon allspice
2 pounds ground beef	½ teaspoon nutmeg
2 eggs	

Grind the apple, pear, and onion, or blend in a blender. Add the ground beef with the rest of the ingredients, and mix well. Form marble-size balls, and place them on a greased foil-lined baking pan. Bake in a 400° oven for 15 minutes. Then place the baking pan under broiler (at the same temperature), and broil for a few minutes just to brown the top of the meatballs. Remove from oven. Make the sauce for the meatballs.

FRUIT SAUCE

2 tablespoons margarine	½ cup applesauce
½ cup blanched almonds, slivered	½ cup dried apricots, cooked and puréed
1½ tablespoons cornstarch	1 tablespoon lemon juice
2 tablespoons brown sugar	1 cup white grapes, seeded
1½ cups chicken soup	

Melt the margarine in a saucepan, and brown the almonds, being careful not to burn them. Remove the almonds and reserve. Blend the cornstarch and sugar with the soup, and place in the saucepan. Bring to a boil, stirring constantly, until clear. Stir in the applesauce, apricot purée, lemon juice, and grapes. Pour over the meatballs, and reheat gently over very low heat. Transfer to a serving dish, and scatter the browned almonds on top. 8 servings.

CURRIED FRUITS

1 large can sliced peaches
1 large can pears, sliced
1 large can sliced pineapple
1 can pie-sliced apples

½ cup maraschino cherries
⅓ cup margarine
¾ cup brown sugar
5 teaspoons mild curry powder

Drain the fruits and arrange them in a large glass baking dish. Melt the margarine in a pan, and add the sugar and curry. Mix, and spoon over the fruits. Bake the fruits for 1 hour in a 350° oven. Serve with meat or chicken. The dish can be baked ahead of time and reheated in a 350° oven for 20 minutes. 12 servings.

*   *   *

TOMATO AND PEPPER SALAD

½ cup vinegar
1 teaspoon whole mustard seed
salt and pepper to taste
1 tablespoon sugar
1 garlic clove, minced

4 large tomatoes, sliced
2 green peppers, sliced
1 red onion, sliced
¼ cup Italian parsley, chopped

Mix the vinegar, mustard seed, salt and pepper, sugar, and garlic in a pot, and bring to a boil.

Place the tomatoes, peppers, and onion in a bowl. Pour the hot vinegar dressing over the vegetables. Refrigerate overnight.

Serve in the bowl with the chopped parsley scattered on top. 6 servings.

*   *   *

COLESLAW

5 cups shredded cabbage (1
    small head)
1 carrot, grated
1 green pepper, sliced
1 red pepper, sliced
1 cup celery, sliced thin
2 scallions, sliced thin

½ cup white vinegar
½ cup water
½ cup mayonnaise
¼ cup sugar
salt to taste
chopped parsley

Wash the cabbage, and cut in half. Put the cabbage in salted cold water to soak for 30 minutes.

Grate or shred the cabbage. Add the carrot, green and red peppers, celery, and scallions, and mix.

Mix the vinegar, water, mayonnaise, sugar, and salt, and pour over the cabbage mixture. Mix well. Correct the seasoning. Add more sugar if desired. Refrigerate for a few hours or overnight. Scatter the chopped parsley over the slaw. 8 servings.

*   *   *

BARLEY AND DRIED FRUIT

½ pound coarse barley
salt to taste
1½ pounds mixed dried fruits
   (prunes, apricots, pears,
   peaches, apples)
½ cup white raisins

½ cup currants
½ teaspoon cinnamon
½ teaspoon powdered ginger
½ cup brown sugar
3 tablespoons margarine

Soak the barley in cold water for a few hours. Cook in the same water, adding salt, for 1 hour. Strain off the water.

Cook the dried fruits in water to cover for 15 minutes. Do not overcook. When removing the fruit, reserve 1 cup of the fruit juice.

In a large greased casserole or glass baking dish, place a layer of the barley, then the dried cooked fruits, raisins, and currants. Mix the cinnamon, ginger, and brown sugar, and sprinkle over the fruits and barley. Cut the margarine in pieces and scatter over the casserole. Add 1 cup of the reserved juice in which the dried fruits were cooked.

Bake in a 350° oven for 1 hour. If barley starts to become dry, cover with foil. Good as a side dish to any meat or fowl or as a dessert. 12 servings.

*   *   *

STRUDEL

2 cups coconut
1 cup white raisins
2 cups walnuts, chopped in
   large pieces
1 cup candied pineapple, cut
   in small pieces
1 cup candied cherries, cut in
   quarters
1 cup jellied candy slices, cut
   in small pieces

1 cup mixed candied fruits
4 cups sugar
2 teaspoons cinnamon
cornflake crumbs or bread
   crumbs
1 pound dried apricots
2 oranges
½ pound margarine or butter,
   melted
½ pound strudel leaves

To prepare the filling, mix the coconut, raisins, nuts, pineapple, cherries, candy slices, and candied fruit with 2 cups of sugar in a large bowl.

Mix the cinnamon with the cornflake crumbs or bread crumbs.

Put the apricots and oranges through a grinder. Add 2 cups of sugar. Mix well. (Any kind of jam can be used instead of the apricot-orange filling.)

Place foil on baking sheets and grease well.

On a slightly damp towel place two sheets of the strudel. (Keep the strudel leaves not being used wrapped well to prevent drying.) Spread some of the margarine or butter over the strudel leaves. Scatter some of the cornflake crumbs over the entire surface. Scatter some of the coconut and fruit mixture. On the end of the strudel leaves nearest to you make a row of the apricot filling, and then roll it up like a jelly roll. Place carefully with the seam down on the baking sheets. Brush with some more melted margarine or butter, and sprinkle with sugar. With a sharp knife, cut into slices, just a little more than half way down. Bend the ends under.

Bake in a 375° oven for 25 to 30 minutes or until light brown. While still warm, cut all the way through. Cool. If stored in a tin, the strudel will keep a few weeks. 40 to 50 slices.

*   *   *

PAREVE COFFEE CAKE

3 cups flour, sifted	1½ cups sugar
2 teaspoons baking powder	5 eggs
1 teaspoon baking soda	1 cup orange juice
1 cup margarine	2 teaspoons vanilla

Sift the flour. Sift again with the baking powder and baking soda.

Cream the margarine with the sugar and add the eggs, one at a time. Mix well. Add the flour, one cup at a time, with the orange juice. Add the vanilla, and mix well.

Pour half the batter into a greased 9 × 12½-inch pan. Sprinkle with half the topping mixture. Cover with the rest of the batter, and sprinkle the rest of the topping mixture on top of the cake.

Bake the cake in a 350° oven for 1 hour or until done.

TOPPING

1 cup walnuts, chopped	¾ cup sugar
2 squares baking chocolate, grated	1 teaspoon cinnamon

Mix all the ingredients together and use for the topping.

PINEAPPLE CAKE

2 cups flour, sifted
2 teaspoons baking soda
½ teaspoon salt
1½ cups sugar

½ cup brown sugar
2 eggs
1-pound 4-ounce can crushed
     pineapple

Mix the flour with the baking soda and salt. Add the sugars, then the eggs together with the crushed pineapple. Mix well, and pour into a 9 × 12-inch greased pan.

Bake in a 350° oven for 30 minutes.

Serve with whipped cream or nondairy topping.

*   *   *

APPLE CANDY

2 pounds apples
sugar

1 teaspoon rose water

Cut the apples in quarters and core but do not peel. Place them in a saucepan. Cover with a little water and bring to a boil. Lower the heat and simmer the apples until very soft.

Blend the apples in a blender or put through a sieve.

For every cup of apple pulp, use 1 cup of sugar. Bring the sugar and the apples to a boil in a pot, lower heat, and simmer for about an hour, stirring every few minutes. When the consistency is like a very thick jam, add the rose water, and pour the mixture into a 9 × 9-inch dish that is sprinkled with sugar. Allow the candy to cool. Cut into squares and sprinkle with more sugar. Let the candy dry at room temperature for a few days.

The same procedure can be followed with peaches, pears, or quinces.

*   *   *

SIMHAT TORAH CAKES (Lekach)

2 eggs
½ cup sugar
1 tablespoon margarine
1¼ cups flour, sifted

1 teaspoon baking powder
1 teaspoon vanilla
coarse sugar

Beat the eggs with the sugar until light in color. Add the margarine.

Sift the flour with the baking powder, and add to the egg mixture. Add the vanilla.

Grease a foil-lined cookie sheet. Drop the mixture on the foil by tablespoons, leaving 4 inches between each cake.

Sprinkle with coarse sugar.

Bake the cakes in a 350° oven until light brown, about 15 to 20 minutes.

* * *

JAM-FILLED BARS

1¼ cups margarine	1 teaspoon baking soda
1¼ cups sugar	1 cup walnuts, chopped
3 cups flour, sifted	1½ cups apricot jam

Cream the margarine with the sugar. With a pastry blender, blend in the flour and baking soda. Add the walnuts and mix lightly. Press half the dough into a 9 × 12½-inch baking pan. Bake this part in a 400° oven for 12 minutes.

Spread the jam over the baked part and sprinkle the rest of the dough all over the jam.

Continue to bake for 25 minutes, or until lightly browned. Cool. Cut into 32 bars.

HANUKKAH

Hanukkah, the Feast of Lights, recalling the dedication of the Temple in Jerusalem following the victory of the Hasmonean Mattathias and his sons over the Syrians, is marked by the kindling of candles. To emphasize the miracle of the cruse of oil found in the Temple, which was sufficient for only one day but burned for eight days, foods fried in oil are served on Hanukkah. Further evidence of the appropriateness of using oil is deduced from the fact that the Hebrew words for Hasmoneans (*Hashmonaim*) and for eight (*shemoneh*), the number of days of the festival, contain the Hebrew letters for oil (*shemen*). Be that as it may, latkes—pancakes fried in oil—have been the distinctive Hanukkah delicacy for centuries. Kalonymus ben Kalonymus, who lived in Italy in the fourteenth century, composed a Hanukkah poem in which he extolled latkes. A folk proverb states: "Hanukkah's latkes teach us that one cannot live by miracles alone." While the variety of latkes is legion, the most popular are those made with grated potatoes. Some are made with cheese, fruits, and yeast. In oriental countries sugar and sesame seeds are added to the pancakes.

According to the *Code of Jewish Law* dairy dishes are featured on Hanukkah to commemorate the heroism of Judith, reputed to be a member of the Hasmonean family. Various legends associate the Apocryphal story of Judith with the Maccabean revolt. Beautiful Judith succeeded in gaining an audience with the enemy general Holofernes, who invited her to a banquet at which she partook only of dairy foods. She fed the general milk and cheese until he was parched and then offered him liberal portions of wine to quench his thirst. When he fell into a drunken stupor, she killed him. Learning that the general was dead, his soldiers took flight and the Jews were saved. Thus the dairy foods serve as a reminder of Judith's valor and the Maccabean triumph.

On the last day of Hanukkah schoolchildren in the Old City of Jerusalem, accompanied by their teachers, used to go from house to house of the well-to-do Jews singing songs and chanting repeatedly, "Buy us a little food" (Genesis 43:2). The householders responded by giving the children fruit, vegetables, fowl, oil, flour, onions, and other foods and sometimes coins with which to purchase food. With whatever they collected they would prepare three meals: one for the poor, another for their teachers, and the third for themselves. Small pieces of dough baked with a meat filling were one of the tidbits served. To add to the merriment of the occasion, however, several pieces of dough were usually stuffed with absorbent cotton.

Similar traditions prevailed in other oriental countries. In the marketplace Yemenite children sold hot potatoes and a drink made with peaches to earn the expenses for their Hanukkah festival meal.

In Hebron the women held their own celebration on the last night of the holiday, at which they made macaroni together and then ate it with salted cheese while engaging in light conversation.

In Turkey the elders of the community, carrying platters of pancakes, visited the affluent Jews to collect Hanukkah gelt for the poor. In exchange for their contributions they were each given three latkes. Bukharan Jews baked cakes with coins inside which they distributed to teachers and indigent relatives.

East European Jews paid special attention to the Sabbath of Hanukkah. On that day they would eat two different kugels—one in honor of the Sabbath and the other for the glory of Hanukkah. Another feature of the Sabbath of Hanukkah was a roast goose or duck from which the schmaltz (fat) was reserved for Passover. *Gribenes* (scraps), stuffed neck roasted and fried with onions, and giblets were also among the popular Hanukkah delicacies of East European Jews.

As Hanukkah is a home festival, many families set a festive table every evening. The enjoyment of the meals is heightened by singing hymns and songs, posing riddles, playing dreidel games, and telling witty stories.

*   *   *

CHICKEN LIVERS IN WINE SAUCE

1 onion, chopped fine
1 tablespoon margarine
1 tablespoon flour
salt and pepper to taste
1 tablespoon sugar
1 cup chicken broth

juice of 1 lemon
1 bay leaf
½ cup white wine
1 pound chicken livers, broiled
parsley, chopped

Sauté the onion in the margarine for 10 minutes, but do not brown. Mix the flour, salt and pepper, and sugar with the chicken broth and lemon juice, and add to the onion, stirring until thick. Add the bay leaf. Cook for 15 minutes over very low heat. Add the wine and the chicken livers, and cook for 5 more minutes. Garnish with the parsley. 6 servings.

*   *   *

LENTIL SOUP

1 pound red lentils	1 onion, chopped
8 cups water	2 tablespoons margarine
1 carrot, sliced	2½ tablespoons flour
2 celery stalks, sliced	salt and pepper to taste

Wash the lentils. Cover with the water, and bring to a boil. Add all the vegetables, lower the heat, and simmer until the lentils are soft.

Strain the soup through a sieve, mashing all the pulp.

In a small saucepan, melt the margarine, add the flour, and brown together; blend into the soup. Season with salt and pepper. Bring to a boil and serve. 8 servings.

*   *   *

GLAZED CORNED BEEF

4 pounds corned beef	½ cup bread crumbs
1 onion	1 teaspoon dry mustard
2 carrots	grated peel of 1 orange
1 bay leaf	grated peel of 1 lemon
½ teaspoon peppercorns	½ cup orange juice
1 teaspoon whole cloves	juice of 1 lemon
½ cup brown sugar	½ cup apple juice

In a large pot, cover the corned beef with cold water; add the onion, carrots, bay leaf, and peppercorns. Simmer covered for 3 hours or until tender. Cool in the broth.

To glaze the corned beef, drain the meat and stud it with the cloves. Combine the sugar, crumbs, mustard, orange peel, and lemon peel, and pat the mixture on top of the meat. Bake for 10 minutes in a 350° oven. Combine the fruit juices, and baste the meat with the juices a few times. Bake for 1 hour. Slice across the grain of the meat. 6 servings.

POT ROAST

2 onions, sliced or chopped	salt and pepper to taste
4 pounds brisket	thyme
garlic powder	paprika
onion powder	potatoes, sliced (optional)

Place the onions in a pot. Lay the meat over the onions. Sprinkle with garlic powder, onion powder, salt and pepper, thyme, and paprika. Cover the pot, and put over very low heat. Cook for about 3 hours or until the meat is tender. (This can be baked in a 350° oven.) No water is necessary.

If desired, sliced potatoes can be added to the roast half an hour before the meat is done. 8 to 10 servings.

*   *   *

CHICKEN FRICASSEE WITH MEATBALLS

2 tablespoons margarine	salt and pepper to taste
chicken giblets	½ teaspoon powdered ginger
2 large onions, chopped	1 garlic clove, mashed
1 3-pound chicken, cut in	1 teaspoon paprika
eighths	3 parsley sprigs
2 carrots, diced	1 bay leaf
2 celery stalks, sliced	broth or water

In a large fryer melt the margarine, and add the giblets and onions; sauté over low heat for 30 minutes. Add the chicken pieces and the vegetables. Sprinkle with the salt and pepper, ginger, garlic, and paprika. Add the parsley and bay leaf. Add broth or water to cover, bring to a boil, lower heat, and simmer for 1 hour. Add the meatballs, and continue to cook for another 30 minutes. 6 servings as main course or 10 as entrée.

MEATBALLS

1 pound ground meat	¼ cup tomato juice
1 egg, beaten	2 tablespoons onion soup mix
¼ cup cornflake crumbs	1 tablespoon parsley, chopped

Mix well the meat with the egg and the rest of the ingredients. Form into small balls, and drop them on top of the chicken fricassee.

PRUNE PUDDING

5 eggs, separated
½ cup sugar
1 cup pitted prunes, sliced
4 ounces unsweetened
   chocolate, grated

½ pound almonds, chopped
3 tablespoons bread crumbs or
   matzah meal
2 teaspoons vanilla

Beat the egg yolks with the sugar until lemon-colored. Add the prunes, chocolate, almonds, crumbs, and vanilla.

Beat the egg whites until stiff, and fold gently into the prune mixture.

Grease a mold or a glass baking bowl, and spoon the pudding into it. Cover the top with foil, securing it all around.

Place the bowl with the pudding on a trivet standing in a kettle with water reaching the top of the trivet. Cover the kettle and steam the pudding for 2 hours over very low heat. Make sure there is always enough water in the kettle.

The pudding can be prepared the day before serving and reheated in the kettle. Be sure to put it on a trivet. Serve with the wine sauce. 8 servings.

WINE SAUCE

1 cup white wine
⅓ cup sugar

3 egg yolks
1 teaspoon vanilla

In the top of a double boiler, put the wine, sugar, and egg yolks. Place the top of the boiler on the lower part which has water reaching to the bottom of the top part. Cook the sauce, stirring constantly until thickened. Add the vanilla. This can be served hot or cold over the pudding.

* * *

FRUIT LATKES

2 cups flour
½ teaspoon salt
3 teaspoons baking powder
1 egg, beaten
⅔ cup orange juice

1 can pie-sliced apples or 1 can
   pineapple chunks
oil for frying
confectioners' sugar

Sift together the dry ingredients. Add the egg and the orange juice. Beat well. Batter will be heavy. Add the well-drained fruit of your choice. Drop by spoonfuls into deep oil at 375°. Fry until brown. Drain on paper toweling. Sprinkle with confectioners' sugar. Serve hot. 6 servings.

*   *   *

SUFGANIOT (Israeli Latkes)

½ package dried yeast
1 cup warm water (105°–115°)
2 cups flour, sifted
2 teaspoons sugar

1 teaspoon salt
1 egg, well beaten
oil for frying

Sprinkle the yeast over the warm water. Let it stand until dissolved. Sift the flour with sugar and salt, and add the egg. Add the yeast, and beat well until the mixture is thoroughly blended. Cover and put in a warm place (85°) to rise until it doubles in bulk.

Place oil in a frying pan to half the height of the pan and heat. When the oil is hot, drop the batter by spoonfuls into the oil. Fry on both sides until latkes are a golden color. Drain well on paper toweling. Sprinkle with granulated sugar. Serve hot. 6 servings.

*   *   *

COTTAGE CHEESE PANCAKES

1 cup cottage cheese
2 eggs, separated
1½ tablespoons cornstarch

½ teaspoon sugar
¼ teaspoon salt

Blend the cottage cheese, egg yolks, cornstarch, sugar, and salt. Beat the egg whites until stiff and fold into the cottage cheese mixture. Drop by tablespoons on a hot, greased griddle. Lower heat and cook on one side until puffed and dry. Then turn with a spatula and brown lightly on the other side. Serve with fruit, berries, sour cream, or jelly. 2 servings.

*   *   *

POTATO PANCAKES

4 large potatoes, grated
3 tablespoons matzah meal
3 eggs, beaten
1 teaspoon salt

¼ teaspoon pepper
1 teaspoon onion powder
oil for frying

Care should be taken to have all the ingredients ready for immediate use before grating the potatoes. (Grated potatoes that are left standing turn brown.) It is desirable to use 2 pans at the same time to expedite frying the pancakes.

Grate the potatoes, and squeeze out as much water as possible. Mix the grated potatoes, matzah meal, eggs, salt, pepper, and onion powder. Heat oil in a frying pan. When the oil is hot, drop the potato mixture by tablespoons into the oil. Fry on both sides until brown. Remove from the oil, and drain on paper toweling.

The pancakes can be fried in advance and frozen. Before serving, lay the pancakes in one layer on a foil-lined cookie sheet and reheat in a 375° oven for about 20 minutes. Serve with applesauce. 6 servings.

* * *

LEMON MERINGUE PIE

CRUST

1 ½ cups flour, sifted
½ cup solid vegetable
  shortening
⅓ cup orange juice

FILLING

1 ¼ cups sugar
6 tablespoons cornstarch
2½ cups water
4 eggs, separated
½ cup lemon juice
peel of 2 lemons, grated
2 tablespoons margarine

With a pastry blender, blend the shortening into the flour, blending until the flour looks pebbly. Add a little less than ⅓ cup of orange juice to hold the flour together. If necessary, use the rest of the orange juice to moisten but do not make a sticky pastry. Wrap in wax paper, and refrigerate overnight or for a few hours for easier rolling.

Roll out the pastry on a large piece of wax paper into a 12-inch circle. Ease the pastry into a 10-inch pie plate by putting the pastry with the wax paper over the plate. Remove the wax paper. Fold the extra dough under the edge of the crust and make a high fluted edge all around.

To prevent shrinkage of the pie shell, place 2 pieces of wax paper (2 × 4 inches each) on opposite sides of the pie shell over the pastry. Now put another pie plate of the same size over the pieces of wax paper. Bake in a 425° oven for 8 minutes. Remove the top plate, and lift out the wax paper carefully. Bake for 8 more minutes, but do not brown. Remove from oven.

To make the filling, mix the sugar with the cornstarch and add the water. Stir to dissolve the cornstarch. Bring the sugar and cornstarch mixture to a boil, stirring constantly until the mixture is thick. Lower the heat and cook for 5 more minutes.

Mix the egg yolks with the lemon juice.

Remove the cornstarch mixture from the heat. Slowly stir the egg and lemon mixture into the cornstarch. Return to the heat and cook, stirring constantly until the mixture again comes to a boil.

Remove from the heat. Add the lemon peel and margarine, and stir until the margarine is melted. Pour into the prepared pie crust.

Make the meringue and pile over the lemon filling, starting at the edges to seal the meringue and to prevent it from shrinking. Swirl the rest of the meringue in the center, covering the entire surface. Bake in a 350° oven for 20 minutes. Turn off the heat and allow the pie to stand in the oven until cool and then remove. Serve at room temperature.

MERINGUE

4 egg whites
dash of salt
10 tablespoons sugar

1 teaspoon lemon juice
1 teaspoon baking powder

Put the egg whites in a medium bowl, and add the salt. Beat until fluffy. Add one tablespoon of sugar and beat until mixed. Add the lemon juice. Continue adding the sugar, 1 tablespoon at a time, and beat until all the sugar is dissolved. Add the baking powder and beat again.

*   *   *

APRICOT BARS

1 orange
1 cup dried apricots
2 eggs
1 cup sugar
⅓ cup oil

1 cup flour, sifted
¼ teaspoon baking powder
¼ teaspoon salt
1 cup nuts, chopped

Cut the orange in quarters, and remove the seeds but not the peel. Put the apricots and orange through a grinder.

Beat the eggs with the sugar, and add the oil. Fold the flour with the baking powder and salt into the egg mixture. Add the apricot and orange mixture. Add the nuts. Mix well.

Spread the mixture into a greased shallow 9 × 13-inch pan, and sprinkle with sugar. Bake in a 350° oven for 25 minutes. While warm, cut into 32 bars.

* * *

CANDIED ORANGE PEEL

peel of 6 oranges
1½ cups sugar

4 tablespoons corn syrup
¾ cup water

Place the orange peel in a saucepan, and cover with water. Bring to a boil, lower the heat, and simmer for 10 minutes. Drain. Cover again with water and bring to a boil. Lower the heat, and simmer for 20 minutes or until the peel is soft. Drain, and slice the peel into long strips.

Bring the sugar, corn syrup, and ¾ cup of water to a boil. Lower the heat, and add the cooked orange peel. Cook the peel in the syrup until most of the syrup is absorbed.

Spread the peel on a foil-lined cookie sheet covered with sugar. Sprinkle more sugar all over the peel. Let dry. Store in a plastic container.

* * *

MENORAH SALAD

lettuce leaves
8 pineapple rings
8 small bananas

lemon juice
8 maraschino cherries

Arrange the lettuce on flat plates for individual salads, or on one large platter. Place the pineapple rings in a line to form the base of a menorah. Cut off the bottom of the bananas so that one end is flat, and scoop out the other end so that it will hold a cherry. Dip the bananas in lemon juice, and stand the flat ends in the pineapple rings. Set the cherries on the banana tops. Serve with cottage cheese and, if desired, sour cream. 8 servings.

CHOCOLATE PEPPERMINT COOKIES

⅔ cup margarine
1 cup sugar
1 egg
2 cups flour, sifted

¼ teaspoon salt
1 teaspoon baking soda
¾ cup cocoa

Beat the margarine with the sugar and egg. Add the flour, salt, baking soda, and cocoa, and mix well. The dough will be soft. If too soft, a little more flour can be added. Refrigerate overnight.

On a lightly floured board, roll out ⅓ of the dough (keep the rest refrigerated) until it is very thin. With a small round cookie cutter or a 1½-inch glass cut the dough into circles. Lay the cookies on an ungreased cookie sheet, and bake in a 325° oven for 8 minutes until cookies are set. Do not overbake.

Continue to make more cookies with the rest of the dough, and then with the scraps of dough.

MINT FILLING

4 tablespoons margarine
2¼ cups confectioners' sugar
1 teaspoon peppermint
   flavoring

1½–2 tablespoons water
a few drops of green food
   coloring

Cream the margarine with the confectioners' sugar, and add the flavoring, water, and food coloring. Beat well for a few minutes.

Spread some of the filling on half of the cookies, and top with another cookie. The cookies will keep well in a tightly covered tin.

*   *   *

TARTS

2 cups flour
4 tablespoons brown sugar

¾ cup margarine   ·
2 eggs, beaten

Mix the flour with the sugar. With a pastry blender, blend in the margarine. Add the eggs to the flour mixture. Mix lightly until a soft dough is formed. Wrap in foil, and refrigerate overnight. The dough will keep for 2 weeks under refrigeration.

Take small pieces of the dough—the size of a large walnut—and pat out each piece to line a cupcake pan. Bake in a 375° oven until lightly browned. Remove carefully from the pan.

In each tart put some of the filling. Place each one in a small cupcake paper. Decorate with nuts or maraschino cherries. Whipped cream and chocolate curls may also be used as a topping. The tarts should be filled just a few hours before serving. 24 small tarts.

FILLING

6 ounces bittersweet chocolate
8 eggs, separated
2 cups confectioners' sugar

2 tablespoons sherry
1 teaspoon vanilla

In the top of a double boiler melt the chocolate over hot water.

Beat the egg yolks with the confectioners' sugar until lemon-colored. Add the sherry, vanilla, and melted chocolate. Whip the egg whites until very stiff, and gently fold them into the chocolate mixture.

*　　　*　　　*

MOCHA ICE CREAM (Pareve)

4 eggs
⅓ cup light brown sugar
1 tablespoon instant coffee
2 tablespoons boiling water

1 10-ounce container nondairy topping
1 tablespoon brandy flavoring

Beat the eggs until double in volume. Add the sugar and continue to beat. Dissolve the coffee in the boiling water; when cool, add it slowly to the egg mixture.

Whip the container of nondairy topping until stiff, and add the flavoring. Gently fold into the egg mixture. Pour into a 9 × 9-inch foil pan, and freeze overnight. 8 servings.

Other flavors can be substituted for coffee and brandy. As an alternative, mix half the egg mixture with one flavor and pour into a pan; then add another flavor to the rest of the egg mixture and pour over the first mixture.

PURIM

The commandment in the Book of Esther to observe Purim as "days of feasting and gladness, and of sending portions one to another, and gifts to the poor" (Esther 9:22) gave rise to the creation of many delicacies directly related to this festival. The tradition of both the *seudah* (Purim meal) and *mishloah manot* (sending of portions) resulted in the introduction of new dishes in the Jewish home. On the occasion of the *seudah*, the Jewish housewife had an opportunity to demonstrate her culinary ability. The portions that were exchanged as well as the gifts to the poor customarily included various types of eatables. In his *Massekhet Purim*, Kalonymus ben Kalonymus, the Jewish parodist who lived in the fourteenth century, lists twenty-four meat and pastry dishes that "were told to Moses on Mount Sinai, all of which one must prepare on Purim."

The Purim culinary art developed differently in the different lands where Jews resided. The most popular Purim dishes today are the hamantashen and kreplach.

The three-cornered hamantashen, baked dough filled with poppy seeds, derives its name from a combination of the two German words —*Mohn* (poppy) and *Taschen* (pockets). Because of the association of this cake with Purim, its original name, *Mohntashen*, became hamantashen, recalling Haman, the enemy of the Jews in the Persian Empire. Some have interpreted the three-cornered delicacy as symbolic of the three-cornered hat said to have been worn by Haman while he was prime minister. More recently it has become a common practice to fill the hamantashen with prunes.

Another favorite Purim dish is kreplach, triangular pieces of dough filled with chopped meat. Purim shares kreplach with two other significant days in the Jewish calendar—the eve of the Day of Atonement and Hoshana Rabbah. The folklorist cleverly gives the following reason for their popularity: Kreplach are eaten on those days on which there is "beating." On the eve of the Day of Atonement men are flogged with forty stripes. Willow branches are beaten on Hoshana Rabbah. During the reading of the Book of Esther on Purim, Haman is beaten whenever his name is mentioned. Support for this explanation is derived from the biblical phrase *HaKeH TaKeH*, "Thou shalt surely smite." The phrase is interpreted as an abbreviation of *Hoshana, Kippur, Haman, Tokhlu Kreplach Harbeh:* "On the days of Hoshana, Atonement, and Haman, thou shalt eat many kreplach."

In some places it is customary to eat cooked beans with salt, usually called *nahit* or *bub*. This vegetarian dish is in remembrance of Esther's diet while she lived in the court of Ahasuerus. This, it is told, was limited to beans and peas so as not to violate the dietary laws, a practice Daniel also followed while in the court of Nebuchadnezzar (Daniel 1:12).

Those who were more punctilious in the observance of Purim were accustomed to eating turkey, which literally translated from Russian means "cock of India," and in Hebrew, *tarnegol hodu*. Eating the "cock of India" is therefore in remembrance of Ahasuerus, "who reigned from India unto Ethiopia" and was a foolish king. The turkey is generally considered the most foolish among fowl.

The place of honor on the table set for the Purim *seudah* is given to the *keylitsh*, an exceptionally large braided loaf of white bread, decorated with raisins. The top of the *keylitsh* is braided with long strands, wide and high in the middle and narrow and low at both ends.

*   *   *

MEATBALLS IN TOMATO SOUP

1 can nondairy tomato soup   *2 tablespoons onion soup mix*
2 carrots, sliced   *¼ cup bread crumbs*
3 celery stalks, sliced   *½ teaspoon garlic powder*
1 large onion, chopped   *3 tablespoons ketchup*
1 pound ground meat   *parsley sprigs*
1 egg, beaten

Bring the tomato soup to a boil together with the carrots, celery, and onion. Cook for 20 minutes over low heat.

While the soup is cooking, mix the meat lightly with the egg, onion soup mix, bread crumbs, garlic powder, and ketchup. Shape the meat mixture into small balls, and add them to the soup. Lower the heat, add the parsley, and cook for 1 hour. 4 servings.

KREPLACH

MEAT FILLING

½ pound ground meat
1 egg
1 small onion, grated
1 tablespoon bread crumbs
salt and pepper to taste

DOUGH

2 eggs, beaten
1½ cups flour (approximately)
½ teaspoon salt

To prepare the meat filling, mix well the meat, 1 egg, onion, bread crumbs, and salt and pepper.

For the dough, beat the 2 eggs in a bowl; add the flour and the ½ teaspoon of salt, and knead until the dough is elastic. A little warm water will help to form a soft dough.

On a floured board or floured wax paper, roll out the dough into a very thin oblong. Cut in squares to size desired. On each square, place a small ball of the filling and quickly fold into a triangle, pinching the edges together. Allow the finished kreplach to stand for 15 minutes.

Bring a large pot of salted water to a boil, add the kreplach, and cover the pot. Cook for 25 to 30 minutes, depending on the thickness of the kreplach. Drain and add to soup.

*   *   *

TONGUE IN CHERRY WINE SAUCE

1 pickled beef tongue
½ cup brown sugar
2 tablespoons cornstarch
¼ teaspoon whole cloves

1 tablespoon lemon juice
1 can pitted sour cherries
2 tablespoons margarine
½ cup red wine

Cook the tongue until tender, and then remove from broth. Reserve 1 cup of the broth. While tongue is still hot, remove the skin, cool, and slice.

Mix the sugar with the cornstarch in a saucepan. Add the cup of tongue broth, cloves, and lemon juice, and bring to a boil, stirring constantly until the sauce is thick. Drain the cherries, and add them to the sauce. Add the margarine and wine.

Arrange the sliced tongue in a baking dish, pour the sauce over the tongue, and bake for 20 minutes in a 350° oven. 12 servings.

ROAST TURKEY

1 12-pound turkey	*powdered ginger*
salt	*thyme*
pepper	*onion powder*
paprika	*garlic powder*

Clean the turkey, and wash and dry it with paper towels. Salt well all over, and sprinkle the cavity with salt. Rub the salt in for a few minutes. Refrigerate overnight.

If stuffing is used, stuff the turkey, truss, and put in a roaster. Sprinkle pepper, paprika, ginger, thyme, onion powder, and garlic powder all over the turkey.

Roast in a 325° oven for 1 hour. Baste with the juice that accumulates in the roaster. Continue to roast and baste the turkey every half hour until the turkey is tender. Time required for cooking depends on size and age of the turkey. Before slicing the turkey, let it stand for 30 minutes for easier carving. 12 or more servings.

BREAD STUFFING

4 cups fresh or stale bread	*½ teaspoon basil*
2 large onions, sliced	*½ teaspoon sage*
4 tablespoons margarine	*½ teaspoon thyme*
2 cups celery, sliced	*½ teaspoon garlic powder*
½ pound mushrooms, sliced	*2 eggs*
1 pound chestnuts, cooked and	*1 bouillon cube (optional)*
shelled	*½ cup water (optional)*
salt and pepper to taste	

Spread the bread on a flat pan, and dry it in a 300° oven for 30 minutes. Soak the bread briefly in water. Squeeze out all the water. Measure 4 cups of bread.

Sauté the onions in the margarine for 10 minutes, but do not brown. Add the celery, and sauté for 5 minutes. Add the mushrooms, and sauté for 2 more minutes. Add the chestnuts, salt and pepper, basil, sage, thyme, and garlic powder. Add the eggs and mix well.

Stuff the turkey cavity, making sure not to stuff it too full; leave room for expansion. Seal the cavity by sewing it with white thread. If there is some stuffing left over, bake it in a small pan. Roast the turkey as directed.

If desired, the stuffing can be baked in a pan rather than stuffed in the turkey or chicken. Melt 4 tablespoons of margarine in a pan, and put the stuffing in the pan. Bake in a 325° for 1 hour. Pour ½ cup of broth (bouillon cube and water) over the stuffing, and continue to bake for 30 minutes. If the stuffing begins to dry, cover with foil.

Individual stuffing balls can also be made by dividing the stuffing in ½-cup measures, putting them on a very well greased cookie sheet, and baking for 30 minutes.

GRAVY

turkey giblets	*a few peppercorns*
1 onion	*salt to taste*
1 carrot	*2 tablespoons flour*
bay leaf	

Cook the giblets in 3 cups of water. Add the onion, carrot, bay leaf, peppercorns, and salt. Cook until the giblets are tender. Remove the giblets, and chop into small pieces. Reserve the giblets. Strain the soup.

Remove 5 tablespoons of the pan dripping in which the turkey was roasted, add to it the flour, and mix well. (For a thicker gravy, use more flour.) Slowly add some of the soup in which the giblets were cooked, and mix well. Add the rest of the soup, and bring to a boil, stirring the gravy until it thickens. Cook for 5 minutes. Add the giblets and serve.

*   *   *

MASHED POTATO KUGEL

4 cups potatoes, mashed	*4 tablespoons margarine,*
salt and pepper to taste	*melted*
4 eggs, beaten	*1 teaspoon onion powder*
2 tablespoons farina or	*ground meat (optional)*
semolina	

To the mashed potatoes, add salt and pepper, eggs, farina or semolina, margarine, and onion powder. Mix well.

Grease well a round baking dish, and put in the potato mixture. Bake in a 375° oven for 45 minutes or until brown. 8 servings.

This potato mixture can be made into individual croquettes. Stuff the mixture with ground meat, and form into long shapes. Fry in oil until golden brown, or bake in a well-greased baking pan in a 375° oven for 20 minutes, depending on the size of the croquettes.

APRICOT DESSERT

½ pound dried apricots
½ cup sugar
½ cup margarine
4 eggs, separated

apricot halves, cooked
prunes, cooked
nondairy topping or whipped
    sweet cream

Cover the apricots with water, and cook until very soft. Blend the apricots in a blender or mash well.

In a saucepan, place the apricots, sugar, margarine, and egg yolks, and cook, stirring constantly, until the mixture is very smooth. Let it cool.

Beat the egg whites until stiff, and fold them into the cooled apricot mixture.

Pour the mixture into a greased baking dish. Set the dish in a deep baking pan and add enough water to reach ¾ of the height of the baking dish; bake for 1 hour in a 325° oven.

Remove from the oven and let cool. Turn out on a serving dish, and decorate with the apricot halves and prunes. Serve with the topping or whipped sweet cream. 8 servings.

*   *   *

NAHIT

1 pound dry chick-peas
1 teaspoon baking soda

salt and pepper to taste

Soak the chick-peas overnight with the baking soda in water to cover. Pour off the water, and rinse twice in cold water. Put in a pot with plenty of cold water. Bring to a boil, and then reduce the heat to simmer. Cover, and cook for 2 hours or until chick-peas are soft. (Be careful not to overcook the chick-peas.) Add some salt.

When soft, strain the chick-peas well. Add pepper and more salt, if desired. Spread out on a clean towel to dry. Keep refrigerated until served.

*   *   *

HAMANTASHEN (pastry dough)

2½ cups flour, sifted
½ teaspoon salt
½ pound margarine

3 egg yolks
3 tablespoons white wine
3 tablespoons white vinegar

Mix the flour with the salt. Add the margarine, and blend with a pastry blender as for pie dough. Mix the egg yolks, wine, and vinegar, and add to the flour mixture. Shape dough into a ball. Refrigerate overnight.

Divide the dough into three pieces. On wax paper, roll out each piece into a thin circle. Cut into circles with a cookie cutter. Place one teaspoon of filling on the dough, and pinch the sides together to form a triangle.

Bake on a ungreased baking sheet in a 400° oven for 20 to 25 minutes, depending on the size of the hamantashen.

APRICOT FILLING

½ pound dried apricots
1½ cups water

1¼ cups sugar

Cook the apricots with the water until they are very soft. Mash or blend the apricots. Add the sugar, and cook over very low heat for 10 more minutes.

*   *   *

HAMANTASHEN (cookie dough)

½ pound margarine
¾ cup sugar
4 eggs
4–5 cups flour, sifted

2 teaspoons baking powder
½ teaspoon salt
1 teaspoon vanilla

Beat the margarine with the sugar until fluffy. Add the eggs, one at a time, beating well. Sift together the flour, baking powder, and salt, and add to egg mixture with the vanilla to form a soft, not sticky, dough.

Roll out on wax paper, and cut with a cookie cutter. Place some of the filling on each cookie. Pinch the sides to form a triangular hamantash. Lay the hamantashen on a greased cookie sheet.

Bake in a 375° oven for 25 to 30 minutes, depending on size of the hamantashen.

MOHN FILLING

¼ pound poppy seeds,*
  ground fine
½ cup sugar
½ cup raisins

¼ cup honey
1 egg
½ teaspoon cinnamon
½ cup ground almonds

Mix the poppy seeds with the rest of the ingredients.

Available in gourmet food shops.

PRUNE FILLING

1 pound prunes	½ cup sugar
½ cup nuts, chopped	1 teaspoon cinnamon
rind and juice of 1 lemon	½ cup raisins

Cook the prunes until they are very soft. Remove the pits. Put the prunes through a grinder or blend in a blender until the prunes are like a thick jam. Add the rest of the ingredients, and mix well.

*   *   *

COCONUT SQUARES

½ cup margarine	**TOPPING**
1 egg	2 eggs
2 tablespoons brown sugar	1 cup brown sugar
1½ cups flour	1 teaspoon vanilla
2 tablespoons orange juice	2 tablespoons flour
	½ teaspoon baking powder
	1½ cups coconut

Beat the margarine with 1 egg in a mixer. Add 2 tablespoons of brown sugar, and continue beating until well mixed. Add the flour with the orange juice to form the dough. Press the dough into an ungreased 9 × 12½-inch baking pan. Bake the dough for 15 minutes in a 375° oven.

While this is baking, prepare the topping. In a mixer, beat well 2 eggs with 1 cup of brown sugar. Then add the vanilla, flour, and baking powder. Mix in the coconut.

Remove the dough from the oven, and spread the topping on it. Reduce the oven temperature to 350°, return to oven, and bake for 30 more minutes. When done, cut into 32 squares.

*   *   *

DATE AND NUT COOKIES

2 eggs, well beaten	1 cup dates, cut in small pieces
1 cup brown sugar	2 cups coconut
2 cups walnuts, chopped	

Beat the eggs with the sugar. Add the other ingredients, and mix well. Wet your hands and shape the mixture into balls; place them on a greased cookie sheet. Bake in a 350° oven for 12 minutes. Do not overbake. Approximately 30 cookies.

SUGAR COOKIES

½ cup margarine
1 cup sugar
1 egg
3¼ cups flour
4 teaspoons baking powder

¼ cup orange juice or white
wine
1 egg white, beaten
nuts, chopped, optional

Cream the margarine with the sugar. Add the egg, and beat well. Add the flour and baking powder together with the juice or wine. Mix into a soft dough.

Roll out very thin, and cut into any shape desired. Brush with egg white, and sprinkle with nuts or sugar. Place on greased cookie sheets. Bake the cookies in a 375° oven for 15 minutes.

* * *

SUMSUM HALVAH (Sesame Candy)

2 cups sesame seeds
1 cup honey

1 cup sugar
1 teaspoon lemon juice

Spread the sesame seeds on a baking sheet. Toast the seeds in a 350° oven, stirring every few minutes. Watch carefully to keep them from burning. When lightly toasted, remove from the oven.

Bring the honey and sugar to a boil. Lower the heat, and cook the syrup about 10 minutes or until a teaspoon of syrup forms a ball when dropped into cold water. Stir in the toasted sesame seeds, and cook for 3 minutes. Add the lemon juice.

Pour the candy on a wet board. With wet hands, flatten out the candy to the size desired. While still warm but not hot, cut the candy with a sharp knife into small squares. When cold, remove from the board to a serving dish. Do not make the candy on a humid day.

* * *

STUFFED PRUNES

1 pound sour prunes
walnut halves
1 cup sugar

1 cup water
juice of 1 lemon
1–2 teaspoons ginger to taste

Pour hot water over the prunes in a strainer. Remove the pits, and stuff each prune with half a walnut.

Bring the sugar and water to a boil. Add the prunes, lemon juice, and ginger. Bring again to a boil and immediately reduce the heat. Allow to simmer for 1 hour. Place the prunes in a jar and cover the jar. The prunes do not need refrigeration and will keep indefinitely.

*   *   *

PEANUT BUTTER PEPPERMINT BARS

½ cup margarine
½ cup brown sugar
1 ¼ cups flour
1 cup creamy peanut butter

TOPPING
6 ounces semisweet chocolate
2 tablespoons corn syrup
2 tablespoons water
¼–½ teaspoon peppermint
   flavoring

Cream the margarine with the sugar until fluffy. Add the flour and mix well. Spread the dough in a 9 × 12½-inch cake pan, and bake in a 350° oven for 20 minutes. While hot, spread the crust with peanut butter.

While the crust is baking, make the topping. Melt the chocolate over hot water. Add the corn syrup and water, and stir to mix well. Add the flavoring.

Spread the chocolate topping over the peanut butter. Let the chocolate set, and then cut into 32 bars.

*   *   *

BLENDER CHOCOLATE DELIGHT

4 eggs
8 ounces semisweet chocolate,
   cut in small pieces

¼ cup nondairy creamer
1 teaspoon vanilla
1 tablespoon rum flavoring

Put all the ingredients in a blender, and blend until all the chocolate is fully blended and the mixture is smooth. The mixture will thicken when refrigerated. Pour into individual serving dishes or into a large bowl. 8 servings. The chocolate delight can be used as a filling or topping for any cake.

PASSOVER

There is a popular saying: "They don't mean the Haggadah but the *kneidlach.*" This folk proverb is undoubtedly not intended to deride the story of Passover but to emphasize the role of the special dishes associated with the festival and the added dimension they give to it. When served during the year, these foods, even if made with Passover ingredients, still lack the *pesachdik* flavor that is tasted only on the holiday.

In past generations Passover preparations went on nearly all year round, starting in the summer months with the harvesting of the wheat for matzah and the making of *vishnik* from cherries. When the grapes were ripe in the fall, the Passover wine was made. By Hanukkah, many housewives had fattened the geese and the ducks, and then they rendered the fat from these fowl for use on Passover. On the morning after Purim, it was already Erev Pesah in many homes. A corner of a room or a closet was cleaned thoroughly and all leaven removed so that the Passover products bought during the coming weeks could be stored there. Urgent consideration was given to the baking of matzot. Beets and water were placed in special large earthenware crocks to ferment for *russel,* a favorite Passover brew. The prohibition to refrain from eating leaven eliminated the use of many foods and resulted in the creation of special foods for Passover. Matzah is not only a staple in place of bread but also, as meal, an ingredient of many Pesah dishes.

Despite the numerous and unusual provisions involved in the observance of Passover (which, incidentally, have been considerably eased in this modern and mechanized age), the joyous festival of freedom and faith is warmly welcomed in Jewish homes. Like all other Jewish festivals, Passover is observed both in the synagogue and in the home. However, it is in the home that the festival assumes its unique role. The entire atmosphere is transformed and permeated with a picturesque charm and a festive spirit.

Especially for Passover, care must be taken to provide for the poor, as the costs for its observance are greater than usual, and they—like all other Jews—should be able to celebrate free of worry. The practice of distributing *maot hittim*, wheat money, or *kimha de-Pisha*, flour for Passover, was instituted to meet the needs of the indigent. This custom has given rise to the creation of special Passover funds in local communities.

The prohibition of leaven, hametz, is stated in the Bible: "Seven days you shall eat unleavened bread; on the very first day you shall remove leaven from your houses" (Exodus 12:15). The prohibition of hametz applies to the fermented products of five kinds of grain: wheat, barley, oats, rye, and spelt. It is likewise forbidden to use any foods that contained hametz. Generally speaking, in order to refrain from hametz, observant Jews do not use those processed foods and food products which do not have a proper rabbinical endorsement for Passover. The removal of hametz also implies the changing of all dishes, silverware, and other kitchen utensils, since they usually absorb leaven. Separate sets of dishes and utensils are provided for Passover, although it is possible for some items to be made fit for use by the process of kashering (ritual scouring).

To be certain that no leaven will be seen or found in the house during Passover and that no one will inadvertently eat thereof, a search for leaven, *bedikat hametz*, is made at the beginning of the evening of the fourteenth day of Nisan. As the home has usually been thoroughly cleaned and rid of all hametz by this time, it is customary to place pieces of bread in several parts of the house—which then become the object of the search, for otherwise hametz might not be found and the benediction that is recited prior to the search would be pronounced in vain. However, as the head of the family does not know where the bread pieces are placed, he must make a thorough search. Before ten o'clock on the morning of the fourteenth day of Nisan, the hametz that remains is burned.

The rabbis recognized the difficulties and hardships of those who possessed leaven in large quantities and would suffer substantial losses if they destroyed all their hametz. To obviate this situation, they instituted *mekhirat hametz*, the transfer of leaven to a non-Jew by a legal bill of sale. Because of the intricacies of the legal formulation, a rabbi is usually designated by his congregants as their agent to execute the transaction. After Passover, the rabbi buys back the leaven from the non-Jew and thus restores it to the possession of the original owners.

As a reminder that the Lord "passed over the houses of the Israelites in Egypt" (Exodus 12:27) and spared their eldest sons on the eve of

Passover, when the firstborn of the Egyptians were slain, the four-teenth day of Nisan is observed as *ta'anit bekhorim*, a fast for the firstborn son of every Jewish family. It is the custom for the firstborn to participate in a *seudat mitzvah*, a religious meal following a *siyyum*, the completion of the study of a tractate of the Talmud. Participation in this study and meal exempts one from the duty of fasting.

The obligation to eat matzah is binding only on the first night of Passover, although eating leaven is forbidden throughout the festival. This accounts for the fact that the special benediction "on eating unleavened bread" is said only at the seder, and *matzah shemurah* (unleavened bread that is watched) is used then. The biblical com-mandment "You shall observe the [Feast of] Unleavened Bread" (Ex-odus 12:17) implies that one must be careful to watch that the dough for the matzah should not become leavened. In preparing matzah, the bakers must take precautions, in the kneading and baking processes, to prevent the dough from becoming fermented and thus leavened. A further precaution is taken by carefully watching the wheat for the matzah, during its harvesting and milling, to assure that rain or damp-ness will not cause fermentation. The unleavened bread that is made with this extra care is known as *matzah shemurah* and is eaten by the more pious throughout the entire festival.

The table for the seder is set before nightfall with a white cloth, beautiful vessels, and the necessary appurtenances, including the *ke'a-rah*, the three matzot in a special three-part cover, wine cups, and the cup for Elijah. The *ke'arah*, a large platter, contains certain unique foods used at the seder: *betzah*, roasted egg, representing the hagigah or festival offering; *zeroa*, roasted bone, a memorial of the paschal lamb offered on the night of Passover in the Temple; maror, bitter herbs; karpas, a green vegetable; haroset, a sweet pap mixture; and salt water.

On Sabbaths and festivals, with the exception of the first two nights of Passover, one is obligated to break bread and say the blessing over two whole loaves of bread. On these two nights a third loaf or cake of unleavened bread is added to fulfill the commandment of eating "the bread of affliction," for the Jewish sages did not want the two loaves used every Sabbath and festival to recall the bread of affliction. The cabbalists called these three matzot by the names of the three divi-sions of Israel—Cohen, Levi, and Israel—to symbolize the unity of the Jewish people.

Each celebrant has a goblet from which he drinks four times during the seder. It is generally stated that drinking the four cups of wine recalls the four expressions of redemption in Exodus 6:6–7, the biblical verses wherein God promised to liberate the Israelites from Egypt.

The seder starts with the leader's chanting the Kiddush, a proclamation of the sanctity of the festival over a cup of wine.

During the seder, a small piece of celery or other green vegetable, karpas, is dipped in salt water, and the benediction for vegetables is said. This unusual practice is for the purpose of arousing the interest of the children. Many people have associated the vegetable symbolically with the joyous festival of spring and the salt water with the tears shed by the Israelites during their years of enslavement in Egypt.

The middle of the three matzot is divided into two. The larger piece, called the afikoman, is then wrapped in a napkin and hidden under the pillow on which the leader reclines. The smaller piece is returned to its place. The purpose of this procedure is to retain the interest of the children throughout the Haggadah ceremony. At the conclusion of the meal, a piece of the afikoman is distributed to all the celebrants so that each may partake of it. The custom has arisen that the children obtain possession of the afikoman during the course of the seder and hold it until it is redeemed with a gift. This may be based on the talmudic statement "they hasten [the eating of] the matzot on the night of Passover so that the children should not sleep," which has been interpreted to mean "they snatch the matzot."

As a reminder that "the Egyptians ruthlessly imposed upon the Israelites. . . . They made life bitter for them with harsh labor at mortar and bricks" (Exodus 1:13–14), it has been ordained that bitter herbs shall be eaten. The bitter herb is dipped into haroset and a blessing recited. Haroset, a mixture of apples, nuts, almonds, cinnamon, and wine, is symbolic of the mortar out of which the children of Israel made bricks in Egypt.

A piece of the third matzah is taken and the bitter herb combined with it to make a sandwich to fulfill the commandment "they shall eat it with unleavened bread and bitter herbs" (Numbers 9:11). The Talmud tells us that this practice was introduced by Hillel during the days of the second Temple.

It is customary to start the meal with an entrée of hard-cooked eggs in salt water, as a symbol of mourning. The egg, also eaten at the mourner's first meal, is said to represent the idea of resurrection. Jewish sages have felt that even joyous occasions should have a symbol of sadness in memory of the destruction of the Temple. This is the prelude to the sumptuous festive meal of the seder.

HAROSET

2 apples
½ cup raisins
½ cup dates
¼ cup almonds, shelled

¼ cup walnuts, shelled
1 teaspoon powdered ginger
1 teaspoon cinnamon
⅓ cup sweet wine

Quarter and core the apples. Grind the apples, raisins, dates, and nuts, and add the ginger, cinnamon, and wine. Mix well. These quantities make 12 portions. The haroset will keep in the refrigerator for a couple of weeks.

* * *

KNEIDLACH (Matzah Balls)

4 eggs
1 teaspoon salt
½ teaspoon cinnamon
 (optional)

½ teaspoon white pepper
6 tablespoons chicken fat or oil
1 cup matzah meal
½ cup soup stock or water

Beat the eggs with the salt, cinnamon, pepper, and chicken fat or oil. Add the matzah meal and the soup or water. Mix thoroughly. Cover and refrigerate the mixture for 1 hour or more.

Bring 4 quarts of salted water to a boil. Shape the mixture into matzah balls, and drop in the boiling water. Cook covered for half an hour. Balls are then ready to be added to soup. 12 large matzah balls.

* * *

SHORT-CUT GEFILTE FISH

4 slices of fresh white fish
4 slices of fresh carp
1 large can or jar gefilte fish

2 onions, sliced
2 carrots, sliced
salt and pepper to taste

Clean and wash the fresh fish. Salt the fish, and refrigerate it a few hours or overnight.

Drain the fish balls, reserving the fish broth.

Place the fish broth in a pot with the onions and carrots, and cook for 10 minutes. Add the fresh fish slices, and cook for 20 minutes or until the fish flakes easily. Do not overcook. Add salt and pepper. Add the fish balls, and cook for 5 minutes.

Remove the fish balls and the sliced fish to a platter. Pour the broth over the fish. Decorate with the carrot slices. Serve hot or cold. 8 servings.

*   *   *

MATZAH FARFEL

2 egg yolks
2 tablespoons margarine,
  melted
1 cup matzah farfel

½ teaspoon salt
¼ teaspoon pepper
¼ teaspoon onion powder

Beat the egg yolks with the margarine, and add the other ingredients. Spread the mixture on a greased foil-lined cookie sheet, and bake in a 350° oven for about 20 minutes until browned. Serve either hot or cold in soup.

*   *   *

ROAST LAMB

3½ pounds shoulder lamb,
  cracked
salt and pepper to taste
6–8 garlic cloves, cut in half
3 tablespoons margarine

2 tablespoons lemon juice
¼ cup white wine or water
3 pounds new potatoes, cooked
¼ cup parsley, chopped

Season the meat with salt and pepper, and insert the garlic with the margarine between the cracked bones, or make incisions in the meat and insert the garlic and margarine.

Place the meat in a roaster and roast for 15 minutes in a 350° oven. Mix the lemon juice and wine or water, and baste the meat with it. Roast the meat for 2½ to 3 hours or until it is tender, basting the meat with the drippings in the pan several times during the roasting. About 30 minutes before the meat is ready, place the potatoes, cut in halves, around the meat, and coat them with the drippings.

Arrange the meat and potatoes on a serving dish and sprinkle with the parsley. 6 servings.

CARROT RING

½ cup matzah meal
¼ cup potato starch
½ teaspoon salt
1 bunch carrots, grated
¼ cup raisins
½ cup sugar
1 teaspoon cinnamon

1 teaspoon powdered ginger
¼ cup lemon juice
grated peel of 1 lemon
½ cup wine
1 egg
¼ cup margarine, melted

Mix the matzah meal with the potato starch and salt. Add the carrots, raisins, sugar, cinnamon, ginger, lemon juice, lemon peel, wine, and egg. Mix well, and stir in the melted margarine. Pour the mixture into a greased ring mold or baking dish, and bake in a 350° oven for 1 hour. Unmold on a plate. 6 servings.

*   *   *

CABBAGE AND FRUIT SALAD

1 cup cabbage, shredded
1 cup carrots, shredded
2 apples, cubed
juice of 1 lemon
1 tablespoon sugar

1 cup uncooked prunes, pitted
  and cut in small pieces
½ cup white raisins
½ cup Brazil nuts or filberts,
  chopped

Mix all the ingredients together. Chill. Mayonnaise or sour cream goes well with this salad. 8 servings.

*   *   *

BORSHT (Beet Soup)

4 medium beets
8 cups water
2 teaspoons salt
¼ cup sugar

6 tablespoons lemon juice
2 eggs
sour cream (optional)

Cook the beets in water to cover until they are soft. Peel the beets, and then grate or shred them. Put the beets into the water, and add the salt. Bring to a boil, and cook for 20 minutes. Add the sugar and lemon juice. Taste the soup, and add more sugar or lemon juice to correct the seasoning.

Beat the eggs with a little water. Add the soup very slowly to the beaten eggs, being careful not to let it curdle. If the meal is a dairy one, sour cream may be added before serving. 10 servings.

MATZAH BREI

4 matzot   1½ teaspoons salt
4 eggs   butter or margarine

Soak the matzot just enough to soften them. Break the eggs in a bowl and beat with the salt. Add the soaked matzot. Heat the butter or margarine in a frying pan over moderate heat. Pour the matzah mixture, and fry until golden on underside, turn over with a spatula and fry on the other side. Serve with sugar and cinnamon. 4 servings.

*   *   *

MATZAH MEAL PANCAKES

4 eggs   1 tablespoon sugar
¾ cup milk or water   1 cup matzah meal
1 teaspoon salt   oil or margarine

Beat the eggs with milk or water. Add salt, sugar, and matzah meal. Beat well. Drop with a spoon into hot oil or margarine, and fry until brown. Turn and brown on other side. Serve with sugar or jam. 4 servings.

*   *   *

TURKEY PANCAKES

1 onion, chopped   1 cup matzah meal
2 tablespoons oil or margarine salt and pepper to taste
½ cup celery, diced   2 cups turkey, cooked and
3 eggs, beaten   cubed
¾ cup soup stock   oil for frying

Sauté the onion in 2 tablespoons of oil or margarine for 10 minutes. Do not brown. Add the celery, and continue to sauté for 5 more minutes. Mix the eggs with the soup stock; add the matzah meal and salt and pepper. Add the turkey and the onions and celery. Mix well.

Drop by tablespoons into hot oil or margarine, and fry until brown. Remove and drain the pancakes on paper toweling. Serve hot with a sauce or gravy. 4 servings.

BAGELS

1 cup water
½ cup oil
2 cups matzah meal

1 tablespoon sugar
1½ teaspoons salt
6 eggs

Place the water in a pot, and add the oil. Bring to a boil. Add the matzah meal, sugar, and salt all at once, and beat with a wooden spoon until all the ingredients are combined. Remove the pot from the heat.

Add the eggs, one at a time, mixing well until the mixture is thick and smooth. Shape the dough into 15 balls, and place them on a greased baking sheet. With the handle of a wooden spoon dipped in cold water, make a round hole in the center of the balls by twisting the handle until the desired bagel shape is formed. Bake in a 375° oven for 1 hour or until nicely browned. 15 bagels.

*   *   *

BLINTZES

3 eggs
1½ cups water
½ teaspoon salt

⅔ cup cake meal
margarine or oil

Beat the eggs with the water and salt. Gradually add the cake meal, stirring constantly to make a smooth batter.

Heat a small frying pan which is greased lightly. When the frying pan is hot, pour about ¼ cup of the batter into the pan and rotate the pan so batter forms a circle. Cook until the edges start to leave the sides of the pan. Turn out on a towel. Continue with the rest of the batter. 8 blintzes.

Fill the blintzes with any desired filling, and cook in margarine or oil.

*   *   *

COCONUT PUDDING

1 fresh coconut, grated
6 eggs, separated
1 cup sugar
juice of 2 lemons

grated rind of 2 lemons
½ cup coconut milk
fresh strawberries

With a sharp instrument make a hole in the soft eye of the coconut. Drain the coconut milk, and reserve. Crack the coconut, and peel with a vegetable knife. Put the coconut pieces through a grinder, blend in a blender, or grate the coconut.

Beat the egg yolks with the sugar until lemon-colored. Add the grated coconut together with the lemon juice and lemon rind. Add the coconut milk. Beat the egg whites until stiff, and fold into the coconut mixture.

Grease a 8 × 8-inch pan, and pour the mixture into it. Bake in a 350° oven for 30 minutes. Sweeten the strawberries, and serve with the pudding. 8 servings.

*   *   *

ALMOND MACAROONS

4 egg yolks   *2 cups ground almonds*
1 cup sugar

Beat the egg yolks well; add the sugar, and beat until lemon-colored. Add the almonds, and mix thoroughly. Chill for easier handling.

Take small pieces of the mixture, and shape into small balls. Place the macaroons on a greased baking sheet. Top with half an almond, if desired. Bake in a 350° oven for 10 minutes. Do not overbake. Approximately 40 macaroons.

*   *   *

COCONUT MACAROONS

4 egg whites   *1 cup coconut, freshly grated*
1 cup sugar   *½ cup walnuts, broken*

Beat the egg whites until frothy. Add the sugar, and beat until stiff. Fold in the coconut and walnuts.

Drop by teaspoons on a baking sheet which is covered with foil. Bake for 30 minutes in a 300° oven. Remove from oven. Let stand a few minutes before removing from baking sheet. Approximately 30 macaroons.

*   *   *

CREAM PUFFS

1 cup water   *½ teaspoon salt*
⅓ cup margarine   *1 cup cake meal*
1 tablespoon sugar   *4 eggs, beaten*

Mix the water with the margarine in a pan. Add the sugar and salt. Bring to a boil. Remove from fire, and pour in the cake meal. Lower heat and return to stove, stirring well to combine the ingredients, until the mixture forms a ball. Remove from the heat, and add ¼ of the eggs until all the eggs are incorporated.

Drop the mixture by teaspoons (or by tablespoons for larger puffs) on a greased baking sheet. Bake in a 400° oven for 20 minutes or until puffed and brown. (It is advisable not to open the oven door during the first 10 minutes of baking.) Allow to cool. Fill with fruits and whipped cream.

*   *   *

BROWNIES

4 ounces bittersweet chocolate   ⅔ cup sugar
¼ cup margarine   ½ cup cake meal
2 eggs   ½ cup walnuts, broken
dash of salt

Melt the chocolate with the margarine over hot water, and allow to cool. Beat the eggs and salt until thick and lemon-colored. Beat in the sugar. Add the chocolate and margarine. Gradually add the cake meal, and blend well. Add the nuts.

Spread the batter evenly in a well-greased 9-inch square pan. Bake in a 350° oven for 35 minutes. Cut into 2¼ × 2¼-inch squares while still hot. Cool in pan. 16 brownies.

*   *   *

CHOCOLATE NUT TORTE

6 eggs, separated   4 ounces semisweet chocolate,
1½ cups sugar   grated
1 cup walnuts, chopped   2 apples, grated
    ½ cup matzah meal

Beat the egg yolks with the sugar until lemon-colored. Add the walnuts, chocolate, apples, and matzah meal.

Beat the egg whites until stiff but not dry, and fold into the egg yolk mixture.

Pour the mixture into a 9-inch springform pan and bake in a 350° oven for 40 minutes or until the cake springs back when touched with a finger. Cool in pan before removing to a serving dish.

SPONGE CAKE

6 eggs, separated
¾ cup sugar
grated peel of 1 lemon

¼ cup orange juice
½ cup cake meal
2 tablespoons potato flour

Beat the egg yolks; add sugar, and beat until lemon-colored. Add the lemon peel and orange juice. Sift together the cake meal and potato flour, and add. Beat the egg whites until stiff, and fold gently into the egg yolk mixture. Pour batter into a round ungreased cake pan. Bake for 45 minutes in a 350° oven.

*   *   *

NUT CAKE

6 eggs, separated
1 cup sugar
2 cups walnuts, chopped

½ cup matzah meal
grated rind of 1 lemon
juice of 1 lemon

Beat the egg yolks, add the sugar slowly, and continue to beat until lemon-colored.

Mix the nuts with the matzah meal and the grated lemon rind, and add to the egg yolks. Add the lemon juice and stir.

Beat the egg whites until stiff. Gently fold half the egg whites into the egg yolk and nut mixture. Fold in the rest of the egg whites, making sure all the egg whites are completely folded in.

Line the bottom of a 9-inch springform cake pan with oiled wax paper. Pour the mixture into the cake pan.

Bake the cake in a 325° oven for 1 hour. Remove from oven and cool.

Run a knife around the sides of the cake. Then release the spring, and remove the cake from the form. Remove the wax paper, and set the cake on a serving dish.

*   *   *

NO-BAKE SEVEN-LAYER CAKE

3½ ounces bittersweet
    chocolate
¼ pound margarine
1 cup fine sugar*

3 eggs, separated
8 whole pieces of egg matzah
sweet wine
½ cup walnuts, chopped

Melt the chocolate over warm water. Allow to cool.

Cream the margarine with the sugar until fluffy and sugar is dissolved. Add the egg yolks, one at a time, and beat well. Beat the egg whites until stiff. Fold the chocolate into the egg yolk mixture and then fold in the egg white mixture.

Dip the matzot, one at a time, in wine, but do not soak too much. Place one matzah on a serving plate. Cover with 1½ tablespoons of the chocolate filling, and continue this process until the eighth matzah is on top. Cover the top and sides with the rest of the filling. Decorate the top with chopped walnuts and chocolate curls. Cover with plastic wrap, and let the cake mellow for 24 hours in the refrigerator. Cut in thin slices, or into small squares for petits fours.

For vanilla seven-layer cake, omit the chocolate, and dip the matzah in white wine. Decorate with chopped almonds.

The chocolate filling can be used as a frosting for other cakes.

To make fine sugar for Passover, put one cup of regular sugar in a blender, and blend the sugar for a few seconds until powdered.

*   *   *

CHEESE PIE

| ½ cup margarine | 3 eggs |
| ½ cup sugar | cake meal |

Cream the margarine with the sugar until fluffy, and then beat in the eggs, one at a time. Add enough cake meal to make a soft dough. Press into 2 9-inch pie pans. Fill with the cheese filling.

Bake the pie in a 325° oven for 40 minutes. When done, leave in the oven until the oven is cool.

This pie crust dough can also be used for lemon meringue pie. For this purpose the shell should be baked in a 350° oven until brown.

FILLING

1½ pounds cottage cheese	1 cup sour cream
4 eggs	2 tablespoons cake meal
¾ cup sugar	juice and rind of 1 lemon

Beat all the ingredients together thoroughly and pour into the unbaked pie crust. Bake as directed.

SOUR CREAM CHOCOLATE FROSTING

6 ounces bittersweet chocolate   *1 cup sour cream*
1 teaspoon instant coffee

Melt the chocolate with the instant coffee over warm water. Add the sour cream, and mix well. The frosting will be sufficient for an 8-inch cake.

*   *   *

COFFEE NUT KISSES

2 egg whites   *½ cup walnuts, chopped fine*
½ cup sugar   *1 tablespoon instant coffee*

Beat the egg whites until frothy. Slowly beat in the sugar, and continue beating until the mixture is stiff. Fold in the nuts and coffee.

Drop by teaspoons on a baking sheet covered with foil. Bake for 25 minutes in a 300° oven. Let stand for a minute before removing from the foil. Approximately 25 kisses.

*   *   *

EINGEMACHTS (Beet Preserves)

1 pound honey   *2 teaspoons powdered ginger*
1 cup sugar   *½ cup walnuts*
4 cups beets, cooked   *juice of 1 lemon*

Bring the honey and sugar to a boil in a deep pot. Cook slowly for 15 minutes. Cut the beets into julienne strips, and add to the mixture of honey and sugar. Cook for 30 minutes. Add the ginger, nuts, and lemon juice, and then cook for 15 minutes longer. Serve cold.

*   *   *

COCONUT JAM

2 cups sugar   *juice of 1 lemon*
2 cups fresh coconut, grated

Boil the sugar with ¼ cup of water until it spins a thread. Add the grated coconut and the lemon juice. Stir constantly until it is quite dry.

DATES IN WINE

1 cup nuts, chopped   **SYRUP**
½ cup sugar   *1 cup red wine*
1 teaspoon cinnamon   *2 cups sugar*
¼ teaspoon powdered ginger   *¼ teaspoon powdered ginger*
1 pound dates, pitted
oil

Mix the nuts with the sugar and spices. Stuff the dates with the mixture. Heat some oil in a frying pan, and when the oil is hot, sauté the dates on all sides.

To make the syrup, mix the wine, sugar, and ginger in a saucepan, and bring to a boil. Lower the heat, and add the dates. Cook until the syrup is absorbed.

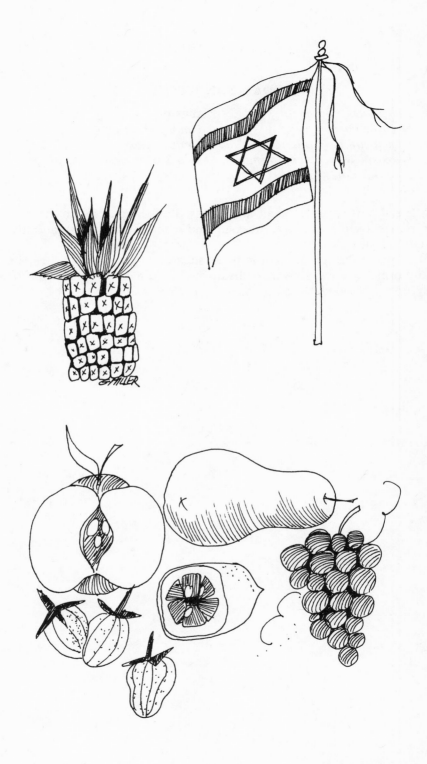

ISRAEL INDEPENDENCE DAY

Israel's Independence Day is celebrated both publicly and privately as a day of rejoicing and thanksgiving. Parades, demonstrations, folk dancing, receptions, and special services in synagogues are the order of the day. In addition, Israelis are encouraged to mark this historic occasion with festive banquets at home celebrations. The Ministry of Education and Culture of the State of Israel has published *Festival Readings for the Independence Day Meal,* on the style of the Passover Haggadah, with provision for drinking four cups of wine.

A service for Independence Day also has been issued with the sanction of the Chief Rabbinate. It includes zemirot (songs) to be sung and selections from the Bible, Talmud, and rabbinic literature to be read at the evening and noon *seudat mitzvah* (meal related to a religious ceremony).

In London a 238-page prayer book entitled *Order of Service and Customs for the Synagogue and Home for Israel Independence Day* was published by Routledge and Kegan Paul. Based on the practice instituted by the rabbis in Israel, the text in Hebrew and English translation by Dr. Moses Friedlander has been adapted for Diaspora Jewry and is preceded by a foreword by former Chief Rabbi Israel Brodie.

On Independence Day the home is decorated with flags, symbols, and flowers, and the table is set in a festive manner with fruit and goodies produced in Israel and twelve twisted loaves, symbolizing the twelve tribes of Israel. Five candles are lit, since the holiday occurs on the fifth day of the month of Iyar. Preceding the meal a special Kiddush over wine is recited. Because Independence Day always falls on the same day of the week as does the seventh day of Passover, when according to tradition the children of Israel crossed the Red Sea, it is appropriate to sing during the meal "The Song of Redemption" by Yehudah Halevi, which is recited on the seventh day of Passover.

The recipes included here are based on the suggestions offered by

Israel's Ministry of Education and Culture. The pancake recipe contains *helmit* (spinach is substituted here), as a reminder of the 1948 siege of Jerusalem, when this wild plant was practically the only vegetable available. The soup with kreplach recalls how Israel beat her enemies in the War of Independence, for, according to Jewish folklore, kreplach are eaten whenever there is beating (see the chapter on Purim).

An assortment of oriental and Western vegetables reminds us of the integration of Jews from many lands into the new nation. Seven Species Cake recalls the seven products of the Holy Land (Deuteronomy 8:8). It is suggested that the cake be cut in square portions to symbolize the ingathering of the exiles from the four corners of the earth.

*   *   *

SPINACH PANCAKES

1 cup spinach, chopped and
  well drained
¼ cup bread crumbs
dash of nutmeg
1 egg

¼ cup onions, chopped
salt and pepper to taste
oil
tomato sauce

Mix all the ingredients, except the oil and tomato sauce. Heat the oil in a frying pan, and drop the spinach mixture by tablespoons into the oil. Fry on both sides until brown. Serve with tomato sauce. 4 servings.

*   *   *

STUFFED CHICKEN

1 cup rice or burghul* *(cracked*
  wheat)
4 tablespoons margarine
1 cup onions, chopped
½ cup celery, sliced
2 tablespoons parsley, chopped

1 teaspoon thyme
salt and pepper to taste
1 4-pound chicken
garlic powder
powdered ginger
paprika

Cook the rice or the *burghul* until soft.

Melt the margarine, and sauté the onions for 10 minutes. Add the celery, and sauté for 5 minutes. Add the parsley, and sauté for 5 more minutes. Add ½ teaspoon of thyme, salt and pepper, and the cooked rice.

Stuff the chicken with the mixture, and sew up the opening. Place the chicken in a roaster, and sprinkle it with salt, garlic powder, ginger, paprika, and ½ teaspoon thyme. Roast the chicken for about 2 hours until tender and nicely browned. 6 servings.

Available in gourmet food shops.

* * *

KLOPS (Ground Meat with Eggs)

1 ½ tablespoons margarine	*1 onion, grated*
2 eggs	*½ teaspoon garlic powder*
½ cup tomato juice	*2 tablespoons parsley, chopped*
½ cup bread crumbs	*salt and pepper to taste*
2 pounds ground meat	*6 hard-cooked eggs*
1 onion, grated	

Grease a roaster with the margarine.

Beat the 2 eggs with tomato juice, and add the bread crumbs. Then add the meat, onion, garlic powder, parsley, and salt and pepper, and mix well.

Pat half the meat mixture in the roaster and place the hard-cooked eggs in a line. Cover with the rest of the meat mixture. Dot with margarine. Bake in a 350° oven for 1 hour.

Individual *klops* can be made by enclosing each egg in some of the meat. To serve, cut the *klops* in half, showing half an egg surrounded with meat. 6 servings.

* * *

SQUASH WITH TOMATOES

1 pound green squash	
1 small onion, chopped fine	*salt and pepper to taste*
2 tablespoons margarine or oil	*1 small clove garlic, mashed*
½ cup fresh or canned	*(optional)*
tomatoes	

Scrape the squash, and dice.

Sauté the onion in the margarine or oil for 10 minutes. Add the squash, and continue cooking for 10 minutes, stirring the mixture to keep it from burning. Add the tomatoes, lemon juice, salt and pepper, and garlic, and cook until the squash is soft. 6 servings.

GEZER HAI (Carrot Salad)

4 large carrots
orange juice
1 orange, peeled and cut up

juice of 1 lemon
sugar or honey to taste
salt to taste

Grate the carrots on a medium grater. Add orange juice to cover. Add the orange pieces, lemon juice, sugar or honey, and salt. Cover and refrigerate overnight. 6 servings.

*   *   *

MIKTZAF SOLET (Farina Lemon Pudding)

2 cups water
juice of 1 lemon
⅓ cup quick-cooking farina
½ teaspoon salt

½ cup sugar
1 package frozen strawberries
or raspberries, defrosted

Bring the water and lemon juice to a boil, and slowly add the farina and the salt. Cook for 10 minutes, stirring a few times. Transfer to a large mixing bowl, and, with beaters at high speed, beat the farina and slowly add the sugar. Beat for 30 minutes until thick and very white. Refrigerate.

Serve cold with the berries as a sauce (or use any other fruit in season). 6 servings.

*   *   *

SEVEN SPECIES CAKE

2 cups flour
1 egg, beaten
1 tablespoon lemon juice
2 tablespoons oil
warm water

12 tablespoons margarine,
melted
¾ cup bread crumbs
confectioners' sugar

FILLING

1 cup figs, cut in small pieces
1 cup raisins
5 tablespoons orange juice
1 cup pitted dates, cut in small
pieces

½ cup chopped almonds or
roasted peanuts
¾ cup sugar
½ cup candied lemon peel, cut
in small pieces

To make the filling, mix the figs and raisins with the orange juice in a saucepan, and simmer over very low heat until the figs are very soft.

Add the dates, almonds or peanuts, sugar, and candied lemon peel, and mix.

To make the dough, mix the flour with the egg, lemon juice, and oil, and add warm water to form the dough. Knead for a few minutes, until the dough is soft but not sticky. Cover with a bowl, and let the dough rest for 20 minutes.

On a floured cloth roll out the dough into a large square. Stretch the dough, being careful not to tear it. Cut into four equal pieces, each to cover a 9 × 13-inch pan. Grease the pan well with 2 tablespoons of margarine, and put in one piece of the dough. Brush with some of the margarine, scatter ¼ cup bread crumbs over the dough and then spread with ⅓ of the filling. Place the second piece of dough on top, repeat the process with the margarine, bread crumbs, and filling. Place the third piece of dough on top, and repeat procedure with the rest of the ingredients. Place the fourth piece of dough on top; pat all around the edge of the pan. Brush the rest of the margarine on top.

Bake the cake in a 375° oven for 45 minutes. Remove, and cover with a clean towel. When the cake is cold, sift confectioners' sugar over it. Cut in squares.

*   *   *

APRICOT CANDY

1½ pounds dried apricots   *1½ cups sugar*

Grind the apricots. Add the sugar, and mix well.

Pat the apricots into a square 9 × 9-inch pan. Let the candy stand for 24 hours. Cut into squares. Sprinkle with additional sugar.

SHAVUOT

In the Bible, Shavuot, the Festival of Weeks, is called the Feast of Harvest and the Day of the Firstfruits, for in ancient times part of the products of the harvest were joyously offered to God as a reminder that everything belongs to Him. Besides being an agricultural festival, Shavuot is associated traditionally with the Season of the Giving of Our Law, marking the birthday of Israel's religion upon receiving the Torah on Mount Sinai.

The colorful ceremony of the offering of the firstfruits in the Temple in biblical times has been symbolically revived in modern times. For many years Hag ha-Bikkurim (Festival of Firstfruits) has been celebrated in Israel with elaborate pageantry. Young and old from villages and colonies converge on Haifa bearing the first products of the season —fruits, sheaves of corn, vegetables, chickens, and sheep—which are offered as gifts to the Jewish National Fund. Kurdistani Jews who were tillers of the soil would bring the firstfruits to their leaders in flower-decorated baskets, while the vineyard owners among them gave to the poor a tithe of the raisins made from the grapes. Synagogues and Jewish homes throughout the world are adorned with flowers, leaves, and tree branches to recall the agricultural aspects of Shavuot.

Rabbi Solomon ben Isaac (1040–1105), the perceptive and erudite Bible and Talmud commentator known as Rashi, said of Shavuot: "One should rejoice on it by eating and drinking to demonstrate that this day on which the Torah was given is acceptable to him" (Pesahim 68b). A folklorist opined: "Shavuot is really far superior to the other festivals. On Passover we are not permitted to eat what we want; on Sukkot we cannot eat where we want; but on Shavuot we may eat what we want, where we want, and even when we want." Accordingly, certain culinary customs have evolved to give due honor to Shavuot.

Dairy dishes characterize the Shavuot meals served on the first day of the festival celebrating the revelation on Mount Sinai. Various rea-

sons have been advanced for this tradition. The Bible itself compares
the Torah to milk and honey. The phrase "honey and milk are under
your tongue" (Song of Songs 4:11) implies that the words of the Torah
shall be as dulcet to one's heart and ear as milk and honey are sweet
to one's tongue. The psalmist declared that "the precepts of the Lord
are . . . sweeter also than honey and the honeycomb" (Psalms 19:9–11).
Hence it is obligatory to partake of honey on Shavuot. Another ra-
tionale for eating these foods on the Feast of the Harvest derives from
the biblical description of the Land of Israel as "a land flowing with
milk and honey" (Exodus 3:8).

Rabbi Moses Isserles (c. 1520–1572) states in the *Code of Jewish Law*:
"It is a universal custom to eat dairy food on the first day of Shavuot.
The reason appears to be that just as on the night of Passover two
cooked dishes are taken in remembrance of the paschal sacrifice and
the festival offering, so one should eat a dairy dish and then a meat dish
[as a reminder of the two sacrifices offered on Shavuot]. It is also
necessary to have two loaves of bread on the table [since it is forbidden
to eat milk and meat with the same loaf], the substitute for the Temple
altar. These are a reminder of the two loaves of bread [made from the
first ears of the new wheat] that were offered on the day of the
firstfruits." A further caution was voiced to avoid mingling meat and
milk foods: "Since one eats dairy foods and also necessarily partakes
of meat, for it is a duty to eat meat in honor of every festival, one
should be scrupulous not to violate a prohibition." On Shavuot the
usual six-hour waiting period to partake of dairy dishes after eating
meat was waived in some communities.

Other commentators maintain that prior to their receiving the
Torah, the children of Israel were permitted to eat nonkosher meat
that was not ritually slaughtered. When the Torah was given on Shavuot, however, they were thenceforth obligated to adhere to the laws
pertaining to ritual slaughter and to forbidden foods. All their cooking
utensils and eating vessels were forbidden; they could not be purged
because the Torah was given on a Sabbath and a festival. Thus they
had no alternative but to eat dairy foods, which were relatively easy
to prepare.

The custom of indulging in dairy fare on Shavuot is also derived
from this biblical verse: *"Minhah hadashah la-Adoshem be-
Shavuotekhem* [your Feast of Weeks, when you bring an offering of
new grain to the Lord]" (Numbers 28:26). The initials of the four
Hebrew words spell *me-halav* (from milk), implying that foods made
from milk are acceptable on Shavuot. Mystics see a reason in the fact
that the numerical equivalent of *halav* (milk) is forty—the number of
days Moses tarried on Mount Sinai. Others find an explanation in the

tradition that the infant Moses refused to suckle from any but a Hebrew nurse. Finally, in Psalm 68, which is read on Shavuot, the mountain on which the Divine Presence rested is called *Gavnunim*, a word akin to *gevinah*, Hebrew for cheese.

Perhaps the most delectable of Shavuot foods are blintzes, rolled pancakes filled with cheese. Among other tempting tidbits are cheese knishes, butter and cheese cakes, and cheese kreplach. The kreplach are three-cornered, based on a talmudic statement: "Blessed be the Merciful One who gave the three-fold Law [Torah, Prophets, Writings] to a people comprising three classes [Cohen, Levi, Israel], through a third-born [Moses, the third child of his parents], in the third month [Sivan]" (Shabbat 88a).

Jewish women in oriental countries took pride in baking for Shavuot a seven-layer cake called *Siete Cielos* (Seven Heavens), symbolic of the traditional seven celestial spheres God traversed to present the Torah to Moses on Mount Sinai. Fashioned in seven circular tiers, each one smaller than the one on which it rested, the cake was decorated with various symbols such as a star of David, the rod of Moses, the two tablets of the Law, manna, Jacob's ladder, and the ark of the covenant. Some topped the cake with a seven-rung ladder to recall Moses ascending Mount Sinai. Similar elaborate pastries, called Sinai Cake, alluded to the mountain. A large cake or bread with raisins, generally known as *pashtudan* or *floden* when baked for Shavuot, was also called Sinai. Some oriental Jewish women baked baklava—a very sweet cake made with nuts, sugar, and honey.

Jews of Kurdistan prepared large quantities of butter and cheese for the festival. Their special dish was ground wheat cooked in sour milk with dumplings of butter and flour. Jewish housewives in Tripoli baked wafers in various shapes: a ladder, to recall that Moses went up Mount Sinai; a hand, denoting hands extended to receive the Torah; the two tablets of the Law; eyeglasses, to see the words of the Torah; and other symbolic forms.

In some communities it was customary to serve matzah remaining from Passover as a reminder that Shavuot is the culmination of the exodus from Egypt. In North Africa the matzah was shredded into bowls of milk and honey.

Some baked long loaves to denote the broad scope of the Torah, regarding which Job said: "The measure thereof is longer than the earth" (Job 11:9). The long hallah sometimes had four heads to signify the four methods of Torah study: *peshat*, the literal meaning; *remez*, interpretation by intimations; *derush*, the homiletical explanation; and *sod*, the mystical meaning. Others baked loaves with seven rings to symbolize the seven celestial spheres mentioned above.

Pious Jews herald Shavuot with an all-night vigil devoted to study of *Tikkun Lel Shavuot,* and partake of cheesecake and coffee to refresh themselves. On the second night of Shavuot, Yemenite Jews read the *Tikkun* in the synagogue. Each brings a choice delicacy, such as spiced coffee or candy, to share with those spending the night in study.

Shavuot was considered the most appropriate season to initiate children in the study of Torah. To endear studying to the children, Hebrew words and letters were written on a slate spread with honey. The children were encouraged to lick the honey and thus sense the Torah's sweetness. At the end of the lesson honey cakes decorated with biblical verses were distributed to the newly initiated pupils.

*   *   *

ALMOND SOUP

¾ cup almonds	salt and white pepper to taste
¼ cup butter or margarine	1 egg, well beaten
1 tablespoon cornstarch	1 cup cream
2 cups water	parsley, chopped
3 bouillon cubes	

Blanch the almonds in boiling water to cover. Remove the skins, and arrange the almonds on a baking sheet. Toast them in a 350° oven until lightly browned. Grind or blend the almonds.

Melt and brown the butter or margarine in a saucepan but do not burn it. Add the almonds. Mix the cornstarch with the water, and add to the saucepan. Add the bouillon cubes. Simmer for 10 minutes. Add the salt and pepper.

Beat the egg with the cream, and slowly add to the soup. Heat the soup, but do not boil. Soup can be served hot or cold with the chopped parsley. 6 servings.

*   *   *

BAKED SALMON

4 pounds salmon, in one piece	½ cup Italian or French
1 medium onion, sliced	dressing
1 lemon, sliced	

EGG SAUCE

3 hard-cooked eggs, chopped
1 cup mayonnaise
1 tablespoon lemon juice

GARNISH

small beets
black olives
cherry tomatoes
white horseradish

Place the salmon on a large piece of foil. Place half the onion slices and half the lemon slices in the cavity of the salmon, and top with half the dressing. Put the rest of the onion and lemon slices on top of the fish, and cover with the rest of the dressing. Fold the foil over the fish, and crimp the edges together tightly.

Place the fish on a flat baking sheet, and bake in a 375° oven for 1 hour or for 15 minutes per pound. Open the foil, and bake for 15 more minutes. Do not overbake. Serve hot or cold with the egg sauce.

To make the egg sauce, mix the chopped eggs with the mayonnaise and lemon juice. Chill. Before serving, pour the sauce over the salmon, or serve the sauce separately.

Garnish with the small beets, black olives, and cherry tomatoes. The beets can be scooped out with a melon baller and filled with white horseradish. 8 to 10 servings as a main dish.

* * *

BEAN SALAD

1 8-ounce can green beans
1 8-ounce can wax beans
1 8-ounce can kidney beans
1-pound can chick-peas
½ cup red onions, chopped
salt and pepper to taste

¼ cup Italian parsley, chopped
½ cup oil
¼ cup wine vinegar
½ teaspoon oregano
½ teaspoon garlic powder

Mix all the ingredients together. Cover and refrigerate overnight. Serve on salad greens. 12 servings.

* * *

FISH MOLD WITH GRAPES

8 pieces fillet of flounder, 8
inches long
juice of 1 lemon
1-pound can red salmon

1 teaspoon onion powder
2 egg whites, stiffly beaten
½ cup heavy cream
salt and pepper to taste

Salt the fish lightly and allow to stand for 1 hour.

Lay the fish in a shallow dish, and pour the lemon juice over it. Let stand while you make the stuffing.

Mash the salmon well, and add the onion powder, egg whites, cream, and salt and pepper. Mix well.

Oil well a ring mold, and lay in it the fish fillets, narrow ends toward the center. Spoon the salmon filling in the center and fold both ends of the fish over the filling. Cover with foil, and place the mold in a shallow pan which contains 1 inch of hot water.

Bake in a 350° oven for 30 minutes. Invert carefully on a serving plate. Reserve the juice left in the mold for the sauce. Keep the fish warm while making the sauce. Make the sauce, and pour over the fish. 8 servings.

SAUCE

2 tablespoons butter	salt and white pepper to taste
2 tablespoons flour	2 egg yolks, beaten
¼ cup white wine	1 small can of white grapes,
juice reserved from the fish	drained
mold	parsley sprigs

Melt the butter in a saucepan; add the flour, and mix well. Add the wine, the juice left in the mold, and salt and pepper, and cook the sauce until it thickens. Stir a little of the hot sauce into the egg yolks, and slowly add it to the sauce. Add the grapes. Heat but do not boil the sauce. Pour the sauce over the fish in the serving plate. Decorate with fresh parsley.

*   *   *

BUREKAS

½ cup butter or margarine	1½ tablespoons white vinegar
½ cup oil	½ cup cold water
3 cups flour	1 egg, beaten with a teaspoon
1 teaspoon baking powder	of water
1 teaspoon salt	sesame seeds

Mix the butter or margarine and oil together with the flour, baking powder, and salt. Add the vinegar with the water, and mix well.

Roll out the pastry very thin on a piece of wax paper. Cut into circles. Put some of the filling on each piece, and fold in half, pinching the edges together with a fork. Lay the *burekas* on a greased foil-lined baking sheet. Brush with the beaten egg, and scatter sesame seeds on top. Prick the top of each *bureka* with a fork. Bake in a 375° oven until nicely browned.

CHEESE FILLING

1 pound farmer cheese	1 cup mashed potatoes
2 egg yolks	salt and pepper to taste

Mash the farmer cheese. Add the egg yolks, potatoes, and salt and pepper, and mix well.

*   *   *

BLINTZES

2 eggs	**FILLING**
dash of salt	½ pound farmer cheese
1 cup flour	½ pound cream cheese
1 cup water	2 egg yolks
1 tablespoon oil	vanilla or lemon flavoring
butter or margarine	1½ teaspoons farina
	sugar to taste

Beat the eggs well with a mixer. Add the salt and flour, and slowly add the water, continuing to mix. Add the oil. The batter will be thin. Let it stand at room temperature for 2 hours. If preferred, use a blender.

To make the filling, mash the farmer cheese well; add all the other ingredients and mix well.

Heat a 7-inch frying pan, and grease lightly. When the frying pan is hot, add two tablespoons of the batter, tipping the pan so that the batter covers the surface of the pan. Cook on one side only, until the top is dry. Turn out, bottom side up, on a clean towel. Continue the process with the rest of the batter. (Two frying pans speed up the work.) When all the pancakes have been made, fill each one with a tablespoon of the filling. Fold over the sides, and then roll the blintzes as you would roll a jelly roll. Fry in butter or margarine.

Serve the blintzes with sour cream, fresh or frozen berries, or other fruits.

The blintzes can also be baked by placing them on a well-greased foil-lined baking sheet and brushing the top of the blintzes with butter or margarine. Bake in a 400° oven until golden brown. Do not over-bake. 8 to 10 blintzes.

NOODLE AND CHEESE PUDDING

*¼ pound medium or fine
  noodles
½ cup butter
2 eggs
⅓ cup sugar
½ cup sour cream*

*¼ pound cream cheese
1 teaspoon vanilla
¼ teaspoon salt
¼ cup white raisins
¼ cup cornflake crumbs
½ teaspoon cinnamon*

Cook the noodles according to directions. To the hot cooked noodles, add ¼ cup of butter.

Beat the eggs with the sugar. Add the sour cream, cream cheese, vanilla, salt, and raisins. Pour the mixture over the noodles and mix well.

Melt the remaining ¼ cup of butter in a 9 × 9-inch baking dish. Pour the noodle mixture into the dish.

Mix the cornflake crumbs with the cinnamon, and sprinkle all over the pudding. Bake in a 350° oven for 40 minutes. Serve hot or cold. 8 servings.

*   *   *

COTTAGE CHEESE MOLD

*1 pound cottage cheese
1 cup heavy sweet cream,
  whipped
3 tablespoons confectioners'
  sugar*

*2 tablespoons lemon juice
2 tablespoons candied ginger,
  cut fine
fresh strawberries*

Mash the cottage cheese. Add the whipped cream to the confectioners' sugar. Mix the cottage cheese with the lemon juice and candied ginger; add the cream, mixing lightly. Pour the mixture into a greased mold or a bowl, and refrigerate overnight.

Unmold on a serving dish. Place the strawberries around the mold and serve. (Any fresh berries or fruit go well with the mold.) 6 servings.

FESTIVAL PUDDING

1 package kosher raspberry
  gelatin
1 package kosher lemon gelatin
1 package instant vanilla
  pudding
1¾ cups nondairy creamer

2 tablespoons sherry
1 large can fruit salad, well
  drained
¼ cup candied ginger, cut fine
1 container nondairy topping
maraschino cherries

Dissolve each package of gelatin in 1½ cups of boiling water. Pour each flavor into a separate square pan, and refrigerate until firm. Cut into small squares.

In a bowl, mix the instant vanilla pudding with the creamer. Add the sherry. Beat until thickened and then refrigerate. It will become thicker upon standing.

In a large glass serving bowl, put the fruit salad mixed with the ginger. Place the raspberry and lemon gelatin squares over the fruit. Pour the cold vanilla pudding over the fruit.

Whip the topping until stiff, and spread over the pudding. Decorate with maraschino cherries and more fruit if desired. Refrigerate overnight or for a few hours. 12 servings.

*　　　*　　　*

BAKED APRICOTS

½ pound dried apricots
1 cup white raisins
2 cups water
⅓ cup sugar, or more to taste

½ cup sherry
¼ cup lemon juice
sour cream

Place the apricots and raisins in a casserole. Cover with the water, and bake in a 325° oven for 1 hour.

Add the sugar, sherry, and lemon juice. Stir to dissolve the sugar. Serve warm or chilled with sour cream. 6 servings.

ROGELACH

1 package dry yeast
¼ cup warm water (105°–115°)
½ cup butter or margarine
⅓ cup sugar
2 eggs

¼ cup sour cream or orange
 juice
3–3¼ cups flour, sifted
½ teaspoon salt
butter or margarine, melted
1 egg white, beaten

FILLING

½ cup sugar
½ cup nuts, chopped

1 teaspoon cardamom or
 cinnamon
½ cup raisins

Mix well the four ingredients for the filling.

Dissolve the yeast in the water.

Cream the butter or margarine with the sugar; add the 2 eggs, sour cream or orange juice, and yeast. Add the flour and salt, and mix well. Knead the dough until it is smooth and does not stick to the hands. Use more flour if dough is sticky. Put the dough in a greased bowl. Cover with plastic wrap, and refrigerate overnight.

Divide the dough into 6 or 8 parts. Roll out each piece of dough into a thin circle. Spread melted butter or margarine on the dough and sprinkle with some of the filling. Cut each circle of dough into 8 wedges. Roll up tightly each wedge of dough from the outer edge of the circle. Place the *rogelach* on a greased baking sheet. Brush the tops with the egg white. Sprinkle with sugar. Let rise in a warm place until double in bulk.

Bake in a 350° oven until nicely browned. Do not overbake. Baking time depends on the size of the *rogelach*. 48 large or 64 small *rogelach*.

*   *   *

CHEESE STRUDEL

1 pound farmer cheese
¾ cup sugar
2 egg yolks
½ cup golden raisins
1 teaspoon vanilla
½ cup butter, melted

6 strudel leaves
1 cup cornflake crumbs or
 bread crumbs
1 cup almonds, chopped
confectioners' sugar

Mix the cheese, sugar, egg yolks, raisins, and vanilla.

Spread some melted butter over three of the strudel leaves. Sprinkle with half the cornflake or bread crumbs and half the chopped almonds. Spread half the cheese filling across one end of the strudel, a few inches from the edge. Fold the dough over the filling and roll up the strudel.

Place the filled strudel on a well-greased cookie sheet, brush with melted butter, and sprinkle with sugar. Cut the strudel in portions but do not cut all the way through. Repeat the process with the other three strudel leaves.

Bake in a 375° oven until nicely browned. Cool and cut the strudel in portions. When cold, sprinkle with confectioners' sugar. 10 servings.

*   *   *

CHEESECAKE

CRUST	FILLING

CRUST

1⅔ cups graham cracker,
 zwieback, or vanilla cookie
 crumbs
½ cup brown sugar
½ cup butter

FILLING

1½ pounds cream cheese
1 cup sugar
4 eggs
1 cup sour cream
¼ cup flour
juice of 1 lemon
grated rind of 1 lemon

Mix the crumbs with the brown sugar and butter. Line a 9-inch springform pan with the crumb mixture.

With a mixer, beat the cream cheese until soft. Add the sugar. Add the eggs, one at a time, beating well. Add the sour cream, flour, lemon juice, and lemon rind. Mix well.

Pour the cheese mixture in the crumb-lined springform pan. Bake the cheesecake in a 325° oven for 1 hour. Turn off the heat, and allow the cake to remain in the oven until cool. Refrigerate.

PINEAPPLE CHEESECAKE

CRUST

1⅔ cups graham cracker
   crumbs
⅓ cup brown sugar
½ cup butter, melted
½ teaspoon cinnamon
½ cup walnuts, chopped

FILLING

1 cup heavy sweet cream
1 cup confectioners' sugar
½ pound cream cheese
1 can pineapple pie filling

Mix the graham cracker crumbs with the brown sugar, butter, cinnamon, and nuts. Spread the crumbs in a flat 11 × 13-inch pan. Bake the crust in a 350° oven for 8 minutes, and then allow to cool.

Whip the sweet cream until thick. Mix the confectioners' sugar and the cream cheese, and stir into the whipped cream. Pour into the cooled graham cracker crust.

Cover with the pineapple pie filling. (Any pie filling may be used.) Refrigerate the cake overnight.

*   *   *

BABKA (Yeast Cake)

1 package dry yeast
¼ cup warm water (105°–115°)
¾ cup sugar
¼ teaspoon salt
3¾ cups flour, sifted
¾ cup warm milk or water

¼ pound butter or margarine
3 eggs
½ cup white raisins
1 teaspoon vanilla
butter or margarine, melted

Dissolve the yeast in ¼ cup of warm water. Add 2 teaspoons of sugar and the salt. Mix 1 cup of flour with ¾ cup warm milk or water, and add to the dissolved yeast. Beat well with a wooden spoon and let it rise until double in bulk.

Cream the butter or margarine with the rest of the sugar until fluffy. Add the eggs, one at a time. Mix in the yeast batter with the rest of the flour and the raisins. Add the vanilla. Mix well by hand or with a wooden spoon. The batter will be thick. Cover the batter with a towel, and let the dough rise until double in bulk (2 to 3 hours).

Spread half the batter in a well-greased angel cake pan, and sprinkle with half the filling. Spread the rest of the batter on top of the filling. Brush the top with melted butter or margarine, and sprinkle with the rest of the filling. Let the *babka* rise again, uncovered, until the dough reaches to the top of the pan. Bake the *babka* in a 375° oven for 40 to 45 minutes.

FILLING

4 tablespoons butter or
   margarine
4 tablespoons flour

¾ cup sugar
1 teaspoon cinnamon
¾ cup nuts, chopped

Mix together all the ingredients.

*　　*　　*

SHAVUOT DOUGHNUTS

6 eggs
2 tablespoons sugar
½ cup butter
2½–3 cups flour
4 teaspoons baking powder

½ teaspoon salt
1 teaspoon vanilla
oil for frying
confectioners' sugar

Beat the eggs with the sugar and butter. Add 2 cups of flour with the baking powder, salt, and vanilla. Dough will be soft. Add enough flour to form a dough which is not sticky. Form the dough into little doughnuts.

Heat the oil. When the oil is hot, drop the doughnuts into the oil. Do not crowd. Fry on one side until brown; turn and fry on the other side. Lift the doughnuts out of the oil, and drain them on paper toweling. Roll in confectioners' sugar.

These doughnuts are best served the day they are made.

*　　*　　*

MOUNT SINAI CAKE

SPONGE CAKE

5 eggs
1 cup sugar
3 tablespoons white wine
1 cup flour, sifted
1 teaspoon baking powder

WINE SAUCE

9 eggs, separated
3 cups white wine
3 teaspoons vanilla
1 cup sugar
1 cup pineapple juice

FILLING

1-pound can pitted dark cherries	*1-pound 4-ounce can pie-sliced apples*
1-pound 4-ounce can pineapple slices, cut up	*1 cup sliced almonds*

Bake the sponge cake a day before assembling the "mountain."

In a medium mixing bowl, beat the eggs with the sugar on high speed until very thick and lemon-colored. Add the wine, and beat a few more minutes.

Reduce the speed of the mixer and slowly mix in the flour sifted with the baking powder.

Line the bottom of a 9-inch springform pan with lightly oiled wax paper. Pour the cake batter into the pan.

Bake the cake in a 350° oven for 30 minutes or until done. Remove from oven, and allow the cake to cool. When cold, run a knife around the cake form, release the spring, and remove the cake. Remove the wax paper.

Drain the fruits for the filling well, saving 1 cup of the pineapple juice for the wine sauce.

To make the wine sauce, put the egg yolks, wine, vanilla, sugar, and pineapple juice in the top of a double boiler, and place over hot but not boiling water. Cook the wine sauce, stirring constantly, until the sauce thickens and coats the spoon. Sauce will be thin. Allow the sauce to cool.

Cut the sponge cake vertically in half, and then cut each half vertically into 6 pieces, each about ¾" wide.

Lay 5 of the longer slices of the cake side by side in an ovenproof dish. On the cake put some of the pineapple, cherries, and apple slices. Pour some of the wine sauce on top, and scatter some almonds. Make a second layer with 4 other slices of cake, some of the fruits, and add some of the wine sauce and almonds. On top of this put 2 of the smaller pieces of the cake, and more fruits, wine sauce, and almonds. Put the last piece of cake on top, and pour the rest of the wine sauce all over the cake and fruits. The cake should resemble a mountain.

Beat the egg whites until very stiff and dry. With a spatula cover the cake with the egg whites, and scatter some of the almonds on the bottom part of the mountain only.

Bake in a 250° oven for 10 minutes just to dry the egg whites. After 10 minutes place a piece of foil on the top part of the cake to keep it from browning. Bake for 10 more minutes until the bottom is a light brown (the top should remain white). The egg whites should resemble snow, and the almonds, stones. Turn off the heat, and leave the cake in the oven for 1 hour. Remove the cake from the oven, and allow to cool at room temperature.

If the cake is to be served the next day, it is advisable to refrigerate it.

Cut a piece of white cardboard into the shape of the two tablets for the Ten Commandments, and place on top of the cake.

*   *   *

WALNUT BARS

½ cup margarine
½ cup brown sugar
½ cup white flour
½ cup whole wheat flour
½ teaspoon vanilla
½ cup apricot or currant jelly

TOPPING
2 egg whites
½ cup sugar
1 cup walnuts, chopped
1 teaspoon vanilla

Cream the margarine with the sugar. Add the flours with the vanilla, and mix well. Spread the dough in a 9 × 13-inch cake pan, and bake in a 350° oven for 15 minutes. While still hot, spread the jelly over the baked crust.

To make topping, beat the egg whites with the sugar until stiff. Add the walnuts and vanilla.

Spread the topping over the jelly layer. Bake for 25 minutes longer. When cool, cut into 32 bars.

*   *   *

CHOCOLATE BARS

½ cup margarine
½ cup brown sugar
½ cup white flour
½ cup whole wheat flour
½ teaspoon vanilla

TOPPING
2 eggs
1 cup brown sugar
1 teaspoon vanilla
2 tablespoons flour
½ teaspoon baking powder
12 ounces chocolate chips
½ cup walnuts, chopped

Cream the margarine with the sugar. Add the flours and vanilla. Mix well. Spread the dough in a greased 9 × 13-inch pan, and bake in a 350° oven for 15 minutes.

To make the topping, beat the eggs with the sugar and vanilla. Add the flour with the baking powder. Add the chocolate chips and walnuts. Spread the topping over the baked crust.

Return to oven and bake for 25 more minutes. While warm, cut into 32 bars.

FOOD FOR THOUGHT

FOOD FOR THOUGHT

THE BOUNTY OF THE LORD

God said, "See, I give you every seed-bearing plant that is upon all the earth, and every tree that has seed-bearing fruit; they shall be yours for food."

GENESIS 1:29

You shall serve the Lord your God, and He will bless your bread and your water.

EXODUS 23:25

He subjected you to the hardship of hunger and then gave you manna to eat, which neither you nor your fathers had ever known, in order to teach you that man does not live on bread alone, but that man may live on anything that the Lord decrees.

DEUTERONOMY 8:3

Bless the Lord, O my soul.
O Lord my God, Thou art very great; . . .
Who causeth the grass to spring up for the cattle,
And herb for the service of man;
To bring forth bread out of the earth,
And wine that maketh glad the heart of man,
Making the face brighter than oil,
And bread that stayeth man's heart.

PSALMS 104:1, 14–15

Go, eat your bread in gladness,
And drink your wine in joy;
For your works were long ago approved by God.

ECCLESIASTES 9:7

I have come to my garden,
My own, my bride;
I have plucked my myrrh and spice,
Eaten my honey and honeycomb,
Drunk my wine and my milk.
Eat, lovers, and drink;
Drink deep of love!

SONG OF SONGS 5:1

Whenever a man does eat and drink and get enjoyment out of all his wealth, it is a gift of God.

ECCLESIASTES 3:13

And they took fortified cities, and a fat land, and possessed houses full of all good things, cisterns hewn out, vineyards, and oliveyards, and fruit-trees in abundance; so they did eat, and were filled, and became fat, and luxuriated in Thy great goodness.

NEHEMIAH 9:25

In the next world a man will be asked to give an account for that which, being excellent to eat, he gazed at and did not eat.

JERUSALEM TALMUD KIDDUSHIN, end

If three men have eaten at the same table and have spoken over it words of Torah, it is considered as if they had eaten at the table of God.

ETHICS OF THE FATHERS 3:4

Honor a festival with food, drink, and clean clothes.

MEKILTA EXODUS 12:16

He who has given teeth will give bread.

FOLK PROVERB

Bless Him, O constant companions,
Rock from whose store we have eaten,
Eaten have we and have left, too,
Just as the Lord hath commanded.
Father and Shepherd and Feeder,
His is the bread we have eaten,
His is the wine we have drunk,
Wherefore with lips let us laud Him,
Lord of the land of our fathers,

Gratefully, ceaselessly chanting,
"None like the Lord is holy."

> Excerpt from TZUR MISHELO, a Sabbath table song
> Unknown medieval poet
> Translated by Israel Abrahams

*   *   *

FEEDING THE HUNGRY

Is not this the fast that I have chosen?
To loose the fetters of wickedness,
To undo the bands of the yoke,
And to let the oppressed go free,
And that ye break every yoke?
Is it not to deal thy bread to the hungry,
And that thou bring the poor that are cast out to thy house?

> ISAIAH 58:6–7

But if a man be just, and do that which is lawful and right . . . and hath not wronged any, but . . . hath given his bread to the hungry, and hath covered the naked with a garment . . . he is just, he shall surely live, saith the Lord God.

> EZEKIEL 18:5–9

I have been young, and now am old;
Yet have I not seen the righteous forsaken,
Nor his seed begging bread.

> PSALMS 37:25

I will abundantly bless her provision;
I will give her needy bread in plenty.

> PSALMS 132:15

He that hath a bountiful eye shall be blessed;
For he giveth of his bread to the poor.

> PROVERBS 22:9

Is not thy wickedness great?
And are not thine iniquities without end? . . .
Thou has not given water to the weary to drink,
And thou hast withholden bread from the hungry.

> JOB 22:5, 7

It is unlawful for a man to eat his own meals before giving food to his beasts, for it is first said [Deuteronomy 11:15], "And I will provide grass in the fields for your cattle," and after it is said, "thus you shall eat your fill."

TALMUD GITTIN 62a

Rabbi Johanan gave his slave a portion of everything he himself ate. He said: "Did not He who made me in the womb make him? And did not One fashion us in the womb?" [Job 31:15].

JERUSALEM TALMUD KETUBOT 5

An Epitaph

Here lies Nachshon, man of great renown,
Who won much glory in his native town;
'Twas hunger that killed him, and they let him die—
They give him statues now, and gaze, and sigh—
While Nachshon lived, he badly wanted bread,
Now he is gone, he gets a stone instead.

ISAAC BEN-JACOB (1801–1863)

The Miser and the Poor

A miser once dreamed he had given away
Some bread to a beggar he met on the way.
In terror he woke, and he solemnly swore
That the rest of his life he would slumber no more.

BEN-ZEEB (1764–1811)

Every man has the right to eat.

HEINRICH HEINE (1797–1856)

If there is sufficient food for six people, there is enough for a seventh person.

FOLK PROVERB

The sated one does not believe the hungry one.

FOLK PROVERB

*   *   *

THE ETIQUETTE OF DINING

When thou sittest to eat with a ruler,
Consider well him that is before thee;
And put a knife to thy throat [use self-restraint],
If thou be a man given to [a large] appetite.

PROVERBS 23:1–2

If you are seated at the table of a great man,
Do not be greedy at it, and do not say,
"There is certainly much upon it!"
Remember that a greedy eye is wrong.
What has been created more greedy than the eye?
That is why it sheds tears on every face.
Do not reach out your hand for whatever you see,
And do not crowd your neighbor at the dish.
Eat like a human being what is set before you.
And do not chew greedily, or you will be hated.
Be the first to stop eating, for the sake of good manners.
And do not be insatiable, or you will give offense.
If you are seated among many persons,
Do not reach out your hand before they do.

APOCRYPHA BEN SIRA 31:12–14, 16–18

People should not talk at meals lest the food go the wrong way, which is dangerous.

TALMUD TAANIT 5b

The pious people of Jerusalem would not sit down to a meal unless they knew who is seated with them.

TALMUD SANHEDRIN 23a

Eat that you may live and forgo excess. Do not believe that excessive eating and drinking strengthen the body and increase understanding, like a sack which is filled by what is put into it. . . .

Work before you eat and rest after you eat. Do not eat ravenously and do not fill your mouth gulp after gulp without breathing space.

MOSES MAIMONIDES (1135–1204)

When one eats he should not talk.

FOLK PROVERB

*　　*　　*

DIETARY LAWS

Every creature that lives shall be yours to eat; as with the green grasses, I give you all these. You must not, however, eat flesh with its life-blood in it.

GENESIS 9:3–4

The choice first fruits of your soil you shall bring to the house of the Lord your God.

EXODUS 23:19

You shall not boil a kid in its mother's milk.

EXODUS 23:19

A physician restricts the diet of only those patients whom he expects to recover. So God prescribed dietary laws for those who have hope of a future life.

LEVITICUS RABBAH 13:2

God forbid that I should believe that the reasons for forbidden foods are medicinal! For were it so, the Book of God's Law would be in the same class as any of the minor brief medical books. . . . Furthermore, our own eyes see that the people who eat pork and insects and such . . . are well and alive and healthy at this very day. . . . Moreover there are more dangerous animals . . . which are not mentioned at all in the list of prohibited ones. And there are many poisonous herbs known to physicians which the Torah does not mention at all. All of which points to the conclusion that the Law of God did not come to heal bodies and seek their material welfare, but to seek the health of the soul and cure its illnesses.

DON ISAAC ABARBANEL (1437–1508)

I maintain that food forbidden by the Law is unwholesome. There is nothing among the forbidden foods whose injurious character is doubted except pork and fat. But also in these cases is the doubt unjustified.

MOSES MAIMONIDES (1135–1204)

The food regulations of Judaism are in principle simple. The use of meat is restricted. Certain animals (e.g., pigs) are not eaten at all; while those permitted are killed in such a way that the minimum of pain is caused and the maximum of blood drained away. They are then subjected to strict examination to ensure their freedom of disease. When declared fit for consumption (kosher), the meat is thoroughly washed in the kitchen and salted in order to extract any blood that remains.

The religious value of these similar observances lies in the spirit in which they are performed; and those who smile at a "kitchen religion" ("pot-and-pan-theism," as it has wittily been called) would do well to ponder the remark of the early Greek philosopher on entering a poor cottage: "Here too are gods." Judaism would seem to hold that the occupation of a housewife is a holy one and that a kitchen too is, or can be made, a place of worship. Holiness is not asceticism, the negation of the world and its fulness. It is rather, in the presence and enjoyment of the world and its fulness, a conscious exercise of self-control; it is a guiding, not an obliteration, of natural desire. All hygienic considerations apart, therefore, food regulations, however irksome, are of deep moral significance. Just as the weekly Sabbath reminds a man that he is not a mere wage-slave, so abstention from certain foods, and a deliberate delay in their preparation, adjure him not to behave as a mere animal, greedily snatching at the first desire of his eyes. Dietary laws and daily prayers, no less than Sabbath and Day of Atonement, foster a life of quality and purpose. They raise the trivialities of the daily round into one continuous act of worship. They are "religion breathing household laws."

LEON ROTH (1896–1963)*

It may appear a minute matter to pronounce the Hebrew blessing over bread, and to accustom one's children to do so. Yet if a Jew, at the time of partaking of food, remembers the identical words used by his fellow Jews since time immemorial and the world over, he revives in himself, wherever he be at that moment, communion with his imperishable people. In contrast to not a few of our co-religionists who have no occasion for weeks and months together to bestow a thought on their creed or their people, the Jew who keeps kashrut has to think of his religious and communal allegiance on the occasion of every meal; and, on every occasion, the observance of those laws constitutes a renewal of acquiescence in the fact that he is a Jew, and a deliberate acknowledgment of that fact.

WALDEMAR HAFFKINE (1860–1930)

*   *   *

THE QUEST FOR FOOD

By the sweat of your brow
Shall you get bread to eat.

GENESIS 3:19

He that tilleth his ground shall have plenty of bread;
But he that followeth after vain things is void of understanding.

PROVERBS 12:11

From Judaism: A Portrait by Leon Roth. Copyright © 1960 by Leon Roth. Reprinted by permission of The Viking Press, Inc.

The righteous eateth to the satisfaction of his desire;
But the belly of the wicked shall want.

PROVERBS 13:25

A woman of valor who can find? . . .
She is like the merchant-ships;
She bringeth her food from afar.
She riseth also while it is yet night,
And giveth food to her household.

PROVERBS 31:10, 14, 15

Send your bread forth upon the waters; for after many days you will find it.

ECCLESIASTES 11:1

It is not possible to compare one who has bread in his basket with one who has not.

TALMUD YOMA 18b

O Lord, give each one his bread, each body what it requires.

TALMUD BERAKOT 29b

The person who expends all his energies on obtaining food and drink will, if he is unable to obtain them legally, endeavor to secure them in whatever manner he can, as the Bible says: "For they eat the bread of wickedness and drink the wine of violence" [Proverbs 4:17].

Therefore it is proper for man to secure only what he requires for his subsistence, that is, enough for sustenance of body. As long as he understands this need, he can give free rein to his appetite for food and drink. However, when he has attained what he requires for subsistence, he should restrain his appetite.

SAADIA GAON (882–942)

The wise man eats to live; the fool lives to eat.

FOLK PROVERB

One has no appetite for food and another has no food for his appetite.

FOLK PROVERB

If one has bread, he should not look for cake.

FOLK PROVERB

BETTER THAN FEASTING

All days of the poor are evil;
But he that is of a merry heart hath a continual feast. . . .
Better is a dinner of herbs where love is,
Than a stalled ox and hatred therewith.

PROVERBS 15:15, 17

Better is a dry morsel and quietness therewith,
Than a house full of feasting with strife.

PROVERBS 17:1

Banished from his home, deprived of his realm, Solomon wandered about in far-off lands, among strangers, begging his daily bread. It happened that once on his peregrinations he met an old acquaintance, a rich and well-considered man, who gave a sumptuous banquet in honor of Solomon. At the meal his host spoke to Solomon constantly of the magnificence and splendor he had once seen with his own eyes at the court of the king. These reminiscences moved the king to tears, and he wept so bitterly that, when he rose from the banquet, he was satiated, not with the rich food, but with salt tears. The following day it again happened that Solomon met an acquaintance of former days, this time a poor man, who nevertheless entreated Solomon to do him the honor and break bread under his roof. All that the poor man could offer his distinguished guest was a meagre dish of greens. But he tried in every way to assuage the grief that oppressed Solomon. The words of his poor host were more grateful to Solomon's bruised heart than the banquet the rich man had prepared for him. It was to the contrast between the consolations of the two men that he applied the verse in Proverbs: "Better is a dinner of herbs where love is, than a stalled ox and hatred therewith."

LOUIS GINZBERG (1873–1953)

*   *   *

GLUTTONY

It is not good to eat much honey.

PROVERBS 25:27

Eat a third [of the capacity of the stomach], drink a third, and leave a third [of your stomach] empty. For if anger overtakes you, there will be room for the expansion of your stomach, and you will not burst.

TALMUD GITTIN 70a

More people die from overeating than from undernourishment.

TALMUD SHABBAT 33a

He who blows away the foam from his glass is not thirsty, and he who says, "what shall I eat with my bread?"—take the bread away from him [for he is not hungry].

TALMUD SANHEDRIN 100b

He who eats foods which do not agree with him violates three prohibitions: he hurts his health, wastes food, and offers a benediction in vain.

ABOT DE R. NATHAN 26

One should not take food except when one is hungry; nor drink unless one is thirsty.

Food should not be taken to saturation; during a meal one should eat one-fourth less than the amount that would give a feeling of satiety.

MOSES MAIMONIDES (1135–1204)

My piteous plight oft makes me weep—
I cannot eat when I am asleep.

M. SCHLESINGER (d. 1829)

If one is a glutton in his youth, he will be a sick beggar in his old age.

FOLK PROVERB

He who has bread wants cake.

FOLK PROVERB

*   *   *

SERVING GUESTS

"Eat and drink," saith he to thee;
But his heart is not with thee.

PROVERBS 23:7

When Rabbi Huna had a meal, he would open wide the door and say: "Let all who are hungry, come and eat."

TALMUD TAANIT 20b

The master of the house [at the commencement of the meal] cuts slices of bread, and the guest pronounces the grace [after meals]. The master of the house breaks bread so that he may do so with a pleasant eye [he serves large pieces which the guest would not cut]; and the guest pronounces the grace in order that he may bless the master of the house.

TALMUD BERAKHOT 46a

What does a good guest say? "How much trouble the host has given himself on my account! How much meat, wine, and cake he has set before me! The care and trouble he has had was for my sake."

What does a bad guest say? "What trouble have I caused the master of the house? I have eaten a piece of bread and a slice of meat and I have drunk a cup of wine. All the trouble he has had was only for the sake of his wife and children."

TALMUD BERAKHOT 58a

A dish tastes best
When served with a guest.

FOLK PROVERB

*   *   *

HORS D'OEUVRES

YIDDISH FOLK PROVERBS

Do not be too sweet, lest you be eaten up;
do not be too bitter, lest you be spewed out.

*   *   *

If one ate yesterday, he is not satiated today.

*   *   *

If the stomach is full, the entire body is happy.

*   *   *

From too much eating, one can die;
from too much fasting, one can die.

*   *   *

For another's celebration one always has a good appetite.

*   *   *

Only at one's own table can one be satiated.

*   *   *

When one brings his own bread, he is a welcome guest.

Tasty is the fish
In another's dish.

*　　*　　*

Guests and fish spoil on the third day.

*　　*　　*

A sick man is asked [if he wants to eat],
but a healthy man is given to eat.

*　　*　　*

If the pot has ingredients, the plate will have food.

*　　*　　*

Where there are many cooks, the food is raw.

*　　*　　*

If one cooks with straw the food remains raw.

*　　*　　*

If chicken is too expensive for you, eat herring.

*　　*　　*

*When a poor Jew eats chicken, it is a sign
that the chicken is sick, or that the poor man is sick.*

*　　*　　*

The poor cook with water.

*　　*　　*

Sweet as honey.

*　　*　　*

Sweet as sugar.

*　　*　　*

For herring one does not need salt.

*　　*　　*

Why do you need honey, if sugar is sweet?

*　　*　　*

When one eats the bagel, the hole remains in one's pocket.

*　　*　　*

One does not need teeth for borsht.

*　　*　　*

From borsht with bread one's cheeks get red.

*　　*　　*

For bread one can always find a knife.

*　　*　　*

Hunger is the best cook.

Hungry? Lick salt and you will be thirsty!

*   *   *

If there is a doctor in the family all are healthy;
and if there is bread, all are satiated.

*   *   *

America—the land of sugar!

*   *   *

When God gives bread, men give butter.

*   *   *

Meat and fish are Sabbath delicacies
and even on weekdays they are not bad.

*   *   *

If one eats kugel a long time he will live long.

*   *   *

What is the good of a beautiful apple if it has a wormy heart?

*   *   *

Sugar in the mouth won't help if you're bitter at heart.

*   *   *

Call me a fool but give me cake.

*   *   *

That only fools love sweet things is an invention of the wise.

*   *   *

Rather than to die of hunger,
it is even better to eat a roast.

*   *   *

Even a shelled egg does not fall by itself into one's mouth.

*   *   *

While love is sweet, it is best with bread.

*   *   *

Love is like butter—it is good with bread.

*   *   *

POTPOURRI

When you are hungry, eat; when you are thirsty, drink.

TALMUD BERAKHOT 62b

Up to forty eating is beneficial; after forty drinking is beneficial.

TALMUD SHABBAT 158a

There is no joyous celebration without eating and drinking.

TALMUD MOED KATAN 9a

It is possible to live without wine but it is impossible without water. Salt is cheap and pepper is dear; yet it is possible to live without pepper but it is impossible without salt.

JERUSALEM TALMUD HORIOT 48c

No scholar should live in a town where vegetables are unobtainable. This implies that vegetables are healthy.

TALMUD ERUVIN 55b

Domestic strife is due only to food.

TALMUD BABA METZIA 59a

When the barley is gone from the jar, strife comes knocking at the door.

TALMUD BABA METZIA 59a

A pot with two cooks is neither hot nor cold.

TALMUD ERUVIN 3a

If hunger makes you irritable, better eat and be pleasant.

BOOK OF THE PIOUS (thirteenth century)

The less you eat, the less you ail.

JOSEPH IBN ZABARA (c. 1140–c. 1200)

You eat to live, you do not live to eat.

SAADIA GAON (882–942)

There is a universal law . . . which none can amend or repeal, and against which no protest or preachment can avail, a law . . . most persistent and inexorable, the law of—eating.

MENDELE MOCHER SEFORIM (c. 1836–1917)

Kugel, this holy national dish, has done more for the preservation of Judaism than all three issues of the magazine *Zeitschrift fuer die Wissenschaft des Judentums.* . . .

It is cholent alone that unites them still in their old covenant.

HEINRICH HEINE (1797–1856)

"Bontche the Silent," a classic story by the Yiddish writer I. L. Peretz, is about a downtrodden Jew who suffered every possible indignity throughout his lifetime without ever murmuring a word of protest. When he died and appeared for judgment before the heavenly court, it was decided to permit him to have any reward he desired. When Bontche realized that the offer was made in good faith, he said, "Well, if it is so, I would like to have—every day, for breakfast—a hot roll with fresh butter."

INDEX OF RECIPES*

*Mrs. Bernice Kremer and Mrs. Kay Powell offered helpful suggestions in the preparation of this index.